AF559798

EVENT TOURISM

EVENT TOURISM

By

Jack Randall

Published by:

DISCOVERY PUBLISHING HOUSE PVT. LTD.
4383/4B, Ansari Road, Darya Ganj
New Delhi-110 002 (India)
Phone : +91-11-23279245; 23253475; 43596065
E-mail : discoverybooksindia@gmail.com
discoverypublishinghouse@gmail.com
namitwasan9@gmail.com
web : www.discoverypublishinggroup.com

First Published: **2011**

Reprinted: **2022**

ISBN: 978-81-8356-896-8

Event Tourism

Printed at:
Infinity Imaging Systems
Delhi

PREFACE

Marketing is necessary in generating awareness and attendance for event tourism. Based on the vast number of distribution channels managed by Whistler's Community Partners and the in-resort expertise in marketing, promotion and communication, there is a great opportunity to develop an integrated marketing and communications strategy that helps grow Whistler's event image and reaches tourists who may or may not have visited Whistler for its events.

Like many other nations, New Zealand wants to pursue the potential rewards resulting from event tourism, or attracting visitors with major events. Part of that strategy is dictated by New Zealand's location, at a distance from many of the tourist-generating countries. Even as they plunge forward, though, the nation's tourism officials should consider how to measure the effects of event tourism, the better to determine what works and what doesn't. The authors offer a framework for developing such a strategy. Gaps that now exist in the nation's event-tourism strategy include, for instance, the lack of coordination among most of the hotel organizations, restaurants, tour operators, and theme parks, and the lack of planning for event-tourism opportunities.

Event planning is the process of planning a festival, ceremony, competition, party, or convention. Event planning includes budgeting, establishing dates and alternate dates, selecting and reserving the event site, acquiring permits, and coordinating transportation and parking. Event planning also includes some or all of the following, depending on the event: developing a theme or motif for the event, arranging for speakers and alternate speakers, coordinating location support (such as electricity and other utilities), arranging decor, tables, chairs, tents, event support and security, catering, police, fire, portable toilets, parking, signage, emergency plans, health care professionals, and cleanup.

Contents

CHAPTER–1

Event Tourism : Various Aspects

A significant motive for year round visits by guests is also event tourism. The Tourist Board of the Primorje-Gorski kotar County has dedicated special attention to this type of tourism by issuing an events calendar titled "From day to day" through the tourist information provider "Kvarner info" which is issued in 8 languages and is the basic source of information about the region and manifestations and is updated and reprinted quarterly.

There is a wide selection of events significant to the enrichment of the tourist offer and extension of the season. From manifestations connected with culture (music festivals, concerts, exhibitions, competitions, press), sport (regattas, endurance, mountain car racing, motorcycling, water skiing, parachuting, cross bowing etc.), tradition (carnivals, folklore, gastronomy), through to development of tourism (support for eco-centres, national parks and nature parks, improvement of places, walking and cycling trails, mountaineering trails) to manifestations connected to the fruits of nature (Marunada – chestnut festival, Days of cherries, Days of asparagus, Days of mountain fruits).

Tourist offer events start in January and February with carnival activities which culminate in one of the largest and most recognisable European carnivals – the Rijeka carnival. The cities of Rijeka and Novi Vinodolski are members of the International Association of Carnival Cities which most vividly indicates the importance, in a tourist sense, of these events founded on traditions and within whose framework are a whole series of traditional manifestations like the zvonc(ari (bell ringing) in Kastav and Matulja, Muna, Žejana...to the Opatija Balinjerade, International Carnival Day and Children's Carnival Promenade. These are followed by entertainment-musical, gastronomy and sports events, which upon the approach of Easter and the pre-season, especially the main tourist season, increase in numbers and grow into a fireworks of attractive tourist events in the summer months.

On one side they are characterised by being an offer for everyone, while on the other hand, being of high quality for even those most demanding of guests. Along with popular fisherman's evenings in most tourist localities, here too are manifestations and festivals like the Osor musical evenings, Summer performances and Festivals of Krk, Rab musical evenings, Lubenic(kih musical evenings, Summers in Frankopan in Kraljevica, International summer carnival in Novi Vinodolski, Liburnia jazz festival in Opatija, Kastaf summer, Rab knightly games, Fruits of the mountain in Gorski kotar, Days of music on Mali Lošinj, events on the Opatija Summer stage, etc. The annual finale of all the events according to tradition is in Mali Lošinj, when in the last four days of the current year the traditional international competition in underwater fishing is held.

NEW ZEALAND BETS ON EVENT TOURISM

Like many other nations, New Zealand wants to pursue the potential rewards resulting from event tourism, or attracting visitors with major events. Part of that strategy is dictated by New Zealand's location, at a distance from many of the tourist-generating countries. Even as they plunge forward, though, the nation's tourism officials should consider how to measure the effects of event tourism, the better to determine what works and what doesn't. The authors offer a framework for developing such a strategy. Gaps that now exist in the nation's event-tourism strategy include, for instance, the lack of coordination among most of the hotel organizations, restaurants, tour operators, and theme parks, and the lack of planning for event-tourism opportunities. Moreover, the government is unable to commit adequate resources to build up the system necessary for promoting event tourism due to uncertainty of desired return on investment. Rather than go event by event, New Zealand would be well advised to take a long view on its strategic approach for attracting international tourists and making event tourism profitable.

EVENT TOURISM: AN EXAMINATION OF MOTIVATIONS AND ACTIVITIES

Festivals, special events, and exhibitions are the cultural resources of an area that make possible the successful hosting of visitors. A large number of organizations and communities throughout North America organize and promote special events to create a positive image of the place and bring in money to the local community. Although there has been substantial research on the economic impact of place-dependent special events, little has been done at the national level to examine motivations and activities of event behavior. This article is intended to examine demographic characteristics, motivations, and activities of those who had gone on a festival/special event/exhibition trip using the U.S. Pleasure Travel Market data. Findings of this study may be of interest to those involved in marketing and management of event tourism.

EVENT TOURISM STRATEGY

Whistler's largest resort partners, Tourism Whistler, the Resort Municipality of Whistler and Whistler Blackcomb Mountains, recognized in March 2007 that there was a need to develop a resort-wide Event Tourism Strategy to help Whistler expand upon its ventures that complement tourism (i.e. events) in an effort to build and stabilize customer visits. This strategy evaluates the role of event tourism (as an economic driver for Whistler, consistent with the Resort's Whistler2020 vision1), explores the impact of event tourism on the Resort's stakeholders, community and its guests, and provides recommendations for Whistler to reach its vision for events ("Whistler is an internationally recognized tourism destination - renowned for its superior quality and diverse events - making it a place to visit again and again"). Specifically, it addresses the following goals for event tourism:

1. Grow and promote a portfolio of events that supports Whistler's brand, values and needs, and enhances Whistler's image (focusing on Whistler's existing events).
2. Develop the infrastructure to support large events in Whistler.
3. Access funding to grow events in Whistler.
4. Streamline Community Partner roles & responsibilities to better serve events.

To date, Whistler has hosted a wide range of events from small local gatherings and regional celebrations, to "signature" events attracting national and international attention. In addition to annual festivals and events, animation has also played an integral role in enlivening the Resort and the guest experience. At the other end of the event scale, Whistler will also be a host venue for the 2010 Olympic and Paralympic Winter Games, a "mega" event that is already garnering international attention for the Resort.

Whistler's stakeholders, specialists in the field of event tourism and destinations that are already engaged in event tourism strategies widely accept that it is necessary to adopt a long-term, strategic approach to event tourism in order to realize the full tourism potential of events. The stakeholders interviewed for this strategy also support an integrated approach that considers both the needs of the guest (or "event tourist" or "tourist") and the community. They unanimously agree that authentic, organic events that celebrate the destination and are aligned with Whistler's brand and values have much greater potential to grow and attract new and repeat visitation.

Since the majority of Whistler's most recognized regional and "signature" events have been established over time, it is important that Whistler's Community Partners continue to focus on nurturing existing events and look for opportunities to grow smaller events into economic generators for the Resort (i.e. attract regional, national and international event tourists). Smaller, grass roots events are typically championed by locals and therefore have already established some level of community buy-in and participation. These events are also more likely to reflect the values, community passion and products of the Resort, and provide a competitive edge over other destinations (e.g. other resorts).

It is also recognized that there are some gaps in Whistler's event portfolio (i.e. specific types of events) and event calendar (i.e. times of the year when there are no events). This provides an opportunity for Whistler to attract and develop new events that can potentially fill these gaps and attract new and repeat visitation during key times of the year. Continuing to focus on Whistler's unique and natural attributes and talents as well as the products that Whistler offers will be key to setting the destination apart from its competitors and ensuring that events remain authentic and aligned with its brand, garnering greater community support and tourism appeal.

Marketing is necessary in generating awareness and attendance for events. Based on the vast number of distribution channels managed by Whistler's Community Partners and the in-resort expertise in marketing, promotion and communication, there is a great opportunity to develop an integrated marketing and communications strategy that helps grow Whistler's event image and reaches tourists who may or may not have visited Whistler for its events.

By leveraging each organization's expertise and resources, and streamlining processes, funding and communication, there is an opportunity to create a centralized event model that will not only help grow existing events, but attract, support and develop new events that fit Whistler's needs. Subsequently, by developing and attracting events that showcase Whistler's core products and talents, and promoting events through an integrated marketing program, Whistler has the potential to generate new and repeat business, and sustain a healthy and engaged community.

To ensure there is sufficient support for third party event producers and that Whistler continues to embrace new event opportunities, it is suggested that the Community Partners primarily focus on areas of event production and support that are aligned with their organizational strengths, resources and responsibilities.

- Event operational planning and on-site support (Resort Municipality of Whistler and Tourism Whistler for resort-wide events; Whistler Blackcomb for on-mountain events; and Whistler Arts Council for arts and culture events).
- New event solicitation (Tourism Whistler, in consultation with other Community Partners, for resort-wide events; RMOW and WB for venue-specific events).
- Community arts and culture programming (Whistler Arts Council).
- Event ticketing and package sales support (Tourism Whistler).
- Supplemental marketing and communications support (Tourism Whistler and Whistler Blackcomb).

With the quantity and diversity of Whistler's events that directly or indirectly involve multiple organizations and individuals, it is recommended that the Community Partners form an Events Working Committee comprising Tourism Whistler, the Resort Municipality of Whistler, Whistler Blackcomb, the Whistler Arts Council, the Whistler Chamber of Commerce and other relevant organizations. The purpose of this committee is to meet regularly and communicate upcoming event activities and opportunities in an effort to streamline support, leverage communication and promotional opportunities, and share event resources and best practices.

It is recommended that the Tourism Whistler and the Resort Municipality of Whistler reconfigure their existing event budgets and resources to develop an environment that provides the necessary funds, roles and skills to nurture, solicit and grow events. Tourism Whistler would be accountable for providing marketing, sales (solicitation), communication and research services and expertise, and ultimately driving tourists to Whistler to experience events. The RMOW and other Resort partners would be responsible for supporting events through resort planning, event operational support, in-kind services, venue use and communication through their respective distribution channels. Recognizing that "mega" events have the potential to generate significant media coverage and usually require an investment from the host resort, e.g. World Cups, it is also recommended that Tourism Whistler, the Resort Municipality of Whistler and Whistler Blackcomb designate annual funds to support these one-off events.

The main findings in this document indicate that there is a need to align and focus on the core competencies of the Resort's key stakeholders in order to support a collaborative approach to event tourism. Specifically, the findings support organizations focusing on their main areas of expertise and utilizing their current resources (funding and staff) to develop and support the growth of events in Whistler.

It is also recognized that there are potential synergies in merging the Whistler Arts Council and Maurice Young Millennium Place. These synergies include housing both teams in one location, streamlining arts and culture programming, and creating greater synergies with existing funding from the Resort Municipality of Whistler and other government bodies. This group would adopt arts and culture events that are currently being produced by organizations that do not necessarily have the adequate resources to produce events, e.g. Canada Day Parade.

Fulfilling the recommended vision for event tourism will help guide the strategy and ensure that all of the stakeholders are working collectively in reaching a common goal for the greater good of the Resort. Once some fundamental ground work has been accomplished, e.g. clarifying roles and responsibilities, developing an Event Framework and reconfiguring resources, Whistler will be better positioned to support the growth of event tourism, specifically filling gaps in Whistler's event calendar, animating the Resort year-round, and identifying opportunities to improve and/or develop new venues for larger events.

EVENT MANAGEMENT

Event management is the application of project management to the creation and development of festivals, events and conferences. Event management involves studying the intricacies of the brand, identifying the target audience, devising the event concept, planning the logistics and coordinating the technical aspects before actually executing the modalities of the proposed event. Post-event analysis and ensuring a return on investment have become significant drivers for the event industry.

The recent growth of festivals and events as an industry around the world means that the management can no longer be ad hoc. Events and festivals, such as the Asian Games, have a large impact on their communities and, in some cases, the whole country. The industry now includes events of all sizes from the Olympics down to a breakfast meeting for ten business people. Many industries, charitable organizations, and interest groups will hold events of some size in order to market themselves, build business relationships, raise money or celebrate.

Marketing Tool

Event management is considered one of the strategic marketing and communication tools by companies of all sizes. From product launches to press conferences, companies create promotional events to help them communicate with clients and potential clients. They might target their audience by using the news media, hoping to generate media coverage which will reach thousands or millions of people. They can also invite their audience to their events and reach them at the actual event.

Services

Event management companies and organizations service a variety of areas including corporate events (product launches, press conferences, corporate meetings and conferences), marketing programs (road shows, grand opening events), and special corporate hospitality events like concerts, award ceremonies, film premieres, launch/release parties, fashion shows, commercial events, private (personal) events such as weddings and bar mitzvahs.

Clients hire event management companies to handle a specific scope of services for the given event, which at its maximum may include all creative, technical and logistical elements of the event. (Or just a subset of these, depending on the client's needs, expertise and budget).

Event Manager

The event manager is the person who plans and executes the event. Event managers and their teams are often behind-the-scenes running the event. Event managers may also be involved in more than just the planning and execution of the event, but also brand building, marketing and communication strategy. The event manager is an expert at the creative, technical and logistical elements that help an event succeed. This includes event design, audio-visual production, scriptwriting, logistics, budgeting, negotiation and, of course, client service. It is a multi-dimensional profession.

The event manager may become involved at the early initiation stages of the event. If the event manager has budget responsibilities at this early stage they may be termed an event or production executive. The early stages include:

- Site surveying
- Client Service
- Brief clarification
- Budget drafting
- Cash flow management
- Supply chain identification
- Procurement

- Scheduling
- Site design
- Technical design
- Health & Safety

An event manager who becomes involved closer to the event will often have a more limited brief. The key disciplines closer to the event are:

- Health & Safety including crowd management,
- Logistics
- Rigging
- Sound
- Light
- Video
- Detailed scheduling
- Security

AS AN INDUSTRY

Event Management is a multi-million dollar industry, growing rapidly, with mega shows and events hosted regularly. Surprisingly, there is no formalized research conducted to assess the growth of this industry. The industry includes fields such as the MICE (Meetings, Incentives, Conventions and Exhibitions), conferences and seminars as well as live music and sporting events.

The logistics side of the industry is paid less than the sales/ sponsorship side, though some may say that these are two different industries.

Technology

Event management software companies provide event planners with software tools to handle many common activities such as delegate registration, hotel booking, travel booking or allocation of exhibition floorspace.

Education

There are an increasing number of universities which offer courses in event management, including diplomas and graduate degrees. In addition to these academic courses, there are many associations and societies that provide courses on the various aspects of the industry. Study includes organizational skills, technical knowledge, P.R., marketing, advertising, catering, logistics, decor, glamor identity, human relations, study of law and licenses, risk management, budgeting, study of allied industries like television, other media and several other areas. Certification can be acquired from various sources to obtain designations such as Certified Trade Show Marketer (CTSM), Certified Manager of Exhibits (CME), Certified in Exhibition Management (CEM), Global Certification in Meeting Management (CMM) and Certified Meeting Professional (CMP).

Career opportunities are in the following Industries :

1. Event Management
2. Event Management Consultancy
3. Hotel, travel and hospitality Industries
4. Advertising Agencies
5. Public Relations Firms
6. Corporations
7. News Media
8. Non-profit organization
9. Integrated Marketing & Communications
10. Event Budgeting and Accounting

Categories of Events

Events can be classified into four broad categories based on their purpose and objective:

1. Leisure events e.g. leisure sport, music, recreation.
2. Cultural events e.g. ceremonial, religious, art, heritage, and folklore.
3. Personal events e.g. weddings, birthdays, anniversaries.
4. Organizational events e.g. commercial, political, charitable, sales, product launch,expo.

EVENT PLANNING

Event planning is the process of planning a festival, ceremony, competition, party, or convention. Event planning includes budgeting, establishing dates and alternate dates, selecting and reserving the event site, acquiring permits, and coordinating transportation and parking. Event planning also includes some or all of the following, depending on the event: developing a theme or motif for the event, arranging for speakers and alternate speakers, coordinating location support (such as electricity and other utilities), arranging decor, tables, chairs, tents, event support and security, catering, police, fire, portable toilets, parking, signage, emergency plans, health care professionals, and cleanup.

Steps to Planning an Event

The first step to planning an event is determining its purpose, whether it is for a wedding, company, birthday, festival, graduation or any other event requiring extensive planning. From this the event planner needs to choose entertainment, location, guest list, speakers, and content. The location for events is endless, but with event planning they would likely be held at hotels, convention centers, reception halls, or outdoors depending on the event. Once the location is set the coordinator/planner needs to prepare the event with staff, set up the entertainment, and keep contact with the client. After all this is set the event planner has all the smaller details to address like set up of the event such as food, drinks, music, guest list, budget, advertising and marketing, decorations, all this preparation is what is needed for an event to run smoothly. An event planner needs to be able to manage their time wisely for the event, and the length of preparation needed for each event so it is a success.

Event Planning as a Career

Event planning is a relatively new career field. There is now training that helps one trying to break into the career field. There must be training for an event planner to handle all the pressure and work efficiently. This career deals with a lot of communication and organization aspects. There are many different names for an event planner such as a conference coordinator, a convention planner, a special event coordinator, and a meeting manager.

Event planners work is considered either stressful or energizing. This line of work is also considered fast paced and demanding. Planners face deadlines and communicating with multiple people at one time. Planners spend most of their time in offices, but when meeting with clients the work is usually on-site at the location where the event is taking place . Some physical activity is required such as carrying boxes of materials and decorations or supplies needed for the event. Also, long working hours can be a part of the job. The day the event is taking place could start as early as 5:00 a.m. and then work until midnight. Working on weekends is sometimes required, which is when many events take place .

Publications and Resources

Many business-to-business trade publications exist to help event planning and production professionals become educated about the issues and trends in their industry. Many are controlled circulation publications available at no cost to qualified event professionals. Qualification is based on multiple variables like job title, company type, industry segment or geographic region, and is at the publisher's discretion.

TRAVEL & TOURISM : INDIA LINE EVENTS

India Travel Mart-Ahmedabad

30-JAN-09 to 01-FEB-09

TBA, Ahmedabad

India's one of the prominent International Travel & Tourism Mart, India Travel Mart (ITM) brings people together to promote Inbound, Outbound and Domestic Tourism in unique style. ITM offer unlimited opportunities for everyone to Explore, Market and Publicize their destination/ product/ organization at one place.

Organizer

India Travel Mart

Secretariat India Travel Mart (itm), e-46, 3rd Floor, Narain Naraina Vihar

New Delhi, Delhi - 110 028 (India)

Phone: +(91)-(11)-25897594/25897596

Fax: +(91)-(11)-25897597

The International Adventure Tourism Show

30-JAN-09 to 01-FEB-09

Palace Grounds, Bangalore

The International Adventure Tourism Show is the best place to showcase adventure tourism products and services. It will serve as a tremendous business opportunity and will bring awareness to the people on Adventure Tourism in the region.

Organizer:

Amazing Global Journeys

No. 52/25, 71st Cross,17th a Main, 5th Block, Rajajinagar

Bangalore, Karnataka - 560 010 (India)

Phone: +(91)-(80)-23142988

Travel & Tourism Fair-Mumbai

07-FEB-09 to 09-FEB-09

World Trade Centre Mumbai,

Travel & Tourism Fair is India's leading exhibition for the travel & tourism industry. Since 1989,it provides an annual opportunity for organisations from India and abroad to showcase their products and services to a large cross section of the travel trade and consumers across major markets in India.

Organizer

Fairfest Media Limited

E-8 Green Park

New Delhi, - 110 016 (India)

Phone: +(91)-(11)-26866874/26866875

Fax: +(91)-(11)-26868073

Travel & Tourism Fair-Delhi

12-FEB-09 to 14-FEB-09

Hotel Ashok, New Delhi

Travel & Tourism Fair is India's leading exhibition for the travel & tourism industry. Since 1989,it provides an annual opportunity for organisations from India and abroad to showcase their products and services to a large cross section of the travel trade and consumers across major markets in India.

Organizer:

Fairfest Media Limited

E-8 Green Park

New Delhi, - 110 016 (India)

Phone: +(91)-(11)-26866874/26866875

Fax: +(91)-(11)-26868073

India Travel Mart-Chandigarh

20-FEB-09 to 22-FEB-09

TBA, Chandigarh

India's one of the prominent International Travel & Tourism Mart, India Travel Mart (ITM) brings people together to promote Inbound, Outbound and Domestic Tourism in unique style. ITM offer unlimited opportunities for everyone to Explore, Market and Publicize their destination/ product/ organization at one place.

Organizer

India Travel Mart

Secretariat India Travel Mart (itm), e-46, 3rd Floor, Narain Naraina Vihar

New Delhi, Delhi - 110 028 (India)

Phone: +(91)-(11)-25897594/25897596

Fax: +(91)-(11)-25897597

India International Travel Mart (IITM Cochin)

20-FEB-09 to 22-FEB-09

TBA, Cochin

India's one of the prominent International Travel & Tourism Mart, India International Travel Mart (IITM) brings people together to promote Inbound, Outbound and Domestic Tourism in unique style. IITM offer unlimited opportunities for everyone to Explore, Market and Publicize their destination/ product/ organization at one place.

Organizer:

Travel Media Networks

473, 2nd Floor, 2nd cross, 9th Main, HAL 2nd Stage, Indira Nagar

Bangalore, Karnataka - 560 0308 (India)

Phone: +(91)-(80)-41152215

Fax: +(91)-(80)-25290708

IAAPI AMUSEMENT EXPO 2009

21-FEB-09 to 23-FEB-09

Bombay Exhibition Centre - NSE Exhibition Complex, Mumbai

Trade Show would be representing to authorities for inclusion of the amusement industry in the tourism sector. The trade show aims at bringing the entire amusement industry under one umbrella.

Organizer:

Indian Association of Amusement Parks & Industries

7, IInd Floor, Radha C. H. S., Telly Gully, Andheri (East)

Mumbai, Maharashtra - 400 069 (India)

Phone: +(91)-(22)-65231643

Fax: +(91)-(22)-26827831

India International Travel Exhibition(IITE-Bhubaneshwar)

28-FEB-09 to 02-MAR-09

TBA, Bhubaneshwar

India International Travel Exhibition (IITE), an exhibition series on Tourism exchange, a platform where the upward moving, high earning Mid level city consumers will interact with your Tourism Board, Travel Partners and Affiliated service providers, thus promoting the beauty and the benefits of your destination. IITE, an annual, travel and tourism exhibition show will be held for the fast growing Net worth consumers of the mid level Indian Cities with respect to their travel and Leisure needs.

Organizer

Global Trade Fairs & Conventions (GTFC)

348, Amar Jyoti

Bangalore, Karnataka - 560 071 (India)

Phone: +(91)-(80)-41483066

Fax: +(91)-(80)-41483066

India Travel Mart- Bhopal

27-MAR-09 to 29-MAR-09

TBA, Bhopal

India's one of the prominent International Travel & Tourism Mart, India Travel Mart (ITM) brings people together to promote Inbound, Outbound and Domestic Tourism in unique style. ITM offer unlimited opportunities for everyone to Explore, Market and Publicize their destination/ product/ organization at one place.

Organizer

India Travel Mart

Secretariat India Travel Mart (itm), e-46, 3rd Floor, Narain Naraina Vihar

New Delhi, Delhi - 110 028 (India)

Phone: +(91)-(11)-25897594/25897596

Fax: +(91)-(11)-25897597

Satte Openworld

24-APR-09 to 26-APR-09

Pragati Maidan, New Delhi

Satte Openworld is the first buyer-seller exchange in the region, the biggest and the best organized travel trade show in India and in South Asia. It has arrived and established itself as a serious business platform for the composite tourism industry. Tourism as a two-way exchange truly took place between India and Nepal, Sri Lanka, Egypt, Malaysia and Kuwait, all of which brought in buyers and sellers.

Organizer:

Cross Section Publications Private Limited

3rd Floor, Rajendra Bhawan 201, Deen dayal Upadhayay

Delhi, - (India)

Phone: +(91)-(11)-3233529/3233588/3233576

Fax: +(91)-(11)-3233569/3233469

CHAPTER–2

EVENTING

Eventing is an equestrian event which comprises dressage, cross-country and show jumping. This event has its roots in a comprehensive cavalry test requiring mastery of several types of riding. It has three main formats: the one-day event (ODE), two-day event and the three-day event (3DE), which in reality now runs four days at some competitions. The sport was once referred to as "Militaire", and there is also a format in which riders complete all three events in one day, called a "horse trial". Also, a "combined test" is a spin-off of eventing which encompasses dressage and show jumping, but leaves out the cross country phase.

The Phases

Eventing is an equestrian triathlon, in that it combines three different disciplines in one competition set out over one day or three days.

Dressage

The dressage phase (held first) comprises an exact sequence of movements ridden in an enclosed arena (20x60m for International 3DE but usually 20x40 for ODE). The test is judged by one or more judges who are looking for balance, rhythm and suppleness and most importantly, obedience of the horse and its harmony with the rider. The challenge is to demonstrate that a supremely fit horse, capable of completing the cross country phase on time, also has the training to perform in a graceful, relaxed and precise manner.

At the highest level of competition, the dressage test is roughly equivalent to the USDF Third Level, and may ask for half-pass at trot, shoulder-in, travers, collected, medium and extended gaits, single flying changes, and counter-canter. The tests may not ask for Grand Prix movements such as piaffe or passage.

Each movement in the test is scored on a scale from 0 to 10, with a score of "10" being the highest possible mark and with the total maximum score for the test varying depending on the level of competition and the number of movements. Therefore, if one movement is poorly executed, it is still possible for the rider to get a good overall score if the remaining movements are very well executed. The marks are added together and any errors of course deducted. To convert this score to penalty points, the average marks of all judges are converted to a percentage of the maximum possible score, multiplied by a co-efficient decided by the governing body and then subtracted from 100.

- Once the bell rings the rider is allowed 45 seconds to enter the ring or is eliminated.
- If all four feet of the horse exit the arena during the test, this results in elimination.
- If the horse resists more than 20 seconds during the test, this results in elimination.
- Errors on course:

  1st Error = minus 2 marks

  2nd Error = minus 4 marks

  3rd Error = elimination

Cross-country

The next phase, cross-country, requires both horse and rider to be in excellent physical shape and to be brave and trusting of each other. This phase consists of approximately 12-20 fences (lower levels), or 30-40 at the higher levels, placed on a long outdoor circuit. These fences consist of very solidly built natural objects (telephone poles, stone walls, etc.) as well as various obstacles such as ponds and streams, ditches, drops and banks, and combinations including several jumping efforts based on objects that would commonly occur in the countryside. Sometimes, particularly at higher levels, fences are designed that would not normally occur in nature. However, these are still designed to be as solid as more natural obstacles. Safety regulations mean that some obstacles are now being built with a "frangible pin system," allowing part or all of the jump to collapse if hit with enough impact. Speed is also a factor, with the rider required to cross the finish line within a certain time frame (optimum time). Crossing the finish line after the optimum time results in penalties for each second over. At lower levels, there is also a speed fault time, incurring penalties for horse and rider pairs completing the course too quickly. Penalties are also incurred if the horse refuses to jump an obstacle or disobeys the rider. Should the horse fall, a mandatory retirement is taken. Should the rider fall off the horse at any point in the competition, compulsory penalties must be added. The penalties for disobediences on cross country are weighted severely relative to the other phases of competition to emphasize the importance of courage, endurance and athleticism. Fitness is required as the time allowed will require a strong canter at the lower levels, all the way to a strong gallop at the higher events.

Horse trials, which may be held over one or two days, have only one phase of cross country. If the trial is held over the course of two days, dressage and show jumping are usually held the first day, with cross country on the second.

In recent years, a controversy has developed between supporters of short and long format three-day events. Traditionally, three day events had dressage, endurance and show jumping. Endurance day consisted of 4 phases, A, B, C and D. Phase A and C were roads and tracks, with A being a medium-paced warm up to prepare the horse and rider for Phase B, a steeplechase format at an extremely fast pace over steeplechase-style fences. Phase C was a slow-paced cool down coming off of Phase B, in preparation for the toughest and most demanding phase, D, or cross-country. Before embarking on Phase D, in the "ten-minute box," horses had to be approved to continue by a vet, who monitored their temperature and heart rate, ensuring that the horse was sound and fit.

Three day events are now offered in the classic format, with endurance day, or short-format, with no steeplechase (phase B)or roads and tracks (phases A & C). The 2004 Olympic Summer Games in Athens, Greece chose the short format, due to lack of facilities, time and financing, which sparked a large debate in the eventing community whether to keep the steeplechase phase or just offer cross-country. Today, most events are run short-format, except for a few one-star competitions.

Due to major injuries at Red Hills and Rolex in 2008, the rules were changed drastically. The change stated that a fall anywhere during the cross-country phase resulted in elimination, even if the rider was galloping on course and not approaching a jump, or in the middle of a combination. Also, a new rule created a $250 fine for riding in jumping phases without a medical arm band carrying information about the rider's medical history, insurance, medications, and blood type.

Scoring

- Refusal, run-out, or circle at an obstacle: 20 penalties
- Second refusal, run-out, circle at the same obstacle: 40 penalties
- Third refusal, run-out, circle on cross-country course: Elimination (E)
- Fall of rider: 60 or 65 penalties
- Fall of horse (shoulder and hind touch the ground): Elimination (E)
- Exceeding Optimum Time: 0.4 penalties per second
- Coming in under Speed Fault Time: 0.4 penalties per second (lower national levels in some countries only)

- Exceeding the Time Limit (twice the optimum time): Elimination (E)

Other Faults

- Competing with improper saddlery: Elimination (E)
- Jumping without headgear or a properly fastened harness: Elimination (E)
- Error of course not rectified: Elimination (E)
- Omission of obstacle: Elimination (E)
- Jumping an obstacle in the wrong order: Elimination (E)
- Jumping an obstacle in the wrong direction: Elimination (E)
- Retaking an obstacle already jumped: Elimination (E)
- Dangerous riding, at determination of the Ground Jury: Elimination (usually with a warning before elimination) (E)
- Failure to wear medical armband: Elimination (at discretion of Ground Jury) (E)

TYPES OF OBSTACLES

Combinations: A combination is always considered one obstacle, and the various elements within the combination are lettered "A", "B", "C" and so on. In Cross-country, the rider need only retake the element they refused rather than the whole complex. So a refusal at element B does not require them to jump A again. However, they have the option of retaking the previous elements if they wish. For example, in a bounce type obstacle it may be physically impossible to approach B without first clearing A. Yet for some in and outs, you can go to B and not have to rejump A.

Many cross-country obstacles have several possible routes to take (for example, at obstacle 5 there may be two A, two B, and two C elements), with one route usually being faster but requiring a more skillful ride or more physical effort from the horse. A rider may take any of the possible routes as long as they pass over each letter once. Additionally, after a refusal, they may jump a different obstacle in its place, as long as it is the same letter. For example, if a refusal occurs at B, the rider may jump an alternative obstacle that is marked B to help avoid a second refusal, but may not jump a second A element in place of the B element.

A refusal at A is a first refusal, and would receive 20 penalties. Whether the rider retakes A or not, a subsequent refusal at B is a second refusal and so on. Three refusals at any one obstacle results in elimination, as does 4 refusals on the entire course.

Veterinary inspection, or "Trot Up"/"Horse Inspection"

Before the beginning of a three-day event, and also before the last phase, horses are inspected by a vet to ensure that they are fit to compete further. It is usually a very formal affair, with well-groomed and braided horses, and nicely dressed riders. It is also a very nerve-racking time, as the "pass" or "fail" determines whether the horse may continue with the competition. A vet can request that a horse is sent to the holding box, when it will then be re-assessed before being allowed to continue.

In lower levels of competition the horse's movement may be analyzed as they finish the cross-country, where they will be asked to trot briefly after crossing the finishing line to satisfy the vet of their soundness.

Show Jumping

Show jumping tests the technical jumping skills of the horse and rider, including suppleness, obedience, fitness and athleticism. In this phase, 12-20 fences are set up in a ring. These fences are typically brightly colored and consist of elements that can be knocked down, unlike cross country obstacles. This phase is also timed, with penalties being given for every second over the required time. In addition to normal jumping skills, eventing show jumping tests the fitness and stamina of the horse and rider, generally being held after the cross-country phase in higher level and international events.

Scoring

- Knocking down an obstacle: 4 penalties
- First Disobedience (refusal, run-out, circle, moving backwards): 4 penalties
- Second Disobedience in the whole round: Elimination (New Rule for 2007)
- First Fall of rider: Elimination
- Fall of horse: Elimination
- Exceeding the time allowed: 1 penalty per second
- Jumping an obstacle in the wrong order: Elimination
- Error of course not rectified: Elimination

An obstacle is defined as having been knocked down if any part of it is lowered. It is therefore possible to knock out a pole below the top pole and receive no penalties.

The winner is the horse and rider with the fewest penalties. Awards are usually presented while mounted, before the placed riders take a lap of honor around the arena.

The Olympic Beginning

Eventing competition that resembles the current three-day were first held in 1902, at the Championnat du Cheval d'Armes in France, but were not introduced into the Olympic Games until 1912. Dressage originally demonstrated the horse's ability to perform on the parade ground, where elegance and obedience were key. Cross-country began as a test of stamina, courage, and bravery over difficult terrain, important for a charger on long marches or if the horse was asked to carry a dispatch across country. The stadium jumping phase sought to prove the horse's continuing soundness and fitness after the difficult cross-country day.

The Olympic eventing competition was originally open only to male military officers in active duty, mounted only on military charges. In 1924, the event was open to male civilians, although non-commissioned Army officers could not participate in the Olympics until 1956. Women were first allowed to take part in 1964; equestrian sports are one of the few Olympic sports in which men and women compete against one another.

Format

The original format, used in the 1912 Olympics, was spread over several days:

- Day 1: Endurance Test - 55 km (33 miles) of roads and tracks (with a time allowed of 4 hours, giving a speed of approx. 230 meters per minute) immediately followed by 5 km of a flagged cross-country course at a speed of 333 meters per minute. Time penalties were given for exceeding the time allowed, but no bonus points were given for being fast.
- Day 2: Rest Day
- Day 3: Steeplechase test of 3.5 km with 10 plain obstacles, at a speed of 600 mpm, with time penalties but no time bonus points
- Day 4: Jumping Test ("Prize Jumping"), which was considered easy by most of the spectators
- Day 5: Dressage Test ("Prize Riding")

The Paris Games in 1924 introduced a format very similar to the one of today: with Day 1 Dressage, Day 2 the Endurance Test, and Day 3 the Jumping Test. The Endurance Test has changed the most since that time. Originally, bonus points could be earned for a fast ride cross-country (less than the optimum time). This helped competitors make up for a poor dressage ride, with a clean, fast cross-country ride. This system, however, was dropped in 1971. The format for the endurance test occurred as below:

- Phase A: Short roads and tracks (with five penalties per 5 seconds over time)

- Phase B: Steeplechase, decreased in speed from 600 mpm to 550 mpm (with 10 penalties added per 5 seconds over the time, 3 bonus points per 5 seconds under time)
- Phase C: Long roads and tracks (with 5 penalties per 5 seconds over time)
- Compulsory Halt (now the 10-minute halt)
- Phase D: Cross-country (with 10 penalties added per 5 seconds over the time, 3 bonus points per 10 seconds under time)
- Phase E: 1¼ mile run on the flat (with 5 penalties per 5 seconds over time).

In 1963, the 10-minute halt was introduced, to occur after the completion of phases A, B, and C. It took place in a marked out area (the 10-minute box), where the horse was checked by two judges and one veterinary official who would make sure the horse was fit to continue onto phase D. If the horse was unfit, the panel would pull it from the competition.

The format of the sport underwent major changes in 2004 and 2005, with the creation of the "short" or "modified format," which excluded phases A, B, and C from endurance day. The primary reason for excluding these phases was that the Olympic Committee was considering dropping the sport of eventing from the Olympics because of the cost and large area required for the speed and endurance phase with a steeplechase course and several miles of roads-and-tracks. To prevent the elimination of the sport from the Olympics program, the "short format" was developed by the FEI. The last Olympic Games that included the long, or "classic", three-day format was the 2000 Summer Games in Sydney, while Rolex Kentucky, the Badminton Horse Trials, and Burghley Horse Trials ran their last long format three-day in 2005. The short format is now the standard for international competition, such as the Olympics and World Equestrian Games.

The change in format has brought about controversy. Some riders support the continuation of the classic format, believing it is the "true test of horse and rider". Others believe the classic format is superior because it teaches horsemanship, due to the extra preparation needed to condition the horse and the care required after the several miles of endurance day. However, some upper-level riders claim to prefer the short format, as they believe it saves wear-and-tear on their horses and allows the horse not only to compete in more three-day events each season, but decreases the chance of injury to the horse. However, this claim has not held true in several recent studies that compared injuries sustained in classic and in short format competitions over equivalent courses. Further, some research indicates that horses are more stressed by the short format than by the careful warm-up inherent in the classic format. Regardless, many upper-level riders prepare their horses for the short format using the same conditioning and training as for the long format. The short format has also been widely urged by breeders of heavier, warmblood-type horses. The long format has remained popular at the Preliminary, or one star, level in the United States, and with riders who feel it maximizes horsemanship.

PENALTY POINT SYSTEM

In 1971, the penalty point system was first introduced into eventing. This system converts the dressage score and all jump penalties on cross-country and show jumping into penalty points, with the horse and rider with the fewest number of points winning the event. Different weight is given for each phase, with the cross-country — the heart of eventing — being the most important, followed by the dressage, and then the show jumping. The intended ratio of cross-country:dressage:show jumping is theoretically 12:3:1. Therefore, an error in cross-country counts heavily. This prevents horses that are simply good in dressage (for example) from winning the event with a poor cross-country test.

In 1971, the following penalty system was instituted:

- Phase A and C: 1 penalty per second over the optimum time
- Phase B: 0.8 penalties per second over
- Phase D: 0.4 penalties per second over

In 1977, the dressage scoring was changed, with each movement marked out of ten rather than out of six. This increased the maximum number of dressage marks from 144 to 240. This number later increased to 250 marks in 1998, after additional movements were added. To keep the correct weight, a formula is used to convert good marks in dressage to penalty points. First, the marks of the judges (if there is more than one) are averaged. Then the raw mark is subtracted from the maximum points possible. This number is then multiplied by 0.6 to calculate the final penalty score.

Show jumping rules were also changed in 1977, with a knock-down or a foot in the water awarded only 5 penalties rather than ten. This prevented the show jumping phase from carrying too much weight, again, to keep the ratio between the phases correct.

Non-Olympic Competition

In its early days, the sport was most popular in Britain, and the British gave the competition a new name, the "Three-Day Event," due to the three day time span of the competition. In America, the sport was also called "combined training," due to the three different disciplines and types of training methods needed for the horse. In the United Kingdom, "combined training" competition includes only the dressage and show jumping phases.

The first annual, Olympic-level event developed was the Badminton Horse Trials, held each year in England. First held in 1949, the Badminton event was created after a poor performance by the British Eventing Team at the 1948 Olympic Games, with the purpose of being a high-class preparation event, and as extra exposure for the military horses, who very rarely had the chance to compete. Initially, only British riders were allowed to compete (although women were allowed, despite being banned from riding in the Olympics), but the competition is now an international open. That is, open to all riders from around the world who have qualified for this level of competition. Badminton is the most prestigious events to win in the world. Currently, the Olympic event is consider a CCI, a rank lower than Badminton which is a CCI.

The second three-day competition to be held at Olympic level each year was the Burghley Horse Trials, first held in 1961. Burghley is the longest running international event.

The first CCI held outside of Britain on an annual basis is the Rolex Kentucky Three Day, held each year in Lexington since 1978.

Importance of Dressage Training

In the early years, the dressage phase was fairly inconsequential in determining the final standings. It was quite possible for a horse to have a terrible dressage test, then run a clean cross-country and show jumping, and still finish near the top of the standings. Since then, correct dressage training has become increasingly important should a horse and rider wish to be placed (complete all sections, and finish in the top 12). This can be traced back to Sheila Willcox who took a particular interest in dressage, becoming abundantly clear when she won Badminton three years running in the 1950s. She had a strong influence on Mary King and Lucinda Green amongst others.

After the 2000 Olympic Games, the FEI hired British eventer and dressage rider Christopher Bartle to write new dressage tests for the upper level events, which would include a greater deal of collection. This has since raised the standard even further in the dressage phase.

Additionally, the cross-country phase has become more technical, asking the horse to be adjustable and supple through combinations. A horse can no longer just be brave and athletic, but must have a good deal of dressage training should his rider wish to successfully negotiate odd distances or bending lines at a gallop. Also, in show jumping, a horse is asked to move with impulsion and engagement; this makes the jump more fluent, the horse to bascule more correctly and is less jarring for both horse and rider.

Safety

Between 1997 and December 2008, at least 37 eventing riders died as a result of injuries incurred while competing in the cross-country phase of eventing at national or international level or at Pony Club, and of these, 18 riders died in the period 2006-2008. These 37 fatal falls have been at all levels of the sport, from domestic one-day events up to regional championships level, and they have occurred in most of the recognized eventing countries around the world, with concentrations in the United Kingdom (14) and the United States (8). At least 25 of these 37 deaths have resulted from a somersaulting (rotational) fall of the horse, with 11 of the 16 deaths in 2007 and 2008 being reported as having resulted from a rotational horse fall.

Information about horse fatalities is difficult to locate, but at least 19 eventing horses, many of them top-level performers, died in 2007 & 2008, most of them in the US.

Over time, course design has become increasingly more focused on the safety of the horse and rider. Fences are built more solidly than in the earlier days, encouraging a bold jump from the horse, which actually helps prevent falls. The layout of the course and the build of the obstacles encourage the horse to have a successful run. This includes a greater use of precision fences, such as corners and "skinny jumps," that are very good tests of the rider's ability and the horse's training, but allow the horse to simply run around the jump if the rider misjudges it. Safety measures such as filling in the area between corner-shaped jumps on cross-country or rails of a fence help prevent the entrapment of the legs of the horse decrease the number of serious falls or injuries.

The newest improvement in cross-country safety is the frangible fence, which uses a pin and other techniques which allow the fence to "break or fall" in a controlled manner to minimize the risk of injury to horse and rider. This can help to prevent the most dangerous situation on cross-country, when the horse hits a solid fence between the forearm and chest, and somersaults over, sometimes falling on the rider. This type of fall has caused the death of several riders, as well as horses.

Leg protection for horses has also improved. Very little was used in the early days, even on cross-country. However, leg protection is now seen on nearly every horse at all levels. Boots have increased in technology, and include materials that either help absorb shock or are very hard and strong to prevent a serious injury.

Rules protecting riders have improved as well. Riders are now required to wear a safety vest (body protector) during cross-country, as well as an ASTM/SEI or ISO approved equestrian helmet equipped with a retention harness, which must be fastened while on the horse. Eventing was one of the first sports to require the use of a helmet with harness when jumping. As of 2010, more riders were wearing air bag vests, which automatically inflate if a rider falls off the horse.

Despite these measures, eventing remains a very dangerous sport, in which horse and rider fatalities do occur occasionally.

The Weight Rule

From the beginning, event horses had to carry a minimum weight of 165 lb (75 kg) (including rider and saddle) during the endurance test, since military horses were expected to be able to carry such weight. Lead weights were carried on the saddle, and the competitor had to be weighed-in with tack immediately following cross-country. The weight was reduced to 154 lb (70 kg) for the 1996 Olympic Games, after a study demonstrated that both the horse's arc over a fence became shallower and the leading leg took a great deal of extra force on landing when the horse was carrying dead weight than when free from the burden. The rule was eventually abolished January 1, 1998. By removing this rule, the stress on the joints and soft-tissue, as well as the chance of a fall, were decreased.

International Competition

International events have specific categories and levels of competition and are conducted under the rules of the FEI. CCI (Concours Complet International, or International Complete Contest) is one such category and defines a three-day event that is open to competitors from any foreign nation as well as the host nation.

- CCI : International Three-day event (Concours Complet International)
- CIC: International One-day event (Concours International Combiné)
- CCIO: International Team Competitions (Concours Complet International Officiel). Includes the Olympics, the World Championships, the Pan Am Games, and other continental championships

The levels of international events are identified by the number of stars next to the category; there are four levels in total. A CCI is for horses that are just being introduced to international competition. A CCI is geared for horses that have some experience of international competition. CCI is the advanced level of competition.

The very highest level of competition is the CCI, and with only six such competitions in the world (Badminton, Burghley, Rolex Kentucky, Adelaide, Luhmuhlen Horse Trials, and the Stars of Pau) it is the ultimate aim of many riders. The World Championships are also considered CCI. Rolex offer a financial prize for any rider who can win three of the biggest competitions in succession. These are Badminton, Burghley and Kentucky. So far, Pippa Funnell is the only rider to do this. Andrew Hoy did come close, however, and in 2010 Oliver Townsend was competing for this coveted "Grand Slam" at Rolex Kentucky when he suffered a fall at obstacle #20 which eliminated him from competition.

One, two and three-star competitions are roughly comparable to the Novice, Intermediate and Advanced levels of British domestic competition, respectively, and to the Preliminary, Intermediate, and Advanced levels of American domestic competition, respectively.

Domestic Competition

Eventing rules and the recognized levels in various nations are similar, but not always identical. While rules usually follow the FEI to some degree, history and tradition of various nations has also influenced competition rules within a given country.

In addition to recognized events that prepare the best riders for international competition, many nations also offer eventing for beginner, youth, and amateur riders through organizations such as Pony Club, 4-H or other riding clubs, where most riders begin their competitive careers. At the most elementary levels, fence heights begin at around 18 inches to 2 ft (0.61 m).

USA

In the United States, Eventing is broken down into the following levels, all of which are recognized by the USEA and are run in accordance to their rules:

- Beginner Novice: X-C fences: 2 ft 7 in (0.79 m), 14-18 efforts XC, ditch 4 ft (1.2 m), drops 3 ft 3 in (0.99 m), 300–350 m/min (meters per minute) on cross country; Stadium fences: 2 ft 7 in (0.79 m), 9-11 efforts.
- Novice: X-C fences 2 ft 11 in (0.89 m), 16-20 efforts, ditch 6 ft 7 in (2.01 m), drops 3 ft 11 in (1.19 m), 350 to 400 m/min; Stadium fences 2 ft 11 in (0.89 m), 9-11 efforts.
- Training: X-C fences 3 ft 3 in (0.99 m), 20-24 efforts, ditch 7 ft 11 in (2.41 m), drops 4 ft 7 in (1.40 m), 420 to 470 m/min; Stadium fences 3 ft 3 in (0.99 m), 10-12 efforts.
- Preliminary: X-C fences 3 ft 7 in (1.09 m), 24-28 efforts, ditch 9 ft 2 in (2.79 m), drops 5 ft 3 in (1.60 m), 520 m/min; Stadium fences 3 ft 7 in (1.09 m), 11-13 efforts.

- Intermediate: X-C fences 3 ft 9 in (1.14 m), 28-32 efforts, ditch 10 ft 6 in (3.20 m), drops 5 ft 11 in (1.80 m), 550 m/min; Stadium fences 3 ft 11 in (1.19 m), 12-14 efforts.
- Advanced: X-C fences 3 ft 11 in (1.19 m), 32-40 efforts, ditch 11 ft 10 in (3.61 m), drops 6 ft 7 in (2.01 m), 570 m/min; Stadium fences 4 ft 1 in (1.24 m), 13-15 efforts.

UK

British Eventing (BE) levels of eventing are as follows:

- BE90 (formerly Introductory): maximum fence height 0.90 m
- BE100 (formerly Pre-Novice): max fence height 1.00 m
- Novice (comparable to the USEA's Preliminary level): max fence height 1.10 m XC, 1.15 m SJ
- Intermediate Novice: max fence height 1.10 XC; 1.20 m SJ
- Intermediate: max fence height 1.15 m XC; 1.25 m SJ
- Advanced Intermediate: max fence height 1.15 m XC; 1.30 SJ
- Advanced: max fence height 1.20 m XC; 1.30 m SJ

Australia

In Australia, where the Equestrian Australia governs eventing competition the levels are as follows:

- Introductory: XC: fences maximum height 0.80 m ditch 1.40 m drops 1.0 m 400 m/min; Stadium fences: 0.8 m
- Preliminary: XC: fences maximum height 0.95 m ditch 2.00 m drops 1.2 m 450 m/min; Stadium fences: 0.95 m
- Pre Novice: XC: fences maximum height 1.05 m ditch 2.40 m drops 1.4, 500 m/min; Stadium fences: 1.05 m
- 1 Star: XC: fences maximum height 1.10 m ditch 2.80 m drops 1.6 m 520 m/min; Stadium fences: 1.15 m
- 2 Star: XC: fences maximum height 1.15 m ditch 3.20 m drops 1.8 m 550 m/min; Stadium fences: 1.20 m

- 3 Star: XC: fences maximum height 1.20 m ditch 3.60 m drops 2.0 m 570 m/min; Stadium fences: 1.25 m.

Ireland

The Irish levels, governed by Eventing Ireland are as follows:

- Intro: X-C - max height with spread 0.90 m, max spread at highest point 1.00 m, max spread at base 1.50 m, max spread without height 1.20 m, max spread over water 2.0 m, max drop 1.20 m. Stadium - 0.90 m.
- Pre-Novice Training CNCP: X-C - max height with spread 1.10 m, max spread at highest point 1.40 m, max spread at base 2.10 m, max spread without height 2.80 m, max spread over water 3.05 m, max drop 1.60 m . Stadium - 1.00 m.
- CNC CNCP:X-C - max height with spread 1.10 m, max spread at highest point 1.40 m, max spread at base 2.10 m, max spread without height 2.80 m, max spread over water 3.05 m, max drop 1.60 m . Stadium - 1.10 m.
- CNC: X-C - max height with spread 1.15 m, max spread at highest point 1.60 m, max spread at base 2.40 m, max spread without height 3.20 m, max spread over water 3.65 m, max drop 1.8 m . Stadium - 1.20 m.
- CNC: X-C - max height with spread 1.20 m, max spread at highest point 1.80 m, max spread at base 2.70 m, max spread without height 3.60 m, max spread over water 4.0 m, max drop 2.0 m . Stadium - 1.25 m.

Canada

The Canadian levels, under the rules of Canadian Eventing, are as follows:

- Entry (equatable to USEA Beginner Novice)
- Pre-Training (equatable to USEA Novice): XC: fences maximum height 0.91 m ditch 1.50 m drops 1.10 m; Stadium fences: 0.96 m

- Training: XC: fences maximum height 1.00 m ditch 1.80 m drops 1.40 m; Stadium fences: 1.05 m.
- Preliminary: XC: fences maximum height 1.10 m ditch 2.80 m drops 1.60 m; Stadium fences: 1.15 m.
- Intermediate: XC: fences maximum height 1.15 m ditch 3.20 m drops 1.80 m; Stadium fences: 1.20 m.
- Advanced: XC: fences maximum height 1.20 m ditch 3.60 m drops 2.00 m; Stadium fences: 1.25 m.

The Horse

In the lower levels, it is possible for any breed of horse, if it has the talent for it, to do well in eventing. Thoroughbreds and part-thoroughbreds currently dominate the sport at the top levels because of their stamina and athletic ability, although many warmbloods and warmblood-thoroughbred crosses also do well. In the UK, Irish sport horses have been popular for many years.

Because larger horses are favored, animals with some draft horse breeding are also seen, notably the Irish Draught and Clydesdale crossbreds. However, smaller horses can also excel; for example, in the 2007 Rolex Kentucky Three Day CCI competition, the third place competitor was a 14.1 hand gelding that was a cross of Thoroughbred, Arabian and Shetland pony breeding.

An event horse must be very responsive to succeed, as a horse that will not listen to a rider on the cross-country phase may end up taking a fall at a jump. The horse should be calm and submissive for the dressage phase, with good training on the flat. For cross-country, the horse must be brave, athletic, and (especially at the higher levels) fast with a good galloping stride and great stamina. The horse does not have to possess perfect jumping form, but should be safe over fences and have good scope. The best event horses are careful over jumps, as those who are not tend to have stadium rails knocked down on the last day. The horse also needs to have sound conformation and good feet.

Riding Attire

Riding attire is different for the three phases. Dressage and show jumping require very conservative attire, following the traditional turnout for each of those disciplines. Cross-country is much less formal, with many riders wearing clothing of personalized colors and the emphasis very much on safety equipment.

Dressage

For the intermediate and advanced levels, dressage attire is similar to that of Grand Prix Dressage. The rider must wear a dark coat (usually black or navy blue), with a shirt, stock tie, and pin. If the rider is riding at FEI level, only then can they wear a shadbelly tailcoat and a top hat. Riding breeches are usually white, although any light colour is permitted.

Gloves are usually white, although other colors are permitted. Spurs of certain lengths and types are required. Riding boots such as field or dress tall boots are usually black, in normal or patent leather.

The lower levels have less restrictive rules on dress. Though navy and black coats are preferred, riders may wear any conservatively colored dark or tweed hunting coat (shadbelly/tail coats are not permitted) with a white shirt and choker or, preferably, stock tie with pin. If a rider wishes to stay within normal requirements for higher-level competition, breeches should be white, but beige or another conservative light color is permissible. A black or navy hunt cap or derby hat may be worn, although many riders use an equestrian helmet, which are considered safer. Boots may be field or dress style, black or brown in color. Gloves and spurs give a polished and professional appearance, but are not required at this level.

Cross-country

The rider is required to wear a protective vest, as well as a ASTM/SEI/BS approved equestrian helmet, properly fastened at all times when jumping (and may be eliminated if this is not done). A medical armband, containing the rider's medicinal history, is required. This is for safety purposes, allowing access to the information should the rider fall, be knocked unconscious, and require medical treatment.

Breeches may be any color, with some riders coordinating it with their shirt or vest color. All shirts must have long sleeves, and light-weight rugby or polo shirts are the most commonly worn type, usually without a stock or tie. Black and/or brown boots may be worn. Riding coats are not worn. This is the event where riders may choose anything from traditional hunter green or navy blue to tie-dye and even zebra stripes or fluorescent colors.

Lastly, many riders also wear a stop-watch to track their time as they go cross-country so that they may adjust their speed as needed to come in as close as possible to the optimum time, if not faster. However, in the UK this is only permitted at Novice level or above.

Show Jumping

Show jumping attire is similar to that of dressage. However, a protective equestrian helmet with harness is required, and riders always wear a short hunt coat, except when weather is unreasonably warm, when, at the discretion of the technical delegate, jackets may be considered optional. If helmet covers are used, they are required to be black or dark blue though some now include national colors where they are entitled to be worn.

As in cross-country, riders wear a medical armband.

Event horses are turned out similarly to dressage horses, with the legs and face (muzzle, jaw, sides of ears, bridle path) neatly clipped. The tail is usually "banged" (cut straight across), usually to a length between the fetlock joint and lower hock. Additionally, most event riders clip the sides of their mount's tails, to give them a finer appearance. The braiding of tails is fairly uncommon, probably because the tail can not be braided if the hairs along the sides of the dock are clipped.

The mane is pulled to about 4 inches in length and is usually braided for dressage as well as the show jumping phase. However, most riders prefer to leave it loose for cross-country in case they need to grab it for security. Some riders also place quarter marks (decorative stenciling) on the hindquarters, although it is not particularly common as of 2007.

Tack

Most event riders have a jumping saddle as well as a dressage saddle, since each places them in a position better-suited for its purpose. At the lower levels, however, a rider can ride all three phases without difficulty in a well-fitted jumping saddle. At the upper levels, riders usually have a saddle specifically designed for cross-country, giving them more freedom for such fences as banks and drops.

Dressage tack is usually black in color, with a white square pad, giving a formal look. Except for the upper levels, where a double bridle is permitted, horses may only be ridden in snaffle bits. There are strict guidelines as to what type of snaffle may be used, and the more severe types (such as any twisted bit) are prohibited. If a double bridle is used, a plain cavesson or crank noseband must be worn. With a snaffle bridle, the rider is also free to use the drop, flash, or figure-eight noseband, with the flash and plain cavesson being the most common. Breastplates are also fairly common in dressage at an event, despite the fact that they are not seen at regular dressage shows. Other forms of equipment, such as martingales, protective boots, gadgets/training devices, bit guards, polo wraps, or tail wraps are not allowed during the test.

In show jumping, the rider uses a jumping saddle, usually with a square or fitted white pad. Rules on tack are less-stringent, and most forms of bridling and bitting are allowed, including the use of gag bits, hackamores, and any type of noseband. Breastplates and protective boots are usually worn. Running martingales are also allowed, but must be used with rein stops. Standing and Irish martingales are not allowed.

For the cross-country phase, the rider usually uses similar tack as for the show jumping. However, protective boots are taped for extra security, to help prevent them from slipping as the horse jumps into water. Most horses that wear shoes are also fitted with horse shoe studs, to prevent slipping. At the upper levels, riders may also apply a grease or lard to the front of the horse's legs, to help the horse slide over fences if they hang a leg. Riders also tend to color-coordinate their cross-country tack to their colors. For example, using the same color saddle pad and tape for their boots, to match their shirt and protective vest.

CHAPTER–3

POTENTIAL OF EVENTS TOURISM

A destination is a town, city or a place which has one or more attractions for tourists. These attractions may be in the form of scenic sights, culture, leisure activities, shopping rebates, food, and excursion. Those attractions are used to accruing revenues from tourists. A tourist has some pre conceived notions about a destination which he might have heard from his surroundings sources like ads, internet and word of mouth from a frien d or family member or may be read in a travel book. A destination image can be positive or negative and is considered an important part of the decision making process of consumers when they consider their destination alternatives. As many of the researcher has explained destination image as is an important determinant (Ritchie, J. and Couch, G. 2000) and also plays an important role in destination selection process (Gunn 1972, LaPage and Cormier, 1977).

In the context of the previously discussed point that there are certain attributes to attract tourists to a destination, EVENTS are the emerging sign of success in the list of these attractions. Events can be defined as a package carried out with a perceived concept, and then customized or modified to achieving the aim of organizing that event. In the new millennium the targeted tou rists are attracted. The key elements of an event can be considered as venue, target audience, media, and event infrastructure.

Venue

Target

Audience

Event

Media

Infrastructure

The above diagram shows how an event involves different attributes with one action. Here venue and infra-structure are directly related to the DESTINATION where an event takes place. Events are capable of delivering:

(1) Key messages about destination.

(2) Community's p ositive image to the world

With growing technologies and advertising scenario, events also include media coverage. This is how the event and destination are two different entities but yet serving each other in a manner. Destination gets a vide media coverage as well as advertising. The participants of the events and the attendees of events visit the destination to take part in the event which bring s lots of fo reign currency to the particu lar destination to entire nation of the event is huge.

Thus an event can be a most powerful way to attract tourists to the destination. The events may be in the form of MICE (meetings, incentives, convections and exhibitions), sporting event, and cultural event or may be award functions like Oscar etc. This is how word Event tourism came into being. Although it is a newer concept but is now widely recognized, having a potential significant contribution to local economies.

In simple terms, an event acts as an attraction for people from outside the local community to visit the location and spend money on accommodation, food and leisure activities at the destination. Events also help to build an image into the minds of tourists who have never visited the place definitely grabs their attention to the destination through media coverage. The tourists have several options and the first thing comes in the mind is the brand names which emerges out of the level of satisfaction.

Key Issues

The goal of this conceptual paper is to enlighten the new horizons of tourism by concept of events tourism. This paper will mainly concentrate on benefits of hosting events:

- Events tourism is useful to attract tourists whether a first time visitor or a repeater.
- How an event an d destination are co -brands.
- To show positive effects of events on a destination

The anticipated outcomes of this paper are showcasing:

- understanding events portfolio.
- growing magnitude of hosting an event in tourism at a destination.
- positive effects of co -branding by image transfer.
- strategies to host an event.

However there are arguments about the image and brand perceptions. Some argue that destination branding is intensely associated with destination image. According to others, image is very different from branding; yet th e brand is created through the image.

Brand vs. Image

Image and Brand are interrelated attributes. Image plays a vital role to develop brand identity and brand is said to have certain images and believes in the mind sets of tourists (Jenson and Kotler). In tourist destination context, there are several different d efinitions of image. Hu nt61 defined country image as people's impressions of countries that they do not reside in. Millman and Pizam62 calls image as the sum of tourism experience-related attributes.

Image Transfer Between Events and Destination:

The image transfer is considered when any benefit that tourist recognise in events becomes benefit for host destination (Meyvis, Janiszewski 2004; Supphellen, Eismann and L.E. Hem, 2004). The co-branding of two brands namely destination and events is very sensitive in nature. Th ey share image tran sfer (use uni assignment govers). The can be positive image transfer or negative image transfer. Th e mere pairing of events and destination is not important rather it is important that which desitnation is paired with which event. It is essential to explore the ev ents brand relation with the destin ation brand to acqu ire desired results (Kim and C.T. Allen (1996); Van Auken and Adams (1999) The image of both brand whilst event and destination play important role while they are paired together (Kim and Allen(1996); Van Auken and Adams (1999); Koernig and Page (2002); McDaniel (1999); Till and Busler (2000)

The poor match of events and destination may lead to negative brand building and may cause transfer of neg ativ e imag e. But if a destination osses a customized event then it can probably be used as brand extensions. In recent years some vents have been developed which are closely related to their destinations' brnad and are recognised by their hosting destinations as to name some Dubai's duty free shopping festival etc. These events often bear the name of their host d estination's name to be more accosiated with the destination brnad. However the literature on branding suggests that it is not that an event should always pssoes a brnad name. It can contribute to the host destination as a feature to make the destination unique in nature and more popular palce to visit (Meyer and Sathi (1985); Ahang and Markman (2001)). By inreasing the freequency of organisisng events, the drawback of short term impact of events can be nulified.

There are different themes and strategies to use events as effective tools to building a brand destination. (Jago et. al. 2003) There should be community support co-operative planning and media support to make most of organsing at a destination. This transfer image between the two. The favourability towards chosing a destination increases visitation aspect (Liping et. al, 2003). Events bring pleasantness and excitement for travelers to return to the destination in future (Kaplanido u, Kyriaki 2007).

Building Destination Brand

The ideation of destination branding is although a newer concept but any of the resources and industry experts has been interests towards destination brand management. Branding is a major issue in product strategy. There is hardly anything that goes unbranded. A brand is a complex symbol that can convey up to six levels of meaning i.e. attributes, benefits, values, values, personality and user (Jennifer) A destination therefore is product which depends o n brand recognition, p erceived, brand quality, strong mental and emotional associations and other assets Consequently, branding focuses on marketing of a product in terms of degree which increases brand equity. As cited by Maureen Atkinson, an eminent industry agent "A brand is a type of shorthand for a product with city branding, what you try to do is create that sh orthand so that when people think of your city, they automatically think of what is best about it."

Thus, a destination brand not only executes name, logo, reputation or status symbol but also the destination's physical attributes, experien ce, quality of services provided, attractions. While branding a city or a reg ion one needs to identify the attraction s and activities to associate them with the destination to build a brand image. In terms of destination's brand equity if a tourist shows inclination towards one destination than the other, it is considered that the brand acceptability of the brand of higher brand equity is more.

Researches in this field prove that image is a key factor in tourism development. When a tourist plans a holiday it is expected that the tourist will have an initial imag e of the destination that might not be visited or might have already been visited. The destination's image plays a vital role because the level of visitation goes down when the same destination is visited frequently that effects the destination branding. Several methods have been used to identify the relevant dimensions of destination image including multi-dimensional scaling, repertory grid. The brand image closely relates to the branding of a destination as it represents the attractions, cultural and benefits to tourists expectations delivering total custo mer satisfaction. The brand makes use of and co-ordinates a full repertoire of marketing activities to build equity.

Branding strategies can vary depending on what kind of a brand is. A functional brand is that brand which involves functions of product. An image brand that involves celebrity associated with a brand. An experimental brand that involves people and place .The empirical research by many quantitative research exp erts acknowledge that the brand perception of tourists to d estination is three dimensional namely sincerity, excitement and conviviality that there is a positive impact on p erceived destination image.

Therefore a strong brand adds unique features to products or services to impart perceptions of quality and value which cultivates market share and customer loyalty. There are various tools for brand- building public relation, sponsorship clubs and consume communities, trade shows, event marketing etc.

Co-branding: (Event vs. Destination)

Co-branding is an effective way to reinforce or change a brand image (Rao and Ruekert (1994); Simonin and Ruth(1998)). In the view of a destination co-branding, the aim objective is to transfer the desired portion of the other brand to destination features. This will require the tow brands to be jointly advertised and promoted. The pairing of two or more brands in a composite brand should match and is paired in such a way that each one of it is perceived when they are paired.

Out of all the brands an even t can be the most effective one as it involves the study of brand prints, understanding what the brand stands for, its positioning and values, identifying the target audience and liaisons with the creative conceptualization to create an event for a perfect mesh with brands personality.

Event involves 5 c's namely con ceptualization of creative idea and ambience, costing which calculates the margins, canvassing for sponsors, customers and networking components, customization of the event according to brand personality, budgets.

Thus events help in creating awareness about the brand highlighting the added features, image building and associating brand personality to target market. In standpoint of destination branding events deliver destination's culture, attractio ns, quality services provided and a long tem impact to visit the destination again to explore it mo re. Events and Festivals have a significant economic impact (Formica, 1998) Community events are expected to increase the number of tourists and the amount of expenditures. (Murphy and Charmich ael, 1991). They are believed to bring social benefits towards community (Getz 1991: Ritchie, 1984) and last but not th e least they lengthen the life cycle of destination. (Getz and Frisby,1998)

The enhancement of co mmunity and creation of positive images (Gets, 1997: Highmian and Ritchie, 2001:

Jago and Shaw, 1998;) improve destination's image. Several researches verified that image improvement is associated with hosting different events (Jeong an d Fau lkner, 19 96 , Mihalik and Sionett, 1998, Pyo, 1995, Ritchie and smith , 1991 and Wicks, 1995).

The basic technique in co-branding a destination with an event is to identify the associating network of competitive destinations and then hosting an event that can reinforce, change or add desirable associations. (Laurence Chalip and Carla A- Costa,). It is important to spot an appropriate events portfolio for a destination that can foster the process of destination branding. As the effects of co-branding depends on the associate event brand with destination brand .By pairing of event's brand with destination brand, it is expected that the elements of event brand will transfer to destinations brand.

Destination marketers can not ignore the pitfalls of co-branding too. If an event, which is well establish ed brand can hamper the host destination's brand image which can result in a reverse or negative effect. The empirical research by Boo and Busser (Event gt.) proved that tourist images after visit was not impacted positively. Moreover festivals participants' images were not changed favorably when compared those of non- participants' image.

Thus, dissimilarity between the event brand and destination brand would render a poor match and would therefore have a negative consequence for the intended transfer of brand image. But d espite of all these44 destination marketers seek to host events (Bramwell, 1997). The only need is to plan a managed event communications that can render a change in destination image (Chalip 1990; Kim and Morrison 2005).

The main objective is not that the event includes the host destination's name rather how consistency is maintained between concepts and features represented by the destination brand extensions and are accepted favorably (Park, Milberg and Lawson 1991). If such events are received open handed by market, then the brand equity of the destination should increase as a consequence of tourists' enhanced perceptions (Swaminathan, Fox and Reddy, 2001).

The core focus should be consistency with the benefits to destination (Kim, (2003)). As ev ents grow, destination marketers need to bulk them into their marketing strategies and they need to take tactical advantages of events when planning the destination's marketing communications campaign. Every possible precaution should be taken while pairing o f events with th e destination, so th at the strong image of th e event may not hamper the destination image.

Mega events are short term events with long term consequences (Roche, 1994) that attract large numbers of international tourists. On the oth er hand the fact states that mega events have negative impacts like housing evictions. Although, these mega events can increase an artificial or temporary spike of accommodation, transport or hospitality while the preceding ben efits of mega events might be short lived.

Therefore, destination marketers who seek to use events to build their brands must construct a portfolio of events (Jago et al.). A single event with a high profile has only a passing effect on the destination brand (Ritchie and Smith, (1991)) but if tourism authorities want it to be long lasting then it is much beneficial to host smaller events through out the year.

Cultural events featuring music, dance, food, shopping, art or any other cultural activities can be supportive to build up a brand image. The effect of events on a destination's brand depends substantially on the reach and the frequency of event mentions and visuals. An event portfolio should appeal to attract tourists of each age group having different interests in different.

Since an event portfolio delivers a destination's image, on grounds like the attractions, services, accessibility, community festivals and the touring experience. Only those events should be included in portfolio that can successfully reinforce the destination's brand. The elevation of destination's brand is by the impact of effective hosting at the destination.

Event and Destination; A Case Review : Quantitative Study by Xiaoyan Xing and Laurence Chalip :

There are arguments that events can hamper the destinations image if not paired well with destin ation. Here is a case to prove this argument worth no ticing. It is within the discussed context Xiaoyan Xing and Laurence Chalip investigate the interaction of both event and destination attributes on a person's intention to visit the destination. An individual's awareness of a destination made up of the cognitive evaluation of experiences, learning, emotions and perceptions related to the destination's image. An event can be defined as something that happens at a given place and time.

Amongst a variety of alternatives, the authors utilized quantitative methods to conclude that how a destination's rating raises when paired with a suitable event or alternatively how an event's rating slows down when not paired with a suitable destin ation. This article particularly discusses that how an image is transferred or shared by two brands, a destination (i.e. city) and an event. The research also investigates how the image transfer affects the intension to visit the destination.

There is a debate in past researches about destination image and destination brand. According to Asli D. A. Tasci and Metin Kozak in the revised form of March 2006 argue that destination branding is overwhelmingly associated with destination image and also image is very different from branding; yet the latter is created through the former. This matter is untouched in the article. Although the research goes along the hypothesis considered but the study seems to be complicated due to many considerations at one instance. Also the researcher may have included an events portfolio rather than a single event. This might hav e justified th e bias towards sporting events.

METHODS:OVERVIEW

The research stands out in terms of its validity and reliability where in an effort to identify possible mismatches between events and their host communities, a quasi-experimental desig n was utilized. Two cities and two events were identified to the extreme ends of th e active-leisurely continuum. Chicago and a NASCAR motor sport event were selected to represent an active city and an active event respectively. The city of Des Monies and a Masters Golf tournament were represented the leisurely end of the continuum.

The design also provided for a no event and a no city option, meaning that nine sets of conditions were possible, but the cell for no city and no event was omitted from the study. These eight conditions were assigned randomly to the participants. Eight mock advertisements were created. In four of these adv ertisements, the destination was central and in the remaining four, the event was central. This alternation of centrality was an important part of the experimental design because this would identify the image transfer effects. That is to evaluate that to what extend the brands pairing help the two brands to be paired together.

Method: Participants

The 317 participants were undergraduate, social science university students. They aged in range from 18 to 41 years. This selection can be biased as their mind sets are much intellectual than the general public. They see very thin g critically than in a way like a general traveler may not do. The sample here does not seem to be justified. The tourists have different age groups and different interests. They have different interests towards sports. Th e selection of the sample group is clearly based on convenience and future research should seek to overcome this important limitation. This could be achieved by sample that more accurately reflects the diversity in the wider community.

Method: Instruments

Participants were exposed to the mock advertisements and were then invited to proceed to the questionnaire. According to the centeredness of the questionnaire were prepared. The condition where the destination was centered the participants had to rate the destination only and the ads where events were centered they had to rate the destinations also. The ratings were on the image scales identified in earlier phase of study mentioned in previous paragraphs. The study does not show any specific questionnaire which makes it difficult for a reader to understand the question line.

Method: Procedures

The three key constru cts measured in this study were 1) image transfer between events and destination; 2) intentions to visit; and, 3) involvement in sports. Image transfer between events and destination was measured using obligatory study to find scales for measuring image transfer by brain storming of various literatures on semantic differential items on brand image, destinations image and general semantic differential model that were relevant to the study.

The common identifiers or adjectives used for the destinations and events were selected under three categories whilst evaluation, activities and potency. There were five dimensions for evaluation and four dimensions for activities. The dimensions for potency were multi-loaded therefore it was eliminated. These dimensions were identified through tests and were proved by a replicate test.

As an argument the even ts and destination image transfer can be affected on political grounds too which are related with the destination. The recent example can be Beijing Olympics and the Tibet issue. Although the sporting event has nothing to do with the political issue but the whole world has been prompted and allegedly forced to speak because of the upcoming Olympics, where more than 157 Countries and 646 Athletes are participating.

Intention to visit was measured by Willingness to Buy scale. The participants rated the destinations on nine pointer scale, which calculate their intentions to visit. This will help to compare the results obtained by the further image transfer scale.

Involvement in sports was measured by Orlick's SSI (Secondary Sport involvement) scale. The participants had to report the frequency at which they watch sports on television. This was considered an important factor to measure because their level of interests towards sports would affect their willingness to visit a destination to where sporting events is on. The sport-events consideration shows only a category from a population who likes sports but researcher would have used other cultural events to see the effects of image transfer in holistic terms of events. Events can't be generally categorized in sports event only. On the other hand, simply keeping a track of how much they read news about sports does not proves their involvement in sports. That can be just out o f the fact that one wants to be informed about happenings around.

ANALYSIS

The data analysis was done through various statistical equations namely MANOVA, this analysis can detect mean differences among a number of different groups on several different measures, while holding one or more variables constant. The method is useful for research studies where there are a variety of segments being assessed on a number of different measures, where one or more variables needs to be controlled for that may potentially bias the results To evaluate the image transfer city to event {3 (city) 2 (event) 2 (gender)} MANCOVA model and to evaluate event to destination {2 (city) 3(event) 2 (gender)} MANCOVA model was used. The two- way three-way and four way interactions analysis was done by multi-variate Roy's largest Root for all the eight conditions. This included gender, city and destination.

The use of statistical method for analyzing the data is strong point for this article to prove its hypothesis but at the same time this massive calculation has made it more complex. The study could have been divided into different research, studying co-branding effect of destination and events one for positive and the other for negative. This could have reduced the complexity of the article.

Results

The results emerged out of the study was interesting to know and might be basis for further studies in effects of sporting events on destination. Out of all the interactions, the four ways and three way interactions h ad no significant result meaning that the holistic effect of gender, sport involvement, city and event was found less significant while two-way interaction was more significant. In the case of where destination was centered, it was found that city when paired with an event had better ratings while involvement of females and males affect the intention to visit. In the case where events were centered, a remarkable result emerged. The event when paired with destination had no significant effect on ratings but it had a significant effect on males and females intentions to visit which was out of the fact that they were more involved with the sporting event than the destination. This proved that nothing matters more than event if event interests people. In other findings it was employed that the ads do not have any direct effects on intension to visit meaning that perceived image plays an important role while planning a trip to destination. The other findings suggests although the ratings of both the destinations improved when paired with events but the ratings were categorized on two dimensions evaluation and activities. The sport-events consideration shows only a category from a population who likes sports but researcher would have used other cultural events to see the effects of image transfer in holistic terms of events. Events can't be generally categorized in sports event only.

Conclusions

The research has proved that mere association of an event with destination had transferred some image as an affect of co-branding. The pairing of brands depends on match up. This match can be in terms of product attributes or interests towards brands. This study suggest that a less active destination provides less activities to tourists but when paired with a sport which is liked by people will definitely improve the destination's perceived image. The researcher further has discussed the co-b randing effects with literature.

It can be added to this research that ways that pairings of event and d estination are interpreted matter (Chalip and Costa 2005).

Events into building brand destination

Events can prove to be as USP for the destination brand. Benchmarking in tourism is characterised by emphasis on improving performance across tourist destinations(Woober, Kozak). Frederic Dimanche put up an idea International Conference of strategic development of tou rism by creating awareness, quality management for the ben efit of the tourism authorities. This study will look in to the deeper effects of events to create a brand equity of destination as events represent the image of cultural and social backgrounds of a destination (Liping A CAI; Bihu, Billy bai) in their reseach article have presented that the level of the visitation to a destination goes down when the same destination is visited freequently.The proposed research will give DMO's an outline to create an event which can fill the gap of satisfaction levels of visitors and will give newer ideas to attract tourists in off seasons too gave a new concept of benchmarking for tourists satisfaction which depends upon quality provided to the tourists.

If planned effectively and used strategically, such events can create economic as well as social benefits for the host community. If events are poorly understood (and planned) communities run the risk of missing an important economic opportunity, while at worst they may even experience some degradation in quality of life and economic costs. Governments have been fast to see the potential of large sporting events to generate economic benefits media attention and the raising of a local area's profile; adding animation and life to existing facilities; encouraging repeat visits; and assisting economic regeneration (Getz, 1991). The majority of the reports trace the flow of spending associated with the event in the host community and identify resultant chang es in sales, tax revenues, inco me and jobs (Lee and Taylor 2003; UK Sport, 2004).

A point of contention in these studies has been the ability to separate between the short-term economic impact of the event (i.e. visitors attending the event) and so-called destination branding events which in turn are assumed to lead to increased tourism in the long—term. Whilst the 'holy grail' appears to be measuring the level of increased tourism to a destination that occurs because of an event, the proposed study seeks to a more modest outcome of determin ing the ability of an event portfolio to in fluence the decision of a tourist to visit a destination. If this can be established it provides impetus to the argument that events are able to induce tourism beyond the timing of th e event itself.

Sport tourism is one of the fastest growing domain s of the leisure tourism market (Chalip & Leyns 2002; Shifflet & Bhatia 1999). Like wise there can be other cultural events too that can be developed considering different interests and different age groups. Events also bring immense benefits to the local community (Getz (1991) and Ritchie (1984)) if they are included in strategic planning of an events tourism.

EVENTS PORTFOLIO

An event portfolio consists of hosting city/cities and event/ events. A marketer should always prepare an events portfolio for a destination while seeking to use events as brand building tool . A mega event may not have long lasting effet on destination but heaps of small events all round the year might increase the interest of people towards a destination. This will lead to focus on different age groups, different in terests like cultural, sports, music etc.

Since events cater those tourists who have interests in entertainment and activities, a marketer or events portfolio desinger should have a target tourist segment. This may consist of families, groups, adventure sporties, individuals, newly wed couples, back paker etc. Events portfolio may contain sporting events, cultural events, business meetings, family festival etc. Thus, the reach of events portfolio depends on targeted tou rists. An events portfolio should reinforce the brand image of destination.

Conclusion: Event Related Marketing Strategies

Past researches prove that there is synergy between a place and its marketing tool. Here destination being a place and events are being a marketing tool. Events are covered by media and the information about the destination where is the event is being hosted automatically market the key features of that destination. The events have the capacity to spread a positive image of a destination. This theory can be said from a range of marketing theories, concepts and strategies.

Media

The brand is affected by advertisement. It increases awareness and may change attitudes towards perceived image of a brand. Promotion for an event as well as destination is required to approach the targeted tourists.

This requires adequate planned publicity campaign by the event marketer to balance the theme and adv ertisements well between destination and event. The print media, radio, internet and television outdoor media should prepare a well organized time and minutes of advertising and their schedules as to when and where the promotions will take place.

Public Relations

Unlike paid advertising for a destination, reporting about an event and a city or a country hosting that event is a purely journalistic activity in terms of coverage. It is absolutely essential that the events are covered for its pre activities, then during the event as well as after event effects. If a large event is covered then it is needless to say that media persons should be invited but when it comes to organize an event with intention to promote a destination then it should be predecided that who will cover the event and how the event and destination will be covered to balance the effect of image transfer. It is thus necessary that PR activities be well planned. Press conferences, press releases, invites to events for impresarios are some means of networking for good public relations. PR personnel have the responsibility to identify and create rapport with press reporters and networking with influences so as to maintain a positive image of the event and destination.

Merchandising

Events have a capability of physical manifestation of destination. Most popular attributes of a destination can be used to be printed on products and the materials which are used for events marketing. The products may bear the destination's name promoting the key features of the host destination. Sports based events hav e traditionally shown the best example of merchandising the destination and event promotion.

Infrastructure

It is thoughtful that does the destination contain a proper infrastructure to hold a big event or there is there a need to develop a new infrastructure to meet such need. It includes proper accessibility to destination via airport, trains or other transfers. High quality hotels should be available for tourists for every class that may at least stand for hygiene and services.

Other Consideration

Hosting an event at a destination may include considerations like institutional or organizational framework. Different permissions from different institutional and tourism bodies like local government and Ministry of Tourism. The laws related to investment and community safety. Hosting an event also involves the social aspects because tourists may be from different cultures and there may be culture shock for the local community. To protect such odd situations the local tourism ministry should set up a body that may keep an eye for any such mishaps that can ruin the sporting spirits of event hosting.

Benefits of Events

It provides off-season benefits to the economy. The tourist may visit the destination if any event is on at the destination. It also adds to increase demand of local business weather hotel bookings, food restaurants, transportation. Events also encourage tourists to stay for a longer time at the destination. Events are also a tool to reach specific target market or a wider market both. They reinforce the destination's image. They help in promotion, positioning and branding a destination. The events help to communicate the destination's awareness. They build brand equity. The long term advantages of hosting an event may be referred as improvement in infrastructure, attractive investment by big companies, quality of life for locals and amazing experience for travelers, destination's brand building and an added value to the city's identity

It can be added further to this research that the co-branding of events with destination or vice-versa can be positive or negative. A huge event may hamper the destination's image as the tourist will be mo re involved with the event than the destination which will not have a long lasting effect whilst a huge event may not have good response if the destination is not well known. Further study can be on terms of that what kind of events can cater the positive impacts on destination. Overall this article puts an undoub ted study in terms of co-branding effects of destination and events.

CHAPTER–4

Sporting Event Tourism

Sports tourism refers to travel for the sake of either viewing or participating in a sporting event staying apart from their usual environment. A sport is an organized, competitive, entertaining, and skillful physical activity requiring commitment and fair play, in which a winner can be defined by objective means. It is governed by a set of rules or customs. In a sport the key factors are the physical capabilities and skills of the competitor when determining the outcome (winning or losing). The physical activity involves the movement of people, animals and/or a variety of objects such as balls and machines or equipment. In contrast, games such as card games and board games, though these could be called mind sports and some are recognized as Olympic sports, require primarily mental skills and only mental physical involvement. Non-competitive activities, for example as jogging or playing catch, are usually classified as forms of recreation.

Physical events such as scoring goals or crossing a line first often define the result of a sport. However, the degree of skill and performance in some sports such as diving, dressage and figure skating is judged according to well-defined criteria. This is in contrast with other judged activities such as beauty pageants and body building, where skill does not have to be shown and the criteria are not as well defined.

Records are kept and updated for most sports at the highest levels, while failures and accomplishments are widely announced in sport news. Sports are most often played just for fun or for the simple fact that people need exercise to stay in good physical condition. However, professional sport is a major source of entertainment.

While practices may vary, sports participants are expected to display good sportsmanship, and observe standards of conduct such as being respectful of opponents and officials, and congratulating the winner when losing.

Etymology and Meaning

"Sport" comes from the Old French desport meaning "leisure." American English uses the term "sports" to refer to this general type of recreational activity, whereas other regional dialects use the singular "sport". The Persian word for "sport" is based on the root bord, meaning "winning". The Chinese term for "sport," tiyu connotes "physical training". The Modern Greek term for sport is athlitismos, directly cognate with the English terms "athlete" and "athleticism."

The oldest definition of sport in English (1300) is of anything humans find amusing or entertaining. Other meanings include gambling and events staged for the purpose of gambling; hunting; and games and diversions, including ones that require exercise. Roget's defines the noun sport as an "Activity engaged in for relaxation and amusement" with synonyms including diversion and recreation. An example of a more sharply defined meaning is "an athletic activity where one competitor or a team of competitors plays against another competitor or group of competitors a conclusive method of scoring...not determined by a judge."

History

There are artifacts and structures that suggest that the Chinese engaged in sporting activities as early as 4000 BC. Gymnastics appears to have been a popular sport in China's ancient past. Monuments to the Pharaohs indicate that a number of sports, including swimming and fishing, were well-developed and regulated several thousands of years ago in ancient Egypt. Other

Egyptian sports included javelin throwing, high jump, and wrestling. Ancient Persian sports such as the traditional Iranian martial art of Zourkhaneh had a close connection to the warfare skills. Among other sports that originate in ancient Persia are polo and jousting.

A wide range of sports were already established by the time of Ancient Greece and the military culture and the development of sports in Greece influenced one another considerably. Sports became such a prominent part of their culture that the Greeks created the Olympic Games, which in ancient times were held every four years in a small village in the Peloponnesus called Olympia.

Sports have been increasingly organized and regulated from the time of the Ancient Olympics up to the present century. Industrialization has brought increased leisure time to the citizens of developed and developing countries, leading to more time for citizens to attend and follow spectator sports, greater participation in athletic activities, and increased accessibility. These trends continued with the advent of mass media and global communication. Professionalism became prevalent, further adding to the increase in sport's popularity, as sports fans began following the exploits of professional athletes through radio, television, and the internet—all while enjoying the exercise and competition associated with amateur participation in sports.

In the new millennium, new sports have been going further from the physical aspect to the mental or psychological aspect of competing. Electronic sports organizations are becoming more and more popular.

CLASSIFICATION OF SPORTS TOURISM

There are several classifications on sports tourism. Gammon and Robinsom suggested that the sports tourism are defined as Hard Sports Tourism and Soft Sports Tourism, while Gibson suggested that there are three types of sports tourism included

Sports Event Tourism, Celebrity and Nostalgia Sport Tourism and Active Sport Tourism.

Hard and Soft Sports Tourism

Hard definition of sports tourism refers to the quantity of people participating at a competitive sport events. Normally these kinds of events are the motivation that attract visitors visits the events. Olympic Games, FIFA World Cup, F1 Grand Prix and regional events such as NASCAR Sprint Cup Series could be described as Hard Sports Tourism.

Soft definition are relatively the tourists travel for participating on recreational sporting, or signing up for an leisure interests. Hiking, Skiing and Canoeing can be described as the Soft Soprts Tourism.

Sport Events Tourism

Sport event tourism refers to the visitors who visit the city with the purpose of watching the events. A good example of this would be during the Olympics. Each Olympic host city receives an immense amount of tourism.

Celebrity and Nostalgia Sport Tourism

Celebrity and Nostalgia Sport Tourism involves in two areas including visits to the sports halls of fame and venue and meeting famous sports personalities in a vacation basis.

Active Sport Tourism

Active Sport Tourism refers to those who really particiapting into the sports or the events.

SPORTSMANSHIP

Sportsmanship is an attitude that strives for fair play, courtesy toward teammates and opponents, ethical behaviour and integrity, and grace in victory or defeat.

Sportsmanship expresses an aspiration or ethos that the activity will be enjoyed for its own sake. The well-known sentiment by sports journalist Grantland Rice, that it's "not that you won or lost but how you played the game," and the Modern Olympic creed expressed by its founder Pierre de Coubertin: "The most important thing . . . is not winning but taking part" are typical expressions of this sentiment.

Violence in sports involves crossing the line between fair competition and intentional aggressive violence. Athletes, coaches, fans, and parents sometimes unleash violent behaviour on people or property, in misguided shows of loyalty, dominance, anger, or celebration. Rioting or hooliganism are common and ongoing problems at national and international sporting contests.

Professional Sports

The entertainment aspect of sports, together with the spread of mass media and increased leisure time, has led to professionalism in sports. This has resulted in some conflict, where the paycheck can be seen as more important than recreational aspects, or where the sports are changed simply to make them more profitable and popular, thereby losing certain valued traditions.

The entertainment aspect also means that sportsmen and women are often elevated to celebrity status in media and popular culture.

Politics

At times, sports and politics can have a large amount of influence on each other.

When apartheid was the official policy in South Africa, many sports people, particularly in rugby union, adopted the conscientious approach that they should not appear in competitive sports there. Some feel this was an effective contribution to the eventual demolition of the policy of apartheid, others feel that it may have prolonged and reinforced its worst effects.

The 1936 Summer Olympics held in Berlin was an illustration, perhaps best recognised in retrospect, where an ideology was developing which used the event to strengthen its spread through propaganda.

In the history of Ireland, Gaelic sports were connected with cultural nationalism. Until the mid 20th century a person could have been banned from playing Gaelic football, hurling, or other sports administered by the Gaelic Athletic Association (GAA) if she/he played or supported soccer, or other games seen to be of British origin. Until recently the GAA continued to ban the playing of soccer and rugby union at Gaelic venues. This ban is still enforced, but was modified to allow football and rugby to be played in Croke Park while Lansdowne Road was redeveloped into Aviva Stadium. Until recently, under Rule 21, the GAA also banned members of the British security forces and members of the RUC from playing Gaelic games, but the advent of the Good Friday Agreement in 1998 led to the eventual removal of the ban.

Nationalism is often evident in the pursuit of sports, or in its reporting: people compete in national teams, or commentators and audiences can adopt a partisan view. On occasion, such tensions can lead to violent confrontation among players or spectators within and beyond the sporting venue. These trends are seen by many as contrary to the fundamental ethos of sports being carried on for its own sake and for the enjoyment of its participants.

Physical art

Sports have many affinities with art. For example, figure skating, artistic gymnastics, dancesport, and Tai chi can be considered artistic spectacles. Similarly, there are other activities that have elements of sport and art in their execution, such as bodybuilding, free running, martial arts, performance art, Yoga, bossaball, dressage, and culinary arts. Perhaps the best example is bull-fighting, which in Spain is reported in the arts pages of newspapers.

All sports involve physical and mental activities that are pursued for more than simply utilitarian reasons. For instance, running, when done as a sport, occurs for reasons beyond simply moving from one place to another. Value is gained from this activity when it is conducted simply for its own sake. This is similar to the concept of aesthetic value, which is seeing something over and above the strictly functional value coming from an object's normal use. For instance, an aesthetically pleasing car is one which doesn't just get from A to B, but which impresses with its grace, poise, and charisma. In the same way, a sporting performance such as jumping doesn't just impress as being an effective way to avoid obstacles. It impresses because of the ability, skill, and style that is demonstrated in its performance.

Art and sports were clearly linked at the time of Ancient Greece, when gymnastics and calisthenics invoked admiration and aesthetic appreciation for the physical build, prowess and 'arete' displayed by participants. The modern term 'art' as skill, is related to this ancient Greek term 'arete'. The closeness of art and sport in these times was revealed by the nature of the Olympic Games, which were celebrations of both sporting and artistic achievements, poetry, sculpture and architecture.

Technology

Technology has an important role in sports, whether applied to an athlete's health, the athlete's technique, or equipment's characteristics.

Equipment - As sports have grown more competitive, the need for better equipment has arisen. Golf clubs, (American) football helmets, tennis racquets, baseball and cricket bats, soccer balls, hockey skates, and other equipment have all seen considerable changes when new technologies have been applied.

Health - Ranging from nutrition to the treatment of injuries, as the knowledge of the human body has deepened over time, an athlete's potential has been increased. Athletes are now able to play to an older age, recover more quickly from injuries, and train more effectively than previous generations of athletes.

Instruction - Advancing technology created new opportunities for research into sports. It is now possible to analyse aspects of sports that were previously out of the reach of comprehension. Being able to use motion capture to capture an athlete's movement, or advanced computer simulations to model physical scenarios has greatly increased an athlete's ability to understand what they are doing and how they can improve themselves.

Terminology

In British English, sporting activities are commonly denoted by the mass noun "sport". In American English, "sports" is more used. In all English dialects, "sports" is the term used for more than one specific sport. For example, "football and swimming are my favourite sports", would sound natural to all English speakers, whereas "I enjoy sport" would sound less natural than "I enjoy sports" to North Americans.

The term "sport" is sometimes extended to encompass all competitive activities, regardless of the level of physical activity. Both games of skill and motor sport exhibit many of the characteristics of physical sports, such as skill, sportsmanship, and at the highest levels, even professional sponsorship associated with physical sports. Air sports, billiards, bridge, chess, motorcycle racing, and powerboating are all recognized as sports by the International Olympic Committee with their world governing bodies represented in the Association of the IOC Recognised International Sports Federations.

Spectator Sport

As well as being a form of recreation for the participants, much sport is played in front of an audience. Most professional sport is played in a 'theatre' of some kind; be it a stadium, arena, golf course, race track, or the open road, with provision for the (often paying) public.

Large television or radio audiences are also commonly attracted, with rival broadcasters bidding large amounts of money for the 'rights' to show certain fixtures. The football

World Cup attracts a global television audience of hundreds of millions; the 2006 Final alone attracted an estimated worldwide audience of well over 700 million. The Cricket World Cup is another sporting event which attracts a global audience. The 2007 Cricket World Cup attracted about 2.3 Billion viewers all over the world. In the United States, the championship game of the NFL, the Super Bowl, has become one of the most watched television broadcasts of the year. Super Bowl Sunday is a de facto national holiday in America; the viewership being so great that in 2007 advertising space was reported as being sold at $2.6m for a 30 second slot.

MULTI-SPORT EVENT

A multi-sport event is an organized sporting event, often held over multiple days, and featuring competition in many different sports between organized teams of athletes from (mostly) nation-states. The first major, modern, multi-sport event of international significance was the modern Olympic Games.

Many regional multi-sport events have since been founded, modeled after the Olympics. Most have the same basic structure. Games are held over the course of several days in and around a "host city," which changes for each competition. Countries send national teams to each competition, consisting of individual athletes and teams that compete in a wide variety of sports. Athletes or teams are awarded gold, silver or bronze medals for first, second and third place respectively. The games are generally held every four years, though some are annual competitions.

History

The Tailteann Games, held near modern Telltown in Ireland, was one of the first multi-sport festivals to be recorded, and its history can be traced back to 1829 BC. These games were a thirty-day meeting which included footraces and stone-throwing events among other events. The Ancient Olympic Games, first held in 776 BC, was the precursor to the Modern Olympic Games, although its first edition only featured a footrace and the number of sporting competitions expanded at later editions.

There were several other "games" held in Europe in the classical era:

- Panhellenic Games:

  The Pythian Games (founded 527 BC) held in Delphi every four years

  The Nemean Games (founded 516 BC) held in Argolid every two years

  The Isthmian Games (founded 523 BC) held on the Isthmus of Corinth every two years
- The Roman Games – Arising from Etruscan rather than purely Greek roots, the Roman Games deemphasized footraces and throwing. Instead, the Greek sports of chariot racing and wrestling, as well as the Etruscan sport of gladiatorial combat, took center stage.

Other multi-sport festivals emerged in the Middle Ages in Europe, including the Cotswold Olimpick Games in England in the 1600s, the Highland games in Scotland, and the Olympiade de la République in France in the 1800s. Other early festivals Canterbury Cricket Week founded in 1842

Olympics

The first modern multi-sport event organised were the Olympic Games, organised by the International Olympic Committee (est. 1894) for the first time in 1896 in Athens, Greece. After some badly organised celebrations (1900, 1904), the Olympics became very popular. The number of sports, initially only a few, is still growing.

The Olympic Games are a major international event featuring summer and winter sports, in which thousands of athletes participate in a variety of competitions. The Games are currently held every two years, with Summer and Winter Olympic Games alternating, although they occur every four years within their respective seasonal games. Originally, the ancient Olympic Games were held in Olympia, Greece, from the 8th century BC to the 5th century AD. Baron Pierre de Coubertin founded the International Olympic Committee (IOC) in 1894. The IOC has since become the governing body of the Olympic Movement, whose structure and actions are defined by the Olympic Charter.

The evolution of the Olympic Movement during the 20th and 21st centuries has resulted in several changes to the Olympic Games. Some of these adjustments include the creation of the Winter Games for ice and snow sports, the Paralympic Games for athletes with physical disabilities, and the Youth Olympic Games for teenage athletes. The IOC has had to adapt to the varying economic, political, and technological realities of the 20th century. As a result, the Olympics shifted away from pure amateurism, as envisioned by Coubertin, to allow participation of professional athletes. The growing importance of the mass media created the issue of corporate sponsorship and commercialization of the Games. World Wars led to the cancellation of the 1916, 1940, and 1944 Games. Large boycotts during the Cold War limited participation in the 1980 and 1984 Games.

The Olympic Movement is comprised of international sports federations (IFs), National Olympic Committees (NOCs), and organizing committees for each specific Olympic Games. As the decision-making body, the IOC is responsible for choosing the host city for each Olympic Games. The host city is responsible for organizing and funding a celebration of the Games consistent with the Olympic Charter. The Olympic program, consisting of the sports to be contested at the Games, is also determined by the IOC. The celebration of the Games encompasses many rituals and symbols, such as the Olympic flag and torch, as well as the opening and closing ceremonies. There are over 13,000 athletes that compete at the Summer and Winter Olympics in 33 different sports and nearly 400 events. The first, second, and third place finishers in each event receive gold, silver, and bronze medals, respectively.

The Games have grown in scale to the point that nearly every nation is represented. Such growth has created numerous challenges, including boycotts, doping, bribery of officials, and terrorism. Every two years, the Olympics and its media exposure provide unknown athletes with the chance to attain national, and in particular cases, international fame. The Games also constitute a major opportunity for the host city and country to showcase themselves to the world.

Ancient Olympics

The Ancient Olympic Games was a series of competitions held between representatives of several city-states and kingdoms from Ancient Greece, which featured mainly athletic but also combat and chariot racing events. During the Olympic games all struggles against the participating city-states were postponed until the games were finished. The origin of these Olympics is shrouded in mystery and legend. One of the most popular myths identifies Heracles and his father Zeus as the progenitors of the Games. According to legend, it was Heracles who first called the Games "Olympic" and established the custom of holding them every four years. A legend persists that after Heracles completed his twelve labors, he built the Olympic stadium as an honor to Zeus. Following its completion, he walked in a straight line for 200 steps and called this distance a "stadion" which later became a unit of distance. Another myth associates the first Games with the ancient Greek concept of Olympic truce. The most widely accepted date for the inception of the Ancient Olympics is 776 BC; this is based on inscriptions, found at Olympia, of the winners of a footrace held every four years starting in 776 BC. The Ancient Games featured running events, a pentathlon (consisting of a jumping event, discus and javelin throws, a foot race and wrestling), boxing, wrestling, and equestrian events. Tradition has it that Coroebus, a cook from the city of Elis, was the first Olympic champion.

The Olympics were of fundamental religious importance, featuring sporting events alongside ritual sacrifices honoring both Zeus (whose famous statue by Phidias stood in his temple at Olympia) and Pelops, divine hero and mythical king of Olympia. Pelops was famous for his chariot race with King Oenomaus of Pisatis. The winners of the events were admired and immortalized in poems and statues. The Games were held every four years, and this period, known as an Olympiad, was used by Greeks as one of their units of time measurement. The Games were part of a cycle known as the Panhellenic Games, which included the Pythian Games, the Nemean Games, and the Isthmian Games.

The Olympic Games reached their zenith in the 6th and 5th centuries BC, but then gradually declined in importance as the Romans gained power and influence in Greece. There is no consensus on when the Games officially ended, the most common-held date is 393 AD, when the emperor Theodosius I declared that all pagan cults and practices be eliminated. Another date cited is 426 AD, when his successor The odosius II ordered the destruction of all Greek temples. After the demise of the Olympics, they were not held again until the late 19th century.

MODERN GAMES

Forerunners

The first significant attempt to emulate the ancient Olympic Games was the L'Olympiade de la République, a national Olympic festival held annually from 1796 to 1798 in Revolutionary France. The competition included several disciplines from the ancient Greek Olympics. The 1796 Games also marked the introduction of the metric system into sport.

In 1850 an Olympian Class, to improve the fitness of locals, was started by Dr William Penny Brookes at Much Wenlock, in Shropshire, England. In 1859, Dr. Brookes renamed the Olympian Class to Wenlock Olympian Games and this annual games continues to this day. The Wenlock Olympian Society was founded by Dr Brookes on November 15, 1860.:28.

Revival

Greek interest in reviving the Olympic Games began with the Greek War of Independence from the Ottoman Empire in 1821. It was first proposed by poet and newspaper editor Panagiotis Soutsos in his poem "Dialogue of the Dead", published in 1833.:1 Evangelis Zappas, a wealthy Greek-Romanian philanthropist, first wrote to King Otto of Greece, in 1856, offering to fund a permanent revival of the Olympic Games.:14 Zappas sponsored the first Olympic Games in 1859, which was held in an Athens city square. Athletes participated from Greece and the Ottoman Empire. Zappas funded the restoration of the ancient Panathenaic stadium so that it could host all future Olympic Games.:14.

Dr. Brookes adopted events from the program of the Olympics held in Athens in 1859 in to future Wenlock Olympian Games. In 1866, a national Olympic Games in Great Britain was organized by Dr. William Penny Brookes at London's Crystal Palace.

The Panathinaiko Stadium hosted Olympics in 1870 and 1875.:2, 13–23, 81 Thirty thousand spectators attended that Games in 1870 though no official attendance records are available for the 1875 Games.:44 In 1890, after attending the Olympian Games of the Wenlock Olympian Society Baron Pierrede Coubertin was inspired to found the International Olympic Committee. Coubertin built on the ideas and work of Brookes and Zappas with the aim of establishing internationally rotating Olympic Games that would occur every four years. He presented these ideas during the first Olympic Congress of the newly created International Olympic Committee (IOC). This meeting was held from June 16 to June 23, 1894, at the Sorbonne University in Paris. On the last day of the Congress, it was decided that the first Olympic Games, to come under the auspices of the IOC, would take place two years later in Athens. The IOC elected the Greek writer Demetrius Vikelas as its first president.:100–105

1896 Games

The first Games held under the auspices of the IOC was hosted in the Panathenaic stadium in Athens in 1896. These Games brought 14 nations and 241 athletes who competed in 43 events. Zappas and his cousin Konstantinos Zappas had left the Greek government a trust to fund future Olympic Games. This trust was used to help finance the 1896 Games.:117 George Averoff contributed generously for the refurbishment of the stadium in preparation for the Games.:128 The Greek government also provided funding, which was expected to be recouped through the future sale of tickets to the Games and from the sale of the first Olympic commemorative stamp set.:128

The Greek officials and public were enthusiastic about the experience of hosting these Games. This feeling was shared by many of the athletes, who even demanded that Athens be the host of the Olympic Games on a permanent basis. The IOC did not approve this request. The committee planned that the modern Olympics would rotate internationally. As such they decided to hold the second Games in Paris.

Changes and Adaptations

Following the success of the 1896 Games, the Olympics entered a period of stagnation that threatened their survival. The Olympic Games held at the Paris Exposition in 1900 and the World's Fair at St. Louis in 1904 were side-shows. The Games at Paris did not have a stadium, however this was the first time women took part in the games. The St. Louis Games hosted 650 athletes, but 580 were from the United States. The homogeneous nature of these celebrations was a low point for the Olympic Movement. The Games rebounded when the 1906 Intercalated Games (so-called because they were the second Games held within the third Olympiad) were held in Athens. These Games are not officially recognized by the IOC and no Intercalated Games have been held since. These Games, which were hosted at the Panathenaic stadium in Athens, attracted a broad international field of participants, and generated great public interest. This marked the beginning of a rise in both the popularity and the size of the Olympics.

Winter Games

The Winter Olympics were created to feature snow and ice sports that were logistically impossible to hold during the Summer Games. Figure skating (in 1908 and 1920) and ice hockey (in 1920) were featured as Olympic events at the Summer Olympics. The IOC desired to expand this list of sports to encompass other winter activities. At the 1921 Olympic Congress, in Lausanne, it was decided to hold a winter version of the Olympic Games. A winter sports week (it was actually 11 days) was held in 1924 in Chamonix, France; this event became the first Winter Olympic Games. The IOC mandated that the Winter Games be celebrated every four years on the same year as their summer counterpart. This tradition was upheld until the 1992 Games in Albertville, France; after that, beginning with the 1994 Games, the Winter Olympics were held on the third year of each Olympiad.

Paralympics

In 1948, Sir Ludwig Guttman, determined to promote the rehabilitation of soldiers after World War II, organized a multi-sport event between several hospitals to coincide with the 1948 London Olympics. Guttman's event, known then as the Stoke Mandeville Games, became an annual sports festival. Over the next twelve years, Guttman and others continued their efforts to use sports as an avenue to healing. For the 1960 Olympic Games, in Rome, Guttman brought 400 athletes to compete in the "Parallel Olympics", which became known as the first Paralympics. Since then, the Paralympics have been held in every Olympic year. As of the 1988 Summer Olympics in Seoul, South Korea, the host city for the Olympics has also played host to the Paralympics.

Youth Games

Starting in 2010, the Olympic Games will be complemented by Youth Games, where athletes between the ages of 14 and 18 will compete. The Youth Olympic Games were conceived by IOC president Jacques Rogge in 2001 and approved during the 119th Congress of the IOC. The first Summer Youth Games were held in Singapore from 14 August - 26 August 2010, while the inaugural Winter Games will be hosted in Innsbruck, Austria, two years later. These Games will be shorter than the senior Games; the summer version will last twelve days, while the winter version will last nine days. The IOC will allow 3,500 athletes and 875 officials to participate at the Summer Youth Games, and 970 athletes and 580 officials at the Winter Youth Games. The sports to be contested will coincide with those scheduled for the traditional senior Games, however there will be a reduced number of disciplines and events.

Recent Games

From 241 participants representing 14 nations in 1896, the Games have grown to about 10,500 competitors from 204 countries at the 2008 Summer Olympics. The scope and scale of the Winter Olympics is smaller. For example, Turin hosted 2,508 athletes from 80 countries competing in 84 events, during the 2006 Winter Olympics. During the Games most athletes and officials are housed in the Olympic village. This village is intended to be a self-contained home for all the Olympic participants. It is furnished with cafeterias, health clinics, and locations for religious expression.

The IOC allows nations to compete that do not meet the strict requirements for political sovereignty that other international organizations demand. As a result, colonies and dependencies are permitted to set up their own National Olympic Committees. Examples of this include territories such as Puerto Rico, Bermuda, Taiwan, and Hong Kong, all of which compete as separate nations despite being legally a part of another country.

International Olympic Committee

The Olympic Movement encompasses a large number of national and international sporting organizations and federations, recognized media partners, as well as athletes, officials, judges, and every other person and institution that agrees to abide by the rules of the Olympic Charter. As the umbrella organization of the Olympic Movement, the International Olympic Committee (IOC) is responsible for selecting the host city, overseeing the planning of the Olympic Games, updating and approving the sports program, and negotiating sponsorship and broadcasting rights. The Olympic Movement is made of three major elements:

International Federations (IFs) are the governing bodies that supervise a sport at an international level. For example, the International Federation of Association Football (FIFA) is the IF for football (soccer), and the Fédération Internationale de Volleyball (FIVB) is the international governing body for volleyball. There are currently 35 IFs in the Olympic Movement, representing each of the Olympic sports.

National Olympic Committees (NOCs) represent and regulate the Olympic Movement within each country. For example, the United States Olympic Committee (USOC) is the NOC of the United States. There are currently 205 NOCs recognized by the IOC.

Organizing Committees for the Olympic Games (OCOGs) constitute the temporary committees responsible for the organization of a specific celebration of the Olympics. OCOGs are dissolved after each Games, once the final report is delivered to the IOC.

French and English are the official languages of the Olympic Movement. The other language used at each Olympic Games is the language of the host country. Every proclamation (such as the announcement of each country during the parade of nations in the opening ceremony) is spoken in these three languages, or the main two depending on whether the host country is an English or French speaking country.

Criticism

The IOC has often been criticized for being an intractable organization, with several members on the committee for life. The leadership of IOC presidents Avery Brundage and Juan Antonio Samaranch was especially controversial. Brundage was president for over 20 years, and during his tenure he protected the Olympics from untoward political involvement. He was accused of both racism, for his handling of the apartheid issue with the South African delegation, and anti-Semitism. Under the Samaranch presidency, the office was accused of both nepotism and corruption. Samaranch's ties with the Franco regime in Spain were also a source of criticism.

In 1998, it was uncovered that several IOC members had taken bribes from members of the Salt Lake City bid committee for the hosting of the 2002 Winter Olympics, to ensure their votes were cast in favor of the American bid. The IOC pursued an investigation which led to the resignation of four members and expulsion of six others. The scandal set off further reforms that would change the way host cities are selected, to avoid similar cases in the future.

A BBC documentary entitled Panorama: Buying the Games, aired in August 2004, investigated the taking of bribes in the bidding process for the 2012 Summer Olympics. The documentary claimed it was possible to bribe IOC members into voting for a particular candidate city. After being narrowly defeated in their bid for the 2012 Summer Games, Parisian Mayor Bertrand Delanoë specifically accused the British Prime Minister Tony Blair and the London Bid Committee (headed by former Olympic champion Sebastian Coe) of breaking the bid rules. He cited French President Jacques Chirac as a witness; Chirac gave guarded interviews regarding his involvement. The allegation was never fully explored. The Turin bid for the 2006 Winter Olympics was also shrouded in controversy. A prominent IOC member, Marc Hodler, strongly connected with the rival bid of Sion, Switzerland, alleged bribery of IOC officials by members of the Turin Organizing Committee. These accusations led to a wide-ranging investigation. The allegations also served to sour many IOC members against Sion's bid and potentially helped Turin to capture the host city nomination.

Commercialization

The IOC originally resisted funding by corporate sponsors. It was not until the retirement of IOC president Avery Brundage, in 1972, that the IOC began to explore the potential of the television medium and the lucrative advertising markets available to them. Under the leadership of Juan Antonio Samaranch the Games began to shift toward international sponsors who sought to link their products to the Olympic brand.

Budget

During the first half of the 20th century the IOC was run on a small budget. As president of the IOC from 1952 to 1972, Avery Brundage rejected all attempts to link the Olympics with commercial interest. Brundage believed the lobby of corporate interests would unduly impact the IOC's decision-making. Brundage's resistance to this revenue stream meant the IOC left organizing committees to negotiate their own sponsorship contracts and use the Olympic symbols. When Brundage retired the IOC had US$2 million in assets; eight years later the IOC coffers had swelled to US$45 million. This was primarily due to a shift in ideology toward expansion of the Games through corporate sponsorship and the sale of television rights. When Juan Antonio Samaranch was elected IOC president in 1980 his desire was to make the IOC financially independent.

The 1984 Summer Olympics became a watershed moment in Olympic history. The Los Angeles-based organizing committee, led by Peter Ueberroth, was able to generate a surplus of US$225 million, which was an unprecedented amount at that time. The organizing committee had been able to create such a surplus in part by selling exclusive sponsorship rights to select companies. The IOC sought to gain control of these sponsorship rights. Samaranch helped to establish The Olympic Program (TOP) in 1985, in order to create an Olympic brand. Membership in TOP was, and is, very exclusive and expensive. Fees cost US$50 million for a four year membership. Members of TOP received exclusive global advertising rights for their product category, and use of the

Olympic symbol, the interlocking rings, in their publications and advertisements.

Effect of Television

The 1936 Summer Olympics in Berlin were the first Games to be broadcast on television, though only to local audiences. The 1956 Winter Olympics were the first internationally televised Olympic Games, and the following Winter Games had their broadcasting rights sold for the first time to specialized television broadcasting networks—CBS paid US$394,000 for the American rights, and the European Broadcasting Union (EBU) allocated US$660,000. In the following decades the Olympics became one of the ideological fronts of the Cold War. Superpowers jockeyed for political supremacy, and the IOC wanted to take advantage of this heightened interest via the broadcast medium. The sale of broadcast rights enabled the IOC to increase the exposure of the Olympic Games, thereby generating more interest, which in turn created more appeal to advertisers who purchased advertising time on television. This cycle allowed the IOC to charge ever-increasing fees for those rights. For example, CBS paid US$375 million for the rights of the 1998 Nagano Games, while NBC spent US$3.5 billion for the broadcast rights of all the Olympic Games from 2000 to 2008.

Viewership increased exponentially from the 1960s until the end of the century. This was due to the use of satellites to broadcast live television worldwide in 1964, and the introduction of color television in 1968. Global audience estimates for the 1968 Mexico City Games was 600 million, whereas at the Los Angeles Games of 1984, the audience numbers had increased to 900 million; that number swelled to 3.5 billion by the 1992 Summer Olympics in Barcelona. However, at the 2000 Summer Games in Sydney, NBC drew the lowest ratings for any Summer or Winter Olympics since 1968. This was attributed to two factors: one was the increased competition from cable channels, the second was the internet, which was able to display results and video in real time. Television companies were still relying on tape-delayed content, which was becoming outdated in the information era. A drop in ratings meant that television studios had to give away free advertising time. With such high costs charged to broadcast the Games, the added pressure of the internet, and increased competition from cable, the television lobby demanded concessions from the IOC to boost ratings. The IOC responded by making a number of changes to the Olympic program. At the Summer Games, the gymnastics competition was expanded from seven to nine nights, and a Champions Gala was added to draw greater interest. The IOC also expanded the swimming and diving programs, both popular sports with a broad base of television viewers. Finally, the American television lobby was able to dictate when certain events were held so that they could be broadcast live during prime time in the United States. The result of these efforts was mixed: the ratings for the 2006 Winter Games, held in Torino, Italy, were significantly lower than those for the 2002 Games, while there was a sharp increase in viewership for the 2008 Summer Olympics, staged in Beijing.

Controversy

The sale of the Olympic brand has been controversial. The argument is that the Games have become indistinguishable from any other commercialized sporting spectacle. Specific criticism was levelled at the IOC for market saturation during the 1996 Atlanta and 2000 Sydney Games. The cities were awash in corporations and merchants attempting to sell Olympic-related wares. The IOC indicated that they would address this to prevent spectacles of over-marketing at future Games. Another criticism is that the Games are funded by host cities and national governments; the IOC incurs none of the cost, yet controls all the rights and profits from the Olympic symbols. The IOC also takes a percentage of all sponsorship and broadcast income. Host cities continue to compete ardently for the right to host the Games, even though there is no certainty that they will earn back their investments.

Symbols

The Olympic Movement uses symbols to represent the ideals embodied in the Olympic Charter. The Olympic symbol, better known as the Olympic rings, consists of five intertwined rings and represents the unity of the five inhabited continents (America, Africa, Asia, Australasia, Europe). The colored version of the rings—blue, yellow, black, green, and red—over a white field forms the Olympic flag. These colors were chosen because every nation had at least one of them on its national flag. The flag was adopted in 1914 but flown for the first time only at the 1920 Summer Olympics in Antwerp, Belgium. It has since been hoisted during each celebration of the Games.

The Olympic motto is Citius, Altius, Fortius, a Latin expression meaning "Faster, Higher, Stronger". Coubertin's ideals are further expressed in the Olympic creed:

The most important thing in the Olympic Games is not to win but to take part, just as the most important thing in life is not the triumph but the struggle. The essential thing is not to have conquered but to have fought well.

Months before each Games, the Olympic flame is lit in Olympia in a ceremony that reflects ancient Greek rituals. A female performer, acting as a priestess, ignites a torch by placing it inside a parabolic mirror which focuses the sun's rays; she then lights the torch of the first relay bearer, thus initiating the Olympic torch relay that will carry the flame to the host city's Olympic stadium, where it plays an important role in the opening ceremony. Though the flame has been an Olympic symbol since 1928, the torch relay was introduced at the 1936 Summer Games, as part of the German government's attempt to promote its National Socialist ideology.

The Olympic mascot, an animal or human figure representing the cultural heritage of the host country, was introduced in 1968. It has played an important part on the Games identity promotion since the 1980 Summer Olympics, when the Russian bear cub Misha reached international stardom. The mascots of the most recent Summer Olympics, in Beijing, were the Fuwa, five creatures that represent the five fengshui elements important in Chinese culture.

CEREMONIES

Opening

As mandated by the Olympic Charter, various elements frame the opening ceremony of the Olympic Games. Most of these rituals were established at the 1920 Summer Olympics in Antwerp. The ceremony typically starts with the hoisting of the host country's flag and a performance of its national anthem. The host nation then presents artistic displays of music, singing, dance, and theater representative of its culture. The artistic presentations have grown in scale and complexity as successive hosts attempt to provide a ceremony that outlasts its predecessor's in terms of memorability. The opening ceremony of the Beijing Games reportedly cost $100 million, with much of the cost incurred in the artistic segment.

After the artistic portion of the ceremony, the athletes parade into the stadium grouped by nation. Greece is traditionally the first nation to enter in order to honor the origins of the Olympics. Nations then enter the stadium alphabetically according to the host country's chosen language, with the host country's athletes being the last to enter. During the 2004 Summer Olympics, which was hosted in Athens, Greece, the Greek flag entered the stadium first, while the Greek delegation entered last. Speeches are given, formally opening the Games. Finally, the Olympic torch is brought into the stadium and passed on until it reaches the final torch carrier—often a well-known and successful Olympic athlete from the host nation—who lights the Olympic flame in the stadium's cauldron.

Closing

The closing ceremony of the Olympic Games takes place after all sporting events have concluded. Flag-bearers from each participating country enter the stadium, followed by the athletes who enter together, without any national distinction. Three national flags are hoisted while the corresponding national anthems are played: the flag of Greece, to honor the birthplace of the Olympic Games; the flag of the current host country, and the flag of the country hosting the next Summer or Winter Olympic Games. The president of the organizing committee and the IOC president make their closing speeches, the Games are officially closed, and the Olympic flame is extinguished. In what is known as the Antwerp Ceremony, the mayor of the city that organized the Games transfers a special Olympic flag to the president of the IOC, who then passes it on to the mayor of the city hosting the next Olympic Games. After these compulsory elements, the next host nation briefly introduces itself with artistic displays of dance and theater representative of its culture.

Medal Presentation

A medal ceremony is held after each Olympic event is concluded. The winner, second and third-place competitors or teams stand on top of a three-tiered rostrum to be awarded their respective medals. After the medals are given out by an IOC member, the national flags of the three medalists are raised while the national anthem of the gold medalist's country plays. Volunteering citizens of the host country also act as hosts during the medal ceremonies, as they aid the officials who present the medals and act as flag-bearers. For every Olympic event, the respective medal ceremony is held, at most, one day after the event's final. For the men's marathon, the competition is usually held early in the morning on the last day of Olympic competition and its medal ceremony is then held in the evening during the closing ceremony.

Sports

The Olympic Games program consists of 26 sports, 30 disciplines and nearly 300 events. For example, wrestling is a Summer Olympic sport, comprising two disciplines: Greco-Roman and Freestyle. It is further broken down into fourteen events for men and four events for women, each representing a different weight class. The Summer Olympics program includes 26 sports, while the Winter Olympics program features 15 sports. Athletics, swimming, fencing, and artistic gymnastics are the only summer sports that have never been absent from the Olympic program. Cross-country skiing, figure skating, ice hockey, Nordic combined, ski jumping, and speed skating have been featured at every Winter Olympics program since its inception in 1924. Current Olympic sports, like badminton, basketball, and volleyball, first appeared on the program as demonstration sports, and were later promoted to full Olympic sports. Some sports that were featured in earlier Games were later dropped from the program.

Olympic sports are governed by international sports federations (IFs) recognized by the IOC as the global supervisors of those sports. There are 35 federations represented at the IOC. There are sports recognized by the IOC that are not included on the Olympic program. These sports are not considered Olympic sports, but they can be promoted to this status during a program revision that occurs in the first IOC session following a celebration of the Olympic Games. During such revisions, sports can be excluded or included in the program on the basis of a two-thirds majority vote of the members of the IOC. There are recognized sports that have never been on an Olympic program in any capacity, including chess and surfing.

In October and November 2004, the IOC established an Olympic Programme Commission, which was tasked with reviewing the sports on the Olympic program and all non-Olympic recognized sports. The goal was to apply a systematic approach to establishing the Olympic program for each celebration of the Games. The commission formulated seven criteria to judge whether a sport should be included on the Olympic program. These criteria are history and tradition of the sport, universality, popularity of the sport, image, athletes' health, development of the International Federation that governs the sport, and costs of holding the sport. From this study five recognized sports emerged as candidates for inclusion at the 2012 Summer Olympics: golf, karate, rugby union, roller sports and squash. These sports were reviewed by the IOC Executive Board and then referred to the General Session in Singapore in July 2005. Of the five sports recommended for inclusion only two were selected as finalists: karate and squash. Neither sport attained the required two-thirds vote and consequently they were not promoted to the Olympic program. In October 2009 the IOC voted to instate golf and rugby union as Olympic sports for the 2016 and 2020 Summer Olympic Games.

The 114th IOC Session, in 2002, limited the Summer Games program to a maximum of 28 sports, 301 events, and 10,500 athletes. Three years later, at the 117th IOC Session, the first major program revision was performed, which resulted in the exclusion of baseball and softball from the official program of the 2012 London Games. Since there was no agreement in the promotion of two other sports, the 2012 program will feature just 26 sports. The 2016 and 2020 Games will return to the maximum of 28 sports given the addition of rugby and golf.

Amateurism and Professionalism

The ethos of the aristocracy as exemplified in the English Independent school greatly influenced Pierre de Coubertin. The independent schools subscribed to the belief that sport formed an important part of education, an attitude summed up in the saying mens sana in corpore sano, a sound mind in a sound body. In this ethos, a gentleman was one who became an all-rounder, not the best at one specific thing. There was also a prevailing concept of fairness, in which practicing or training was considered tantamount to cheating. Those who practiced a sport professionally were considered to have an unfair advantage over those who practiced it merely as a hobby.

The exclusion of professionals caused several controversies throughout the history of the modern Olympics. The 1912 Olympic pentathlon and decathlon champion Jim Thorpe was stripped of his medals when it was discovered that he had played semi-professional baseball before the Olympics. His medals were restored by the IOC in 1983 on compassionate grounds. Swiss and Austrian skiers boycotted the 1936 Winter Olympics in support of their skiing teachers, who were not allowed to compete because they earned money with their sport and were thus considered professionals.

As class structure evolved through the 20th century, the definition of the amateur athlete as an aristocratic gentleman became outdated. The advent of the state-sponsored "full-time amateur athlete" of the Eastern Bloc countries further eroded the ideology of the pure amateur, as it put the self-financed amateurs of the Western countries at a disadvantage. Nevertheless, the IOC held to the traditional rules regarding amateurism. Beginning in the 1970s, amateurism requirements were gradually phased out of the Olympic Charter. After the 1988 Games, the IOC decided to make all professional athletes eligible for the Olympics, subject to the approval of the IFs. As of 2004, the only sport in which no professionals compete is boxing, although even this requires a definition of amateurism based on fight rules rather than on payment, as some boxers receive cash prizes from their National Olympic Committees. In men's football (soccer), only three players over the age of 23 are eligible to participate per team in the Olympic tournament.

CONTROVERSIES

Boycotts

The Olympic Council of Ireland boycotted the 1936 Berlin Games, because the IOC insisted its team needed to be restricted to the Irish Free State rather than representing the entire island of Ireland. There were three boycotts of the 1956 Melbourne Olympics: Netherlands, Spain, and Switzerland refused to attend because of the repression of the Hungarian uprising by the Soviet Union; Cambodia, Egypt, Iraq and Lebanon boycotted the Games because of the Suez Crisis; and China (the "People's Republic of China") boycotted the Games because Taiwan (the "Republic of

China") was allowed to compete in the games. In 1972 and 1976 a large number of African countries threatened the IOC with a boycott to force them to ban South Africa and Rhodesia, because of their segregationist regimes. New Zealand was also one of the African boycott targets, because its national rugby union team had toured apartheid-ruled South Africa. The IOC conceded in the first two cases, but refused to ban New Zealand on the grounds that rugby was not an Olympic sport. Fulfilling their threat, twenty African countries were joined by Guyana and Iraq in a Tanzania-led withdrawal from the Montreal Games, after a few of their athletes had already competed. Taiwan also decided to boycott these Games because the People's Republic of China (PRC) exerted pressure on the Montreal organizing committee to keep the delegation from the Republic of China (ROC) from competing under that name. The ROC refused a proposed compromise that would have still allowed them to use the ROC flag and anthem as long as the name was changed. Taiwan did not participate again until 1984, when it returned under the name of Chinese Taipei and with a special flag and anthem.

In 1980 and 1984, the Cold War opponents boycotted each other's Games. Sixty-five nations refused to compete at the Moscow Olympics in 1980 because of the Soviet invasion of Afghanistan. This boycott reduced the number of nations participating to 81, the lowest number since 1956. The Soviet Union and 14 of its Eastern Bloc partners (except Romania) countered by boycotting the Los Angeles Olympics of 1984, contending that they could not guarantee the safety of their athletes. Soviet officials defended their decision to withdraw from the Games by saying that "chauvinistic sentiments and an anti-Soviet hysteria are being whipped up in the United States". The boycotting nations of the Eastern Bloc staged their own alternate event, the Friendship Games, in July and August.

There had been growing calls for boycotts of Chinese goods and the 2008 Olympics in Beijing in protest of China's human rights record, and in response to Tibetan disturbances and ongoing conflict in Darfur. Ultimately, no nation supported a boycott. In

August 2008, the government of Georgia called for a boycott of the 2014 Winter Olympics, set to be held in Sochi, Russia, in response to Russia's participation in the 2008 South Ossetia war. The International Olympic Committee responded to concerns about the status of the 2014 games by stating that it is "premature to make judgments about how events happening today might sit with an event taking place six years from now".

Politics

The Olympic Games have been used as a platform to promote political ideologies almost from its inception. Nazi Germany wished to portray the Nationalist Socialist Party as benevolent and peace-loving when they hosted the 1936 Games. The Games were also intended to show the superiority of the Aryan race; a goal that was not met due in part to the achievements of athletes such as Jesse Owens, who won four gold medals at this Olympics. The Soviet Union did not participate until the 1952 Summer Olympics in Helsinki. Instead, starting in 1928, the Soviets organized an international sports event called Spartakiads. Other communist countries organized Workers Olympics during the interwar period of the 1920s and 1930s. These events were held as an alternative to the Olympics, which were perceived as a capitalist and aristocratic event. It was not until the 1956 Summer Games that the Soviets emerged as a sporting superpower and, in doing so, took full advantage of the publicity that came with winning at the Olympics.

Individual athletes have also used the Olympic stage to promote their own political agenda. At the 1968 Summer Olympics, in Mexico City, two American track and field athletes, Tommie Smith and John Carlos, who finished first and third in the 200 meter sprint race, performed the Black Power salute on the victory stand. The second place finisher Peter Norman wore an Olympic Project for Human Rights badge in support of Smith and Carlos. In response to the protest, IOC President Avery Brundage told the United States Olympic Committee (USOC) to either send the two athletes home or withdraw the track and field team. The USOC opted for the former.

Currently, the government of Iran has taken steps to avoid any competition between its athletes and those from Israel. An Iranian judoka did not compete in a match against an Israeli during the 2004 Summer Olympics. Although he was officially disqualified for excessive weight, Arash Miresmaeli was awarded US$125,000 in prize money by the Iranian government, an amount paid to all Iranian gold medal winners. He was officially cleared of intentionally avoiding the bout, but his receipt of the prize money raised suspicion.

Use of Performance Enhancing Drugs

In the early 20th century, many Olympic athletes began using drugs to improve their athletic abilities. For example, the winner of the marathon at the 1904 Games, Thomas J. Hicks, was given strychnine and brandy by his coach. The only Olympic death linked to doping occurred at the Rome Games of 1960. During the cycling road race, Danish cyclist Knud Enemark Jensen fell from his bicycle and later died. A coroner's inquiry found that he was under the influence of amphetamines. By the mid-1960s, sports federations were starting to ban the use of performance enhancing drugs; in 1967 the IOC followed suit.

The first Olympic athlete to test positive for the use of performance enhancing drugs was Hans-Gunnar Liljenwall, a Swedish pentathlete at the 1968 Summer Olympics, who lost his bronze medal for alcohol use. The most publicized doping-related disqualification was that of Canadian sprinter Ben Johnson, who won the 100 meter dash at the 1988 Seoul Olympics but tested positive for stanozolol. His gold medal was subsequently stripped and awarded to runner-up Carl Lewis, who himself had tested positive for banned substances prior to the Olympics.

In the late 1990s, the IOC took the initiative in a more organized battle against doping, by forming the World Anti-Doping Agency (WADA) in 1999. There was a sharp increase in positive drug tests at the 2000 Summer Olympics and 2002 Winter

Olympics. Several medalists in weightlifting and cross-country skiing were disqualified because of doping offenses. During the 2006 Winter Olympics, only one athlete failed a drug test and had a medal revoked. The IOC-established drug testing regimen (now known as the Olympic Standard) has set the worldwide benchmark that other sporting federations around the world attempt to emulate. During the Beijing games, 3,667 athletes were tested by the IOC under the auspices of the World Anti-Doping Agency. Both urine and blood tests were used to detect banned substances. Several athletes were barred from competition by their National Olympic Committees prior to the Games; only three athletes failed drug tests while in competition in Beijing.

Violence

The Olympics have not brought lasting peace to the world, even during celebrations of the Games. In fact, three Olympiads had to pass without a celebration of the Games because of war: the 1916 Games were cancelled because of World War I, and the summer and winter games of 1940 and 1944 were cancelled because of World War II. The South Ossetia War between Georgia and Russia erupted on the opening day of the 2008 Summer Olympics in Beijing. Both President Bush and Prime Minister Putin were attending the Olympics at that time and spoke together about the conflict at a luncheon hosted by Chinese President Hu Jintao. When Nino Salukvadze of Georgia won the bronze medal in the 10 meter air pistol competition, she stood on the medal podium with Natalia Paderina, a Russian shooter who had won the silver. In what became a much-publicized event from the Beijing Games, Salukvadze and Paderina embraced on the podium after the ceremony had ended.

Terrorism has also threatened the Olympic Games. In 1972, when the Summer Games were held in Munich, Bavaria, Germany, eleven members of the Israeli Olympic team were taken hostage by the terrorist group Black September in what is now known as the Munich massacre. The terrorists killed two of the athletes soon after they had taken them hostage and killed the other nine during a failed liberation attempt. A German police officer and 5 terrorists also perished. During the Summer Olympics in 1996 in Atlanta, a bomb was detonated at the Centennial Olympic Park, which killed 2 and injured 111 others. The bomb was set by Eric Robert Rudolph, an American domestic terrorist, who is currently serving a life sentence for the bombing. The 2002 Winter Olympics were the first Olympic Games held since September 11, 2001, which meant security at every Olympic games since then have been ramped up further to avoid a terrorist attack.

Champions and medalists

The athletes or teams who place first, second, or third in each event receive medals. The winners receive gold medals, which were solid gold until 1912, then made of gilded silver and now gold-plated silver. Every gold medal must contain at least six grams of pure gold. The runners-up receive silver medals and the third-place athletes are awarded bronze medals. In events contested by a single-elimination tournament (most notably boxing), third place might not be determined and both semifinal losers receive bronze medals. At the 1896 Olympics only the first two received a medal; silver for first and bronze for second. The current three-medal format was introduced at the 1904 Olympics. From 1948 onward athletes placing fourth, fifth, and sixth have received certificates, which became officially known as victory diplomas; in 1984 victory diplomas for seventh- and eighth-place finishers were added. At the 2004 Summer Olympics in Athens, the gold, silver, and bronze medal winners were also given olive wreaths. The IOC does not keep statistics of medals won, but National Olympic Committees and the media record medal statistics as a measure of success.

HOST NATIONS AND CITIES

The host city for an Olympic Games is usually chosen seven years ahead of their celebration. The process of selection is carried out in two phases that span a two-year period. The prospective host city applies to its country's Olympic Committee; if more than one city from the same country submits a proposal to its NOC, the national committee typically holds an internal selection, since only one city per NOC can be presented to the International Olympic Committee for consideration. Once the deadline for submission of proposals by the NOCs is reached, the first phase (Application) begins with the applicant cities asked to complete a questionnaire regarding several key criteria related to the organization of the Olympic Games. In this form, the applicants must give assurances that they will comply with the Olympic Charter and with any other regulations established by the IOC Executive Committee. The evaluation of the filled questionnaires by a specialized group provides the IOC with an overview of each applicant's project and their potential to host the Games. On the basis of this technical evaluation, the IOC Excutive Board selects the applicants that will proceed to the candidature stage.

Once the candidate cities are selected, they must submit to the IOC a bigger and more detailed presentation of their project as part of a candidature file. Each city is thoroughly analyzed by an evaluation commission. This commission will also visit the candidate cities, interviewing local officials and inspecting prospective venue sites, and submit a report on its findings one month prior to the IOC's final decision. During the interview process the candidate city must also guarantee that it will be able to fund the Games. After the work of the evaluation commission, a list of candidates is presented to the General Session of the IOC, which is assembled in a country that must not have a candidate city in the running. The IOC members gathered in the Session have the final vote on the host city. Once elected, the host city bid committee (together with the NOC of the respective country) signs a Host City Contract with the IOC, officially becoming an Olympic host nation and host city.

By 2016, the Olympic Games will have been hosted by 44 cities in 23 countries, but by cities outside Europe and North America on only eight occasions. Since the 1988 Summer Olympics in Seoul, South Korea, the Olympics have been held in Asia or Oceania four times, a sharp increase compared to the previous 92 years of modern Olympic history. The 2016 Games in Rio de Janeiro will be the first for a South American country. No bids from countries in Africa have ever succeeded.

The United States has hosted four Summer and four Winter Olympics, more than any other nation. Among Summer Olympics host nations, the United Kingdom has been the host of two Games, and will host its third Olympics in 2012 in London, making London the only city ever to host three times. Germany, Australia, France, and Greece are the other nations to have hosted the Summer Olympics twice.

Concerning the Winter Olympics, France has hosted three Games, while Switzerland, Austria, Norway, Japan, and Italy have hosted twice. The most recent Games were held in Vancouver, Canada's second Winter Olympics and third overall. The next Winter Games will be in Sochi, Russia in 2014, which will be the first time this nation has hosted.

OTHER EVENTS

At the beginning of the 20th century, another multi-sport event, the Nordic Games were first held. These Games were held in Scandinavia, and the sports conducted were winter sports such as cross-country skiing and speed skating. The Nordic Games were last held in 1926, after which the 1924 Winter Sports Week in Chamonix was declared the first Olympic Winter Games.

In the 1920s, all kinds of other multi-sport events were set up. These were usually directed for a selected group of athletes, rather than everybody, which was - basically - the case with the Olympic Games. The Soviets organised the first Spartakiad in 1920, a communist alternative to the 'bourgeois' Olympic Games, and in 1922 the University Olympia was organised in Italy, the forerunner of the World University Games, meant for students only. Regional Games were another kind of multi-sport event that was established, such as the Far Eastern Championship Games or the Central American and Caribbean Games.

Central Audiences

Since the establishment of the Olympics, most serial multi-sport events have been organized for specific audiences and participating countries or communities:

- regional, such as the East Asian Games and the South American Games.
- political, such as the Spartakiad and the GANEFO.
- historic or historicultural roots, such as the Commonwealth Games (for members of the Commonwealth of Nations) and the Jeux de la Francophonie (for members of La Francophonie).
- ethnocultural or ethnoreligious, such as the Pan-Armenian Games (for ethnic communities of Armenians both in Armenia and in other countries) and the Maccabiah Games (for communities of Jews of both ethnic and religious origins).
- religious, such as the Islamic Solidarity Games and the previously mentioned Maccabiah Games.
- occupational, such as the Military World Games, the World Police and Fire Games and the Universiade.
- physical structure, such as the Paralympics, the Deaflympics and the Special Olympics World Games.
- human age, such as the World Masters Games, Commonwealth Youth Games and the Senior Olympics.
- gender and sexual orientation, such as the Women's Islamic Games and the Gay Games.

List of Major International Competitions

The Olympic Games are still the largest multi-sport event in the world in terms of worldwide interest and importance (though no longer in participation), but several others also have significance.

Worldwide Events

Multi-sports events for non-Olympic sports

- World Games, held first in 1981, stage many sports (though not all) that are not Olympic sports. The World Games is therefore sometimes also unofficially called Olympics for non-Olympic sports. (They cannot be called "Olympic" games without infringing on the Olympic committees' trademarks.).
- World Mind Sports Games, first held in 2008 for games of skill (e.g. chess, go, etc.).
- The X Games and Winter X Games, which highlight extreme action sports.

By Occupation

- World University Games (also called Universiade), held first in 1923, for students at universities worldwide.
- Military World Games, held first in 1995, for military athletes from over 100 countries.
- World Police and Fire Games, begun in 1985, for law enforcement officers and firefighters worldwide; third only to the World Masters Games and Summer Olympics in number of participants.

By Organisation and Language

- Commonwealth Games, held first in 1930 (although similar games in 1911) for all nations from the Commonwealth of Nations.
- Commonwealth Youth Games, began in 2000.
- Francophone Games, held first in 1989, for nations that speak French.
- Lusophony Games, begun in 2006, for Portuguese-speaking countries.

- Islamic Solidarity Games, first held in 2005, for all nations from the Organisation of the Islamic Conference.
- Women's Islamic Games, began in 1993.

By political and historical allegiance

- Bolivarian Games, began in 1938, for countries liberated by Simón Bolívar.
- Games of the Small States of Europe held first in 1985, for eight small states in Europe.
- Island Games, first held in 1985, fcr teams from several islands and other small territories.
- Goodwill Games, held first in 1986, held as an alternative after the boycotted Olympics of 1980 and 1984. (Final edition was held in 2001).
- Spartakiad, a defunct event involving athletes from the Soviet Union.
- Games of the New Emerging Forces, held first in 1963 in Jakarta, Indonesia, for the so-called "emerging nations" (mainly newly independent socialist states).

By Ethnicity

- Maccabiah Games, first held in 1932, for Jewish athletes worldwide.
- Pan Arab Games, held first in 1953, for Arabic nations.
- Pan-Armenian Games, began in 1999.

Other

- Gay Games and World OutGames held first in 1982 and 2006, for the worldwide gay community.
- World Masters Games, first held in 1985, for mature athletes. Most participants of any multi-sport event, with

approximately twice as many competitors as the Summer Olympics.

- World Sport for All Games, first held in 1992, by TAFISA.

Regional Events

- All-Africa Games, held first in 1965, for all African nations.
- Pan American Games, held first in 1951, for all nations of the Americas.
- Central American and Caribbean Games, held first in 1926, every 4 years for nations in the Caribbean, Central America and/or borderind the Caribbean sea.
- South American Games, began in 1978.
- Arafura Games, held first in 1991 and hosted in the Oceania region.
- Asian Games, held first in 1951, for all Asian nations.
- Southeast Asian Games, held first in 1959, for nations in Southeast Asia.
- East Asian Games, for nations in East Asia.
- West Asian Games, for nations in West Asia.
- Central Asian Games, for nations in Central Asia.
- South Asian Games, for nations in South Asia
- European Youth Olympic Festival (EYOF), for youth athletes from Europe, began in 1991 (summer) and 1993 (winter).
- Mediterranean Games, held first in 1951, for all nations bordering the Mediterranean Sea.
- South Pacific Games, held first in 1963 for countries around the South Pacific.
- Central American Games, held first in 1973 for countries in the Central America.

- Caribbean Games, proposed to be held first in June 2009 for countries in the Caribbean sea, suspended by the swine flu fears, it still to determinate the next edition for 2011.
- Arctic Winter Games, held first in 1970, an international biennial celebration of circumpolar north and artic sports and culture.

National Events

- National Games of the People's Republic of China, perhaps the oldest national games with a history dating back to 1910.
- Korean National Sports Festival, held first in 1920, for provinces in South Korea.
- National Sports Festival of Japan.
- Palarong Pambansa in the Philippines.
- Canada Games.
- SUKMA Games in Malaysia.

Disability

Other Games are intended for handicapped or disabled athletes. The International Silent Games, held in Paris in 1924, were the first Games for deaf athletes. The Stoke Mandeville Wheelchair Games, incepted in 1948 in England, were the first Games for wheelchair athletes. In 1960, the first Paralympic Games were held, connected with the Olympic Games. The Special Olympics World Games, for athletes with intellectual disabilities, were first held in 1968.

CHAPTER–5

Media Event Tourism

A media event, as loosely defined by evolving modern usage, is an occasion or happening, spontaneous or planned, that attracts prominent coverage by mass media organizations, particularly television news and newspapers in both print and Internet editions. The element of immediacy (as in "breaking news") is crucial in spontaneous media events, while in planned events like a major speech by a national leader or a public demonstration against a government action, the prime importance of the subject matter itself is relied upon to elevate the occasion to true media event status. When individuals or groups attempt to generate publicity for themselves through a contrived media event, the occasion almost never captures widespread interest in the way a "naturally" occurring event does—such attempts are usually thought of as instances of "spin" or media manipulation, despite the use of the term "media event" by advertising agencies or other planners.

OVERVIEW

Media events in the serious contemporary sense of the term have been happening roughly since the early 1940s, when the ubiquity of movie-house newsreels joined with the established presence of newspapers and commercial radio to form a communications convergence able to give the man-or-woman-on-the-street the sense that everywhere he or she looked or listened, the same "story" was before them. This media saturation was greatly furthered by television, invented in the late 1920s and reaching millions of households by 1950. Starting around 1980, 24-hour cable television news operations debuted with great fanfare, with their signature use of new civilian satellite links that made on-camera live or near-live reporting from almost any spot on earth feasible while the event was still underway or its immediate aftermath continued to affect those involved. Finally, the emergence of the World Wide Web in 1994, allowing for instant global reporting, debating, polling and blogging, completed the communications environment of today, wherein a media event of global significance, or even one of limited geographical scope but consisting of particularly unusual or affecting content, can literally claim the time and attention of most of the world's people as events unfold.

Media events can hold sway on many levels, from a small city television viewership up to the entire planet, sometimes occupying a smaller audience non-stop while a larger audience is fed sporadic updates. For instance, the dramatic twists and turns of Viktor Yushchenko's 2005 bid for the Ukrainian presidency, featuring poisoning plots, voter intimidation, outraged citizens demonstrating in the capital city and other tense, "newsworthy" developments, easily constituted an extensive media event within Ukraine itself even as international mass media followed it closely but did not grant it uninterrupted coverage. By contrast, the September 11, 2001 attacks did reach the plateau of a sustained, planet-wide media event, due mostly to the unprecedented realtime visuals, the involvement of citizens and perpetrators from many different countries and cultures, and a single-day intentional taking of human life not seen at such levels in the developed world since the end of World War II.

The coverage of global and national media events has become a pillar of large news organizations, which often operate at scant profitability in-between these major occurrences. Public opinion, and even baseline attitudes of one culture towards another, can be largely determined by what is seen and heard during a major media event, and the entire careers of journalists can be made (or unmade) by their conduct during these iconic situations. In the United States, the first full bore post-WWII media event was the 1963 assassination of President John F. Kennedy, and it, to a great extent, determined the unwritten hierarchy of American journalists and "news personalities" for the succeeding 40 years. The development of "glasnost" and the ensuing fall of Communism in Russia was a similar determinant for journalists there.

Parallel instances for almost every nation or region can be found, with the major media event corresponding to the shared memory of a "defining moment" often felt in personal, yet nationalistic, terms. The fall of the Berlin Wall in November, 1989 was such a moment for Germans on both sides; the resolution of the Chinese Civil War in 1950 still resounds in that nation; the achievement of independence from Great Britain in 1980 by Zimbabwe (formerly Rhodesia) was a defining moment which dominated news reporting on several continents at the time; the invasion, starting on March 20, 2003, that deposed Iraq's Saddam Hussein was one of the few modern media events capturing the attention of a majority of the planet's adults and will likely be commemorated in Iraq, in celebration or infamy, for generations, accompanied by news footage first transmitted that day. The distinguishing characteristic of all these is a day or other short period of time during which changes of great importance came to a head, lending themselves to breaking news-style media coverage.

MEDIA CIRCUS

Media circus describes a news event where the media coverage is perceived to be out of proportion to the event being covered, such as the number of reporters at the scene, the amount of news media published or broadcast, and the level of media hype. The term is meant to critique the media by comparing it to a circus and, as such, is an idiom and not an objective observation. Media hype, orgy, and feeding frenzy are similar terms used in reference to a critique of news and entertainment media.

Although the idea is older, the term media circus began to appear around the mid 1970s. An early example is from the 1976 book by author Lynn Haney, in which she says "Their courtship, after all, had been a media circus". A few years later The Washington Post had a similar courtship example in when it said "Princess Grace herself is still traumatized by the memory of her own media-circus wedding to Prince Rainier in 1956." The term has become increasingly popular with time since the 1970s.

Reasons for being critical of the media are as varied as the people who use the term. However, at the core of most criticism is that there may be a significant opportunity cost when other more important news issues get less public attention as a result of coverage of the hyped issue.

Media circus is the central plot device in the 1951 movie Ace in the Hole about a self-interested reporter covering a mine disaster. It cynically examines the relationship between the media and the news it reports. It was originally called The Big Carnival, with "carnival" referring to what we now call a "circus".

Events described as a media circus include:

United Kingdom

- The suicide of Dr David Kelly
- The Disappearance of Madeleine McCann
- The Cheriegate property scandal
- The Russell Brand Show prank telephone calls row
- The February 2009 Great Britain and Ireland snowfall
- The life, death and funeral of Jade Goody

United States of America

- David Gelman, Peter Greenberg, et al. in Newsweek on January 31, 1977: "Brooklyn born photographer and film producer Lawrence Schiller managed to make himself the sole journalist to witness the execution of Gary Gilmore in

Utah....In the Gilmore affair, he was like a ringmaster in what became a media circus, with sophisticated newsmen scrambling for what he had to offer."

- The Death Of Elvis Presley, Aug.16 1977
- The rescue of Jessica McClure, October 14-16, 1987
- The O. J. Simpson trial, from 1994-1995
- The Blizzard of '96 (1996). "...this storm ...so hyped by the media in the same way that the O. J. Simpson murder case became hyped as the "Trial of the century". (Elizabeth Davis, The Daily Beacon, January 12 1996).
- Y2K Hype
- The 2001 Summer of the Shark
- The trial of Martha Stewart (2004). "The stone-faced Stewart never broke stride as she cut a path through the media circus." (Newsweek, "Martha's Fall", March 15 2005)
- The Clinton-Lewinsky scandal, from 1998-1999
- The 2004 Super Bowl XXXVIII halftime show controversy
- The 2005 People v. Jackson
- The 2005 divorce of Brad Pitt and Jennifer Aniston
- The 2005 Runaway bride case
- The Eliot Spitzer prostitution scandal
- The 2009 flu pandemic
- The 2009 Death of Michael Jackson
- The 2009 Balloon boy hoax
- The 2009 Tiger Woods scandal
- The 2009–2010 Toyota vehicle recalls
- The 2010 Deepwater Horizon oil spill
- The Brett Favre retirement saga in 2009 and 2010

Aruba

- The disappearance of Natalee Holloway

Australia

- The 2005 Cronulla riots
- The Beaconsfield Mine collapse
- The information of Swine influenza
- Jessica Watson's return to Sydney in May 2010 after her "solo round the world trip"

Brazil

- The murder of Isabella Nardoni

Pakistan

- The Shoaib Sania Marriage

Peru

- Joran van der Sloot and the death of Stephany Flores Ramírez

Sensationalism

Sensationalism is a manner of over-hyping events, being deliberately controversial, loud, self centred or acting to obtain attention. It is also a form of theatre.

In Mass Media

The term is commonly used in reference to the mass media. Critics of media bias of all political stripes often charge the media with engaging in sensationalism in their reporting and conduct. That is, the notion that media outlets often choose to report heavily on stories with shock value or attention-grabbing names or events, rather than reporting on more pressing issues to the general public.

In the extreme case, the media would report the news if it makes a good story, without much regard for the factual accuracy or social relevance. Thus, a press release including ridiculous and false pseudoscientific claims issued by a controversial group is guaranteed a lot of media coverage. Two examples are claims of human cloning by Clonaid and claims of cold fusion by Pons and Fleischmann.

Such stories are often perceived (rightfully, or mistakenly) as partisan or biased due to the sensational nature in which they are reported. A media piece may report on a political figure in a biased way or present one side of an issue while deriding another, or neutrally, it may simply include sensational aspects such as zealots, doomsayers and/or junk science. Complex subjects and affairs are often subject to sensationalism. Exciting and emotionally charged aspects can be drawn out without providing elements such as pertinent background, investigative, or contextual information needed for the viewer to form his or her opinion on the subject.

Mainstream media may choose a comedy site as a news source and then proceed to display its content without any factual checks. One widely reported example involved The Onion's story on Harry Potter.

One presumed goal of sensational reporting is increased (or sustained) viewership or readership, which can be sold to advertisers, the result being a lesser focus on proper journalism and a greater focus on the "juicy" aspects of a story that pull in a larger share of audience.

History of Sensationalism

Mitchell Stephens, in his account of "The History of News", illustrates that sensationalism can be found in the Roman Acta, and was spread with enthusiasm by preliterate societies. Sensationalism can be found in books of the 16th and 17th century; however, it is asserted that sensationalism in this era was used to teach moral lessons.

Sensationalism is further believed by Stephens to have brought the news to a new audience. He discusses the heavy use of sensationalism aimed towards the lower class, as they have less of a need to understand politics and the economy. Through this, the audience is further educated and encouraged to take more interest in the news.

However, Stephens notes, "when journalists confine themselves to the search for the violent or the miraculous, not only do they paint a grotesque face on the world, but they deprive their audiences of the opportunity to examine subtler occurrences with larger consequences".

Sensationalism in Broadcasting

Sensationalism is often blamed for the 'infotainment style' of many of the news programs broadcast over radio and television. Yet the news has always been enjoyed for as long as it has been exchanged. The debate of sensationalism used in the mass medium of broadcasting is based on a misunderstanding of its audience, especially the television audience. Thompson explains that the term 'mass' which is connected to broadcasting, suggests a 'vast audience of many thousands, even millions of passive individuals'. When sensationalism used through broadcasting is combined with this concept of the passive mass audience, it is assumed the audience consumes all information fed to them. However, Thompson continues that the recipients of a message, no matter how sensationalized it is, ' make with it what they will, and the producer is not there to elaborate or to correct possible misunderstanding'. Thus it is the misinterpretation of the broadcast audience as passive consumers which is problematic for the use of sensationalism.

Furthermore, while the newspaper is often seen as a more credible source than television news because of televisions use of footage over spoken information, they are both sensationalized to the same extent. Television news is restricted to showing the scenes of crimes rather than the crime itself because of the unpredictability of events. Whereas newspaper writers can always recall what they did not witness. "No act of violence is beyond the reach of the still formidable magic of words". Furthermore, television news writers have room for fewer words than their newspaper counterparts. Their stories are measured in seconds, not column inches, and thus even with footage, television stories are undeniably shallower than most newspaper stories. And because their words are intended for a less acute, less painstaking sense — hearing — television news writers must forswear the more complex formulations a newspaper reporter might hazard.

Sensational spellings are common in advertising and product placement. In particular, brand names such as Cadbury's "Creme Egg" (standard English spelling: cream) or Kellogg's "Froot Loops" (fruit) may use unexpected spellings to draw attention, and also to make an everyday word patentable. The inscription "Fish 'n' chips" above a chip shop is similar. Sensational spelling may take on a cult value in popular culture. An example of this is the heavy metal umlaut. In esoteric circles, magic is often spelled magick to differentiate it from stage magic.

It is also often used in teenybopper media including that targeting children including Miley Cyrus, Hilary Duff, and other teen celebrities.

CHAPTER–6

Festival Event Tourism

A festival is an event, usually and ordinarily staged by a local community, which centers on and celebrates some unique aspect of that community.

Among many religions, a feast is a set of celebrations in honour of God or Gods. A feast and a festival are historically interchangeable. However, the term "feast" has also entered common secular parlance as a synonyms for any large or elaborate meal. When used as in the meaning of a festival, most often refers to a religious festival rather than a film or art festival.

In the Christian liturgical calendar there are two principal feasts, properly known as the Feast of the Nativity of our Lord (Christmas) and the Feast of the Resurrection, (Easter). In the Catholic, Eastern Orthodox, and Anglican liturgical calendars there are a great number of lesser feasts throughout the year commemorating saints, sacred events, doctrines, etc.

For a list of festivals in the USA, please see List of festivals in the United States.

ETYMOLOGY

The word fest derives from the Middle English, from Middle French word festivus, from the Latin word festivus. Festival was first recorded as a noun in 1589. Before it had been used as an adjective from the fourteenth century, meaning to celebrate a church holiday. The etymology of feast is very similar to that of festival. The word "feste" (one letter different from "fest") comes from Middle English, from Middle French, from the Latin word festa. Feast first came into usage as a noun circa 1200, and feast was used as a verb circa 1300. A festival is a special occasion of feasting or celebration, that is usually religious. There can be many different types of festival, like Halloween and Christmas.

Function

Festivals, of many types, serve to meet specific needs, as well as to provide entertainment. These times of celebration offer a sense of belonging for religious, social, or geographical groups. Modern festivals that focus on cultural or ethnic topics seek to inform members of their traditions. In past times, festivals were times when the elderly shared stories and transferred certain knowledge to the next generation. Historic feasts often provided a means for unity among families and for people to find mates. Select anniversaries have annual festivals to commemorate previous significant occurrences.

Types of festivals

There are numerous types of festivals in the world. Though many have religious origins, others involve seasonal change or have some cultural significance. Also, certain institutions celebrate their own festival (often called "fests") to mark some significant occasions in their history. These occasions could be the day these institutions were founded or any other event which they decide to commemorate periodically, usually annually.

Seasonal festivals

Seasonal festivals are determined by the solar and the lunar calendars and by the cycle of the seasons. The changing of the season was celebrated because of its effect on food supply. Ancient Egyptians would celebrate the seasonal inundation caused by the Nile River, a form of irrigation, which provided fertile land for crops. In the Alps, in autumn the return of the cattle from the mountain pastures to the stables in the valley is celebrated as Almabtrieb. A recognized winter festival, the Chinese New Year, is set by the lunar calendar, and celebrated from the day of the second new moon after the winter solstice. An important type of seasonal festivals are those related with the agricultural seasons. Dree Festival of the Apatanis living in Lower Subansiri District of Arunachal Pradesh is one such important festival, which is celebrated every year from July 4 to 7 praying for bumper crop harvest.

VARIOUS TYPE OF FESTIVEAL

Arts Festival

An arts festival is a festival that focuses on the visual arts in all its forms, but which may also focus on or include other arts. Arts festivals in the visual arts are exhibitions and are not to be confused with the commercial "art fair". Artists participate in the most important of such festival exhibitions by invitation, and these exhibitions (e.g. the Venice Biennale) are organised by internationally recognized curators chosen by a committee of peers. These international exhibitions must be distinguished from art fairs, market-oriented gatherings of art dealers and their wares, which have recently emerged as among the most important art-world venues for promoting artists and sales of contemporary art in the present-day super-heated art market.

Probably the two oldest festivals are in England. The Three Choirs Festival in the West of England was established as a "yearly musical assembly" by 1719. The other is the Norfolk and Norwich Festival which first took place in 1772 The largest arts festival in England today is the Brighton Festival.

Leading arts festivals include the Edinburgh Festival in Edinburgh, which is the largest arts festival, Adelaide Festival of Arts in Adelaide, the Biennale of Sydney, and Festival d'Avignon in Avignon, France. One-off arts festivals have included the Liverpool 08 European Capital of Culture in 2008 and the current

Larkin 25 festival celebrating the life of the English poet Philip Larkin in Kingston-upon-Hull.

Beer Festival

A Beer Festival is an organised event during which a variety of beers (and often other alcoholic drinks) are available for tasting and purchase. Beer festivals are held in a number of countries. A Beer Exhibition is usually synonymous with a Beer Festival but, whilst a beer festival may involve a limited range of beer styles or manufacturers, with an emphasis on entertainment, use of the term "beer exhibition" places emphasis on sampling or tasting a wide range of beers, usually craft-brewed in a variety of different styles by various brewers. There may be a theme; for instance beers from a particular area, or a particular brewing style such as winter ales. Beerex is a commonly used portmanteau word coined in 1977 as an abbreviated form of Beer Exhibition.

Notable British Beer Festivals

- The Great British Beer Festival held annually in August in London is the largest beer festival in the UK organised by CAMRA. The "GBBF",founded in 1977, was attended by over 66,000 people in 2006 when 350,000 pints of ale were consumed over the five days.
- The CAMRA National Winter Ales Festival; held at New Century Hall, Manchester, is designed to showcase beer styles which may not be readily available during the summer festival. Taking place every January, it has also been celebrated in Glasgow and Burton-on-Trent.
- The Luton Beer Festival, organised by South Beds CAMRA, is one of the first major beer festivals of the UK calendar year. With over 100 beers, ciders and perries usually available. Takes place 18–20 February 2010 and is currently in its 27th year.
- The Peterborough CAMRA Beer Festival held in three giant marquees on the Embankment, Peterborough, PE1

1EF has been running since 1978 and is the largest outside of London with 35,000 visitors, 400+ draught real ales, 80+ ciders and perries and 100+ bottled beers. Live music every evening. Takes place on the Tuesday to Saturday in the week before August Bank Holiday.

- The Nottingham Robin Hood Beer Festival in Nottingham, has been held annually in October since 1977 (before 2008 styled Nottingham Beer Festival). It is held in the grounds of Nottingham Castle in the city having moved there from the Victoria Leisure Centre. It has grown to 15,000 people attending in 2008 with 57,500 pints of real ale consumed.
- The Farnham Beer Exhibition in Surrey, having been held every year since 1977 at the Farnham Maltings, is the longest-running beer festival to be held annually on a single site in the United Kingdom, and every year sells over 29,000 pints of real ale during its 3 day opening.
- The Cambridge Beer Festival, held since 1974, is the longest running beer festival, although it has changed venue three times. Currently, it is held for a week each May in a large marquee erected on Jesus Green in Cambridge. It is the second largest festival outside of London and had 32,000 people attending in 2007.
- The Reading Beer Festival was first held in 1994, and has now grown to one of the largest beer festivals in the UK. 4 days immediately preceding the May Day Bank Holiday every year. It is now the third largest festival outside London, after Cambridge.
- The Telford Beer Festival, otherwise known as Britain's biggest pub-based, cooled hand-pulled beer festival happens twice a year at the Crown Inn in Oakengates, Telford, Shropshire. Typically held on the Last weekend in April and the First weekend in October lasts 5 days with 34 individually

cooled hand pulls Ales, Ciders or Perries.

Other festivals are held in Portsmouth known as the Pompey Beer Festival, London, Nottingham, Peterborough, St Albans, Norwich and in many other places. They are both very large and offer an interesting and distinctive selection of British and foreign beers.

The largest German Beer Festival to be held in Britain takes place each year at Alexandra Palace as part of their Fireworks celebrations. Known as The Alexandra Palace German Beer Festival the 2009 event takes place on Saturday 7 November and includes performances from Chas n Dave and a host of traditional German acts.

Comedy festival

A comedy festival is a celebration of comedy with many shows, venues, comedy performers (such as stand up comics, sketch troupes, variety performers, etc.) and is held over a specific block of time. Normally, each festival has a diverse range of comedy themes and genres.

Some comedy festivals are the Edinburgh Fringe, the Melbourne International Comedy Festival, Sydney Comedy Festival, FunnyFest Calgary Comedy Festival, Cologne Comedy Festival, Just For Laughs, the Iowa Comedy Festival, Winnipeg Fringe Theatre Festival, the HK International Comedy Festival, the Kilkenny Cat Laughs Comedy Festival and the New Zealand International Comedy Festival.

Japanese Cultural Festival

The Japanese Cultural Festival is an annual event held by most schools in Japan, from Nursery schools to universities at which their students display their everyday achievements. People who want to enter the school themselves or who are interested in the school may come to see what the schoolwork and atmosphere are like. Parents may also want to see what kind of work their children have been doing.

The Cultual Festival are originally held to display the students' daily learning, but many people who visit the cultural festivals come to the festivals just for fun. Food is served, and often classrooms or gymnasiums are transformed into temporary restaurants or cafés. Dances, concerts and plays may be performed by individual volunteers or by various school "clubs" such as the dance club, the orchestra club, the band club and the drama club.

The Cultural Festivals are intended to be a fun event, but it is also the only opportunity each year for students to see what life is like in other schools. It is also intended to enrich people's lives by increasing social interaction. Cultural festivals are frequently depicted in anime and manga.

Esala Perahera festival

Esala Perahera (the festival of the tooth) is the grand festival of Esala held in Sri Lanka. It is very grand with elegant costumes. Happening in July or August in Kandy, it has become a unique symbol of Sri Lanka. It is a Buddhist festival consisting of dances and nicely decorated elephants. There are fire-dances, whip-dances, Kandian dances and various other cultural dances. The elephants are usually adorned with lavish garments. The festival ends with the traditional 'diya-kepeema'.

The Esala Perahera in Kandy is believed to be a fusion of two separate but interconnected "Peraheras" (Processions) – The Esala and Dalada. The Esala Perahera which is thought to date back to the 3rd century BC, was a ritual enacted to request the gods for rainfall. The Dalada Perahera is believed to have begun when the Sacred Tooth Relic of the Buddha was brought to Sri Lanka from India during the 4th Century AD. The TOOTH RELIC was take in procession to Sri Lanka by Princess Hemamala & Prince Dantha.

The Modern Perahera dates back to the reign of the Kandyan King Kirthi Sri Rajasinghe (1747 – 1781 AD). During these times, the Tooth Relic was considered private property of the

King and the public never got a chance to worship it. However, King Rajasinghe decreed that the Relic be taken in procession for the masses to see and venerate.

After the Kandyan Kingdom fell to the British in 1815, the custody of the Relic was handed over to the Maha Sanga (the Buddhist Clergy). In the absence of the king, a lay custodian called the "Diyawadana Nilame" was appointed to handle routine administrative matters.

The Kandy Esala Perahera begins with the Kap Situveema or Kappa, in which a sanctified young Jackfruit tree (Artocarpus integrifolia) is cut and planted in the premises of each of the four Devales dedicated to the four guardian gods Natha, Vishnu, Katharagama and the goddess Pattini. Traditionally it was meant to shower blessing on the King and the people.

Film Festival

A film festival is an organised, extended presentation of films in one or more movie theaters or screening venues, usually in a single locality. The films may be of recent date and, depending upon the focus of the individual festival, can include international releases as well as films produced by the organisers' domestic film industry. Sometimes there is a focus on a specific film-maker or genre (e.g., film noir) or subject matter (e.g., gay and lesbian film festivals). A number of film festivals specialise in short films, each with its defined maximum length. Film festivals are typically annual events.

The first major film festival was held in Venice in 1932; the other major film festivals of the world (Berlin, Edinburgh, Cannes, Moscow, and Karlovy Vary) date back to the 1930s, 1940s and 1950s.

The Edinburgh International Film Festival in the UK was established in 1947 and is the longest continually running film festival in the world. Raindance Film Festival is the UK's largest celebration of independent film-making and is taking place in London in October.

The first North American high film festival was the Columbus International Film & Video Festival, also known as The Chris Awards, held in 1953. According to the Film Arts Foundation in San Francisco, "The Chris Awards (is) one of the most prestigious documentary, educational, business and informational competitions in the U.S; (it is) the oldest of its kind in North America and celebrating its 54th year."

It was followed four years later by the San Francisco International Film Festival held in March 1957 whose emphasis was on feature-length dramatic films. The festival played a major role in introducing foreign films to American audiences. Among the films shown in its founding year were Akira Kurosawa's Throne of Blood and Satyajit Ray's Pather Panchali.

Today there are thousands of film festivals around the world, ranging from high profile festivals such as Sundance Film Festival (Park City, UT) to horror festivals such as Terror Film Festival (Philadelphia, PA).

Digital feature film distribution began in 2005, along with the arrival of the world's first online film festival, the GreenCine Online Film Festival, sponsored by DivX.

Significant or notable festivals

The three most prestigious film festivals are commonly regarded to be that of Berlin, Cannes and Venice; these festivals are sometimes called the "Big Three." Polish director Krzyszt of Kies'lowski's The Three Colors Trilogy were each made for these festivals, with Blue for Venice, White for Berlin, and Red for Cannes.

- "A" Festivals: The festivals in Cannes, Venice, Toronto, Berlin, Shanghai, Moscow, San Sebastián, Montréal, Locarno (since 2002), Karlovy Vary, Mar del Plata, Cairo, Tokyo, and Warsaw are listed as "A festivals", or "category one" by the International Federation of Film Producers Associations (FIAPF).

- Experimental films: Ann Arbor Film Festival was started in 1963. It is the oldest continually operated experimental film festival in North America and has become one of the premiere film festivals for independent and, primarily, experimental filmmakers to showcase their work.
- Independent films: In the US, Telluride Film Festival, Sundance Film Festival, Austin's South by Southwest, and New York City's Tribeca Film Festival, are all considered significant festivals for independent film. The biggest independent film festival in the UK is Raindance Film Festival.
- Latin American significance: The Cartagena Film Festival, founded by Victor Nieto in 1960, is the oldest film festival in Latin America. The Festival de Gramado (or Gramado Film Festival) Gramado, Brazil along with the Guadalajara International Film Festival in Guadalajara, Mexico are considered to be the most important film festivals of Latin America. It was first held in 1973, awarding Latin American films. The Huelva Ibero-American Film Festival has been held since 1975 in that Spanish city. While the Expresión en Corto International Film Festival is the largest competitive film festival in Mexico, specializing in emerging talents, and is held each year during the last week of July in the two colonial cities of San Miguel de Allende and Guanajuato. Among Spanish speaking countries the Dominican International Film Festival is held annually in Puerto Plata, DR, the Valdivia International Film Festival is held annually in the city of Valdivia. It is arguable the most important film festival in Chile.
- North American significance: The San Francisco International Film Festival, started in 1957, is the oldest continuously running film festival in the Americas. It highlights current trends in international film and video production with an

emphasis on work that has not yet secured U.S. distribution. The Toronto International Film Festival, begun in 1976, is now the major North American film festival and the most widely attended worldwide. Toronto's Hot Docs is the leading North American documentary film festival. The largest festival, in terms of the number of features shown, is the Seattle International Film Festival, screening 270 features, and approximately 150 short films. Meanwhile, the New York Film Festival only shows a few films in each year, but it still has big impact in the United States. The Sundance film festival is a major festival for independent film.

- Animation: Founded in 1960, the Annecy International Animated Film Festival is the oldest international film festival dedicated exclusively to animation. The others are: Zagreb (f. 1972) Ottawa (f. 1976), Hiroshima (f. 1985), KROK (f. 1989), and Anima Mundi (f. 1992). There are also a variety of regional festivals in various countries.
- Environmental Significance: The Environmental Film Festival in the Nation's Capital was founded in 1993 by Flo Stone. 2009 marks the inaugural year of the Environmental Film Festival at Yale University, featuring feature-length documentaries and short films intended to raise awareness and encourage discussion about the world's most pressing environmental issues.
- International Digital Film Festival /2007 / Bucharest / International / Kinofest is the first digital film festival in Romania. Kinofest has the explicit goal of promoting young film-makers, artists and their work - film, music and visual art-wise; and also, to cultivate the interest in and promote the arts and media culture among the general public through independent film, video and new media making / http://kinofest.com/

- Traveling Film Festivals: Dawn Breakers International Film Festival is a recent notable international film festival among Gadabout, UNAFF, United Nations Association Film Festival and Media That Matters Film Festival.
- Asian Film Festival: Most notable amongst the Asian Film Festivals are the Osian's-Cinefan Film Festival, which was recently expanded to include Arab Cinema as well, and the Pusan International Film Festival (PIFF).

Fire Festival

Beltane or Beltaine is pronunciation: Scottish Gaelic Bealltainn, the Gaelic name for either the month of May or the festival that takes place on the first day of May.

Bealtaine was historically a Gaelic festival celebrated in Ireland, Scotland and the Isle of Man. Bealtaine and Samhain were the leading terminal dates of the civil year in Ireland though the latter festival was the more important. The festival survives in folkloric practices in the Celtic Nations and the Irish diaspora, and has experienced a degree of revival in recent decades.

Bealtaine is a cross-quarter day, marking the midpoint in the Sun's progress between the spring equinox and summer solstice. Since the Celtic year was based on both lunar and solar cycles, it is possible that the holiday was celebrated on the full moon nearest the midpoint between the spring equinox and the summer solstice. The astronomical date for this midpoint is closer to 5 May or 7 May, but this can vary from year to year.

In Irish Gaelic, the month of May is known as Mí Bhealtaine or Bealtaine, and the festival as Lá Bealtaine ('day of Bealtaine' or, 'May Day'). In Scottish Gaelic, the month is known as either (An) Cèitean or a' Mhàigh, and the festival is known as Latha Bealltainn or simply Bealltainn. The feast was also known as Céad Shamhain or Cétshamhainin from which the word Céitean derives. Beltane was formerly spelled 'Bealtuinn' in Scottish Gaelic; in Manx it is spelt 'Boaltinn' or 'Boaldyn'. In Modern Irish, Oidhche Bealtaine or Oíche Bealtaine is May Eve, and Lá Bealtaine is May Day. Mí na Bealtaine, or simply Bealtaine is the name of the month of May.

Folk Festival

A Folk festival celebrates traditional folk crafts and folk music.

Notebal Flok Festival

Australia

- National Folk Festival (Australia)

Canada

- Calgary Folk Music Festival
- Canmore Folk Music Festival
- Edmonton Folk Music Festival
- Jasper Folk Festival
- Wild Mountain Music Fest

Ontario

- Barriefolk (Barrie)
- Blue Skies Festival (Clarendon)
- Canterbury Folk Festival (Ingersoll)
- City Roots Festival (Toronto)
- Festival du Loup (Penetanguishene)
- Hillside Festival (Guelph)
- Home County Folk Festival (London)
- Mariposa Folk Festival (Orillia)
- Mill Race Festival of Traditional Folk Music (Cambridge)
- Northern Lights Festival Boréal (Sudbury)
- Ottawa Folk Festival (Ottawa)

- Red Rock Folk Festival (Red Rock)
- Shelter Valley Folk Festival (Grafton)
- Stewart Park Festival (Perth)
- Summerfolk Music and Crafts Festival (Owen Sound)
- TD Canada Trust Sunfest (London)
- Twisted Pines Music and Arts Festival (Penetanguishene)
- Winterfolk Roots and Blues Festival (Toronto)

Manitoba

- Brandon Folk, Music & Art Festival
- Folklorama
- Winnipeg Folk Festival

Nova Scotia

- Celtic Colours (Cape Breton)
- Deep Roots Music Festival (Wolfville)
- Lunenburg Folk Harbour Festival (Lunenburg)
- Stan Rogers Folk Festival (Canso)

Saskatchewan

- Regina Folk Festival
- Saskatoon FolkFest

Denmark

- Tønder Festival

Festival Interceltique de Lorient

France

- Festival Interceltique de Lorient

Germany

- TFF.Rudolstadt

Spain

- Interceltic Festival of Avilés

  The 2004 Interceltic Festival of Avilés in Asturias, Spain

USA

- A laska Folk Festival
- American Folk-Blues Festival
- Florida Folk Festival
- Folkmoot USA
- New Jersey Folk Festival
- Philadelphia Folk Festival
- Pittsburgh Folk Festival
- Northwest Folklife Festival
- Norsk Høstfest
- National Folk Festival (USA)
- Newport Folk Festival Tour

UK

- Chippenham Folk Festival
- White Horse Folk Festival
- The Green Man Festival
- Cambridge Folk Festival
- Beverley Folk Festival
- Sidmouth Folk Week
- Stroud Festival
- Celtic Connections

- Folk and Roots - guide to UK Folk Festivals
- Middlewich Folk and Boat Festival

National

- National Folk Festival, UK
- National Folk Festival (Australia)
- National Folk Festival (USA)

Food Festival

A food festival is a festival, usually held annually, that uses food, often produce, as its central theme. "These festivals have always been a means of uniting communities through celebrations of harvests and giving thanks for a plentiful growing season. They can be traced back thousands of years to celebrating the arrival of harvest time, the autumnal equinox, and the honoring of earth gods." The largest one in the United States (and the world) is the Taste of Chicago held in Chicago, Illinois.

Literary Festival

A literary festival, also known as a book festival or writers' festival, is a regular gathering of writers and readers, typically on an annual basis in a particular city. A literary festival usually features a variety of presentations and readings by authors, as well as other events, delivered over a period of several days, with the primary objectives of promoting the authors' books and fostering a love of literature and writing. Writers' conferences are sometimes designed to provide an intellectual and academic focus for groups of writers without the involvement of the general public. There are many literary festivals held around the world. A non-exhaustive list is set out below, including dates when a festival is usually held.

Mela Festival

Melas are south Asian events which have spread around the world from the south Asian subcontinent. Mela means 'gathering' and can describe festival, market, trade event, religious gathering and more.

Melas are distinguished by their bringing together of south Asian cultures and those of other countries when promoted by south Asian Diasporas abroad.

Mela are celebrated with music, dance, theatre, fashion, food and stalls, these are days for the whole family, to join in and embrace south Asian culture.

The European Mela Network is the networking organisation for melas in Europe. It seeks to promote mela activities and provide support for mela organisers and initiate new mela developments.

Music Festival

A music festival is a festival oriented towards music that is sometimes presented with a theme such as musical genre, nationality or locality of musicians, or holiday. They are commonly held outdoors, and are often inclusive of other attractions such as food and merchandise vending machines, performance art, and social activities. The Pythian Games at Delphi included musical performances, and may be one of the earliest festivals known. During the Middle Ages festivals were often held as competitions.

Many festivals are annual, or repeat at some other interval. Some, including many rock festivals, are held only once. Some festivals are organized as for-profit concerts and others are benefits for a specific cause.

Another type of music festival is the educative type, organised annually in local communities, regionally or nationally, for the benefit of amateur musicians of all ages and grades of achievement. While entrants perform prepared pieces in the presence of an audience which includes competitors, the essential feature of this type of festival is that each participant receives verbal and written feedback, there and then, from a highly qualified, professional adjudicator — someone who they might never meet in any other way. They also usually receive a certificate, classified according to merit, and some may win trophies. The competitive element is often played down, however, as the important aspect is that participants can learn from one another. Such festivals aim to provide a friendly and supportive platform for musicians to share in the excitement of making music. For many they provide a bridge between lessons & examinations and performing confidently in public.

The world's largest music festival is Summerfest, which is held for eleven days every year in Milwaukee, Wisconsin. Each year, it attracts between 800,000 and 1,000,000 spectators. The Woodstock Festival in 1969 drew nearly 500,000 attendees.

Peanut Festival

The National Peanut Festival (NPF), the United States' largest peanut festival, is held each fall in Dothan, Alabama, to honor peanut growers and to celebrate the harvest season. The fairgrounds are located on Highway 231 South, three miles south of the Ross Clark Circle. The festivities include games and amusement rides on a large midway, animal acts, agricultural displays, an outdoor amphitheater with live music concerts by national recording artists, beauty pageants, arts and crafts displays, contests, food and a two-hour parade. The National Peanut festival also sponsors and holds field crop exhibits with prizes awarded to each exhibitor. The peanut festival also has other competitions, including but not limited to: Sewing Cake Decorating Photography Cooking Art.

Religious Festival

A religious festival is a time of special importance marked by adherents to that religion. Religious festivals are commonly celebrated on recurring cycles in a calendar year or lunar calendar.

Ancient Roman Religious Festivals

Ludi—Although the ancient Roman holiday of "Floralia", celebrated by the set of games and theatrical presentations known as the "Ludi Florales," began in April, it was really an ancient May Day celebration. Flora, the Roman goddess in whose honor the festival was held, was a goddess of flowers, which generally begin to bloom in the spring. The holiday for Flora (as officially determined by Julius Caesar when he fixed the Roman calendar) ran from April 27 to May 3.

Roman public games or "ludi" were financed by minor public magistrates known as "aediles." The curule aediles produced the Ludi Florales. The position of curule aedile was originally (365 B.C.) limited to patricians, but was later opened up to plebians, too. The ludi could be very expensive for the aediles who used the games as a way of winning the affection and votes of the people.

The Floralia Festival

The Floralia festival began in Rome in 238 B.C., to please the goddess Flora into protecting the blossoms. The Floralia fell out of favor and was discontinued until 173 B.C., when the senate, concerned with wind, hail, and other damage to the flowers, ordered Flora's celebration reinstated as the Ludi Florales.

The Ludi Florales included theatrical events, including mimes, naked actresses and prostitutes. In the Renaissance, some writers thought that Flora had been a human prostitute who was turned into a goddess, possibly because of the licentiousness of the Ludi Florales or because, according to David Lupher, Flora was a common name for prostitutes in ancient Rome.

The celebration in honor of Flora included Florida wreaths worn in the hair much like modern participants in May Day celebrations. After the theatrical performances, the celebration continued in the Circus Maximus, where animals were set free and beans scattered to insure fertility.

The Saturnalia

Saturnalia is the feast at which the Romans commemorated the dedication of the temple of the god Saturn, which took place on December 17. Over the years, it expanded to encompass the whole week, up to December 24.

The Saturnalia was a large and important public festival in Rome. It involved the conventional sacrifices, a couch (lectisternium) set out in front of the temple of Saturn and the untying of the ropes that bound the statue of Saturn during the rest of the year. Besides the public rites there were a series of holidays and customs celebrated privately. The celebrations included a school holiday, the making and giving of small presents (saturnalia et sigillaricia) and a special market (sigillaria). Gambling was allowed, even for slaves; however, although it was officially condoned only during this period, one should not assume that it was rare or much remarked upon during the rest of the year. It was a time to eat, drink, and be merry. The toga was not worn, but rather the synthesis, i.e. colorful, informal "dinner clothes"; and the pileus (freedman's hat) was worn by everyone. Slaves were exempt from punishment, and treated their masters with disrespect. The slaves celebrated a banquet: before, with, or served by the masters. A Saturnalicius princeps was elected master of ceremonies for the proceedings. Saturnalia became one of the most popular Roman festivals which led to more tomfoolery, marked chiefly by having masters and slaves ostensibly switch places. The banquet, for example, would often be prepared by the slaves, and they would prepare their masters' dinner as well. It was license within careful boundaries; it reversed the social order without subverting it.

The customary greeting for the occasion is a "io, Saturnalia!" — "io" (pronounced "ee-oo") being a Latin interjection related to "ho" (as in "Ho, praise to Saturn").

Buddhist Religious Festivals

- Asalha Puja
- Kathina
- Magha Puja
- Pavarana
- Uposatha
- Vassa
- Vesakha Puja

Christian Religious Festivals

The central festival of Christianity is Easter, on which Christians celebrate their belief that Jesus Christ rose from the dead on the third day after his crucifixion. Even for Easter, however, there is no agreement among the various Christian traditions regarding the date or manner of the observance, less for Christmas, Pentecost, or the various less widely recognized holy days listed as Category:Christian festivals and holy days.

Hindu Religious Festivals

- Diwali
- Gudi padwa
- Pongal
- Holi
- Navratri
- Ganesh Chaturthi
- Raksha Bhandan
- Krishna Janmashtami
- Dussehra
- Dasara
- Onam
- Vijayadashami
- Ugadi

Sikh Religious Festivals

- Sangrand
- Poonai
- Maghi
- Guru Nanak Javanthi
- Guru Gobind Javanthi

- Holi/Hola Mohalla
- Diwali
- Vaisakhi

Islamic Religious Festivals

- Eid ul-Adha
- Eid ul-Fitr

Messianic Jewish Religious Festivals

Messianic Judaism derives most of its liturgical influences directly from Judaism. It adds additional elements from the Christian tradition, since most outsiders would consider it a form of Christianity. Appointed times, called mo'edim, follow the standard Jewish liturgical calendar, though additional hermenuetical applications are derived in light of the teachings Jesus of Nazareth (Yeshua among other transliterations).

External Links

Overview of the Mo'edim from a Messianic perspective

Jewish Religious Festivals

Jewish holiday, (or Yom Tov or chag in Hebrew) is a day that is holy to the Jewish people according to Judaism and is usually derived from the Hebrew Bible, specifically the Torah, and in some cases established by the rabbis in later eras. The holidays always occur on the Hebrew calendar only. There are a number of festival days, fast days (ta'anit) and days of remembrance, collectively known as "Jewish holidays" in English, ("Yamim Tovim" or "chagim" in Hebrew).

Renaissance Festival

A Renaissance fair, Renaissance faire, or Renaissance festival is an outdoor weekend gathering, usually held in the United States, open to the public and typically commercial in nature, which emulates a historic period for the amusement of its guests. Some are permanent theme parks, others are short-term events in fairgrounds or other large public or private spaces. Renaissance fairs generally include an abundance of costumed entertainers, musical and theatrical acts, art and handicrafts for sale, and festival food. Some even offer camping, for those who wish to stay more than one day. Most Renaissance fairs are set during the reign of Queen Elizabeth I of England. Some are set earlier, during the reign of Henry VIII, or in other countries, such as France, and some include broader definitions of the Renaissance which include earlier periods, such as the Vikings, or later, such as 18th Century pirates, and some engage in deliberate "time travel" by encouraging participants to wear costumes representing several eras in a broad time period. Renaissance fairs encourage visitors to enter into the spirit of things with costumes and audience participation. Most tolerate, and many welcome, fantasy elements such as wizards and elves.

Chicago journalist Neil Steinberg said (of the Bristol Renaissance Faire), "If theme parks, with their pasteboard main streets, reek of a bland, safe, homogenized, whitebread America, the Renaissance Faire is at the other end of the social spectrum, a whiff of the occult, a flash of danger and a hint of the erotic. Here, they let you throw axes. Here are more beer and bosoms than you'll find in all of Disney World."

Rock Festival

A rock festival, or a rock fest, is a large-scale outdoor rock music concert, featuring multiple acts, often spread out over several days. The first rock festivals were put on in the late 1960s and were important socio-cultural milestones. In the 1980s a minor resurgence of festivals occurred with charity as the goal.

Today, many rock festivals are annual events sponsored by major corporations. Besides rock, many feature multiple genres of music such as pop, dance, and electronic. Some owners of radio stations produce radio festivals that only include bands of a specific style of rock . The size of these events means that large temporary infrastructures are installed, supplying amenities like water-based ablution facilities.

Science Festival

A science festival is a public event featuring a variety of science- and technology-related activities—from lectures, exhibitions, workshops, live demonstrations of experiments, guided tours and panel discussions to cultural events such as theater plays, readings and musical productions, all with the aim of involving the general public in explorations of the different facets of science. Many science festivals are annual events, and for most of them, the actual festival takes place over a period between a few days and more than a week.

Modern science festivals have a number of different roots. The British Association for the Advancement of Science's Festival of Science evolved out of the society's annual meetings, first held in 1831, which were originally meant to provide a discussion forum for scientists, but later became a public showcase of science. The oldest science festival in the modern sense appears to be the Edinburgh International Science Festival, which was first held in 1988.

As science organizations and funding bodies put ever more emphasis on outreach to foster public understanding both of the results and the wider relevance of science, recent years have seen the creation of a number of new science festivals. Since 2002, there is an umbrella organization for European science festivals and similar events, the European Science Event Association.

The US has been something of a latecomer as far as regular science festivals are concerned, although the annual meeting of the American Association for the Advancement of Science includes a number of public events. Focusing on one particular science, the physics festival "Mastering the Mysteries of the Universe", was held in Atlanta, Georgia, in 1999 in association with the centennial of the American Physical Society. Since 2004, there has been a science festival in Pittsburgh (the SciTech festival; from 2005 on known as the SciTech Spectacular), and new science festivals have been held in Cambridge, Massachusetts (the Cambridge Science Festival, first held in April 2007) and in New York City (the World Science Festival held at the end of May 2008) and in March 2009, San Diego hosted the first west coast science festival, the San Diego Science Festival.

As of 2009 the Science Festival Alliance, formed with a 3-year NSF grant, has supported the growth of independent regional science festivals, with an initial emphasis on celebration in communities throughout the US.

Planned for October 2010, the USA Science and Engineering Festival is positioned as the "country's first national science festival." This national emphasis is based partly on encouraging local events to coincide with the major event in Washington DC. Such satellite events are planned for: Austin, Texas; Chapel Hill, NC; Berkeley, CA; Buenos Aires, Argentina, South America; Champaign,IL; Columbus, OH; DeKalb, IL; Flushing Meadows Corona Park, Queens, NY; Houston, Texas; Middle River, MD; New Jersey; Oceanside, CA; Pocatello, ID; Pondicherry, India; Raleigh, NC; Ruskin, FL; Santa Ana, CA; Sewell, New Jersey (South Jersey); Clifton, New Jersey (The New Jersey Science and Engineering Festival); Stamford, CT; Tucson, AZ; Vancouver, WA; Portland,OR; Wichita, KS.

Festivals can vary greatly in size and scope. A university might stage a small festival in its hometown; on the other end of the scale, the 2006 British Association Festival of Science held on September 2–9 in Norwich, England, was attended by more than 174,000 visitors.

Typical Festival Events

Science festivals feature a great variety of events. A classic format is to have a series of lectures, with topics ranging from cutting-edge research to unusual perspectives on science. For instance, the 2007 Edinburgh festival Big Ideas series includes talks on what makes racing cars fast, the molecular basis of food preparation, the neurobiology of love and beauty and the properties of quarks. Most science festivals include hands-on activities similar to those found in science centers. Another popular theme is the interaction of science and culture.

Science festivals are also aimed at playing an important, if informal part in secondary science education. Many have events specifically aimed at students and/or teachers, such as workshops or offering curriculum-linked workshops and science shows to regional schools throughout the year.

Sindhi Festivals

One of the oldest civilizations of human history, the Sindhis have a rich and clearly distinct cultural heritage are very festive. Their most important festival is the birthday of Lord Jhule lal, Cheti Chand. Besides this, they celebrate Akhandi (Baisakhi) and Teejari (Teej).

1. Cheti Chand, Celebration of the birth of Water god (Varun Devta) Sai Uderolal, popularly known as Jhulelal . So much has been said and written about it that it would be superfluous to repeat the event. In Sindh the beginning of the New Year was considered Cheti Chand . Some businessmen opened new account books; many however, did that on the eve of Diwali. On the full moon day, people used to go to a river or lake and offer 'Akho' with a pinch of rice mixed with milk and flour. If there was no river or 'Darya' , the ritual was performed at a well. Even Sikhs went to temples or Gurdwara , because Guru Nanak's birthday also took place on Purnima .

2. Sagra (Sacred thread) Sindhi Bhaibands often lived in foreign countries; therefore, their wives were always worried about the good health of their husbands. For this purpose they performed pooja and fasted on four Mondays of Sawan month, after which they perform pooja , distribute sweet rice and then had the sacred thread tied on the wrist by the priest (Bandhan). Here in India, the priests have made a show business which costs nearly 500-800 rupees, a gimmick to knock out money.

3. Mahalakshmi's Sacred Thread (Mahalakshmi-a-jo-Sagro) This sacred thread had 16 strips and 17 days. On the day when the sacred thread was to be untied, it was celebrated as an important day and special savouries like satpura and pakwan of Suji & Maida were made and distributed firstly to the priests and the poor and afterwards the remaining savouries were used by family members.

4. Fasts In Sindhis, generally Mondays & Saturdays, Giyaras or Umaas were observed as fasts (vrats). During the fast of Satyanarayan and nine days of Ekaanaas , only one time meal was generally taken.

5. Teejri, This festival takes place in the month of Sawan when married women and girls paint their hands and feet with Mehndi , go on fast for the whole day, during which they used to play games , swing in Jhulas and sing love songs. In the night after making an offering to the moon, they would break the fast.

6. Akhan Teej, On this day new earthen pots of water(matkas) were kept and everyone was offered clean and cool water. The significance of this day was to offer water to the thirsty. Hence at every nook and corner, sharbat , with pieces of apple in it, was offered to passersby along with 'prasad' . On this day, it was also customary to send new earthen pots and fruits to priests and Gurdwara.

7. AUnn-Matyo In the month of Sawan , on the Baaras of Krishna Paksha, cereals were changed in food, i.e. instead of wheat and rice, chapatis made of gram flour (Besan) were eaten.

8. Ban Badhri During the month of 'Bado' , during the Baaras of Shukla Paksha , god Varun had taken avtaar . In lieu of that small insects like ants etc. were fed Gur (jaggery) and Musti . Married daughters are invited by their parents for meals.

9. Somavati Umaas During certain months Umaas takes place on a Monday. That day is considered important for having a "dumb dip' in the waters; without talking to anyone early in the morning. It is also, called 'Gungee Umaas" .

10. Nandhi and Vaddi Thadri Both of these take place in the month of Sawan . On the day before Thadree day, people cook

lola (sweet flour cakes) and rote (fried cakes) because there has to be no lighting of fire in the house on the Thadree day. The lolas and Rotes are eaten with curd or pickle. On that day drops of water are also sprinkled on the cooking fire to appease Sitladevi Mata.

11. Janamashtami, Ram Navmi and Shivratri Since Krishna was born after midnight, on Janamashtami , bhajans and kirtan are held in temples till midnight. On Ram Navmi , Lord Rama's birthday is celebrated. On Shivratri people drink 'Thaadhal' with some 'bhang' in it, after making offering of it in the Mahadev temple. In the villages and cities, big pots of 'Taahri' (sweet rice) are prepared and distributed among all.

12. Tirmoori On this festive day parents send ladoos & chiki (Laaee) made of Tils to their married daughters. On the Makar Sankrant day the sun moves from south to north. It is therefore also called 'utraan' or 'Tirmoori' . In Mahabharat battle Bhisham Pitamah did not breathe his last till ' utraan' since on this day there happens flush of light in Dev Lok .

13. Dassehra Few days before Dassehra there used to be Ramlila program which was attended by throngs of people. On the Dassehra day colourful effigies of Ravana, Kumbhkarna and Meghnath were burnt.

14. Diyaaree Two days before Diwali, Sindhis start lighting Diyaas (earthen lamps) from 'Dhan Teras' . The bazaars are full with prospective consumers. Friends and relatives meet one another with affection and extended pleasantries and sweetmeats. In the night, Laxmi Poojan takes place when all the members of the family pray with reverence and respect. In the night, people used to take in their hands a stick to which a rag dipped in oil was tied which was burnt. It was called 'Mollawaro' ; everyone shouted 'Mollawaro..... Mollawaro'....

15. The Giyaras of Kati Before partition, on this day people in Sindh used to be engaged in giving charity. The whole bazaar would be full with hundreds of beggars and the needy, who would spread a cloth before them, on which people, according to their

mite, would throw money, Bhugra , fruits etc. The jugglers used to arrange their Tamashas on the road with monkeys and bears dancing on the tunes played by the jugglers. An atmosphere of gaiety and gay prevailed all through the day.

16. Navratra During this days devotees of Devi ate one meal a day and did not even shave and cut hair. Ladies sang bhajans . In Nagarparkar they used to dance like Garba in Gujrat.

17. Lal Loi, Celebrated on the 13th of January every year, during Lal Loi kids used to bring wood sticks from their grand parents and aunties and like a fire camp burnt these sticks in the night with people enjoying, dancing and playing around fire. Some ladies whose wishes were fulfilled offered coconuts in the fire and distributed prasad 'Sesa' ; this continued till midnight.

18. Rakhri, During the Purnima of Sawan month sisters tied a Rakhi to their brothers. This day is called "Rakhree Bandhan'. Even the near cousin sisters used to put Rakhis on cousin brothers . Sisters used to come from far off places and towns to specially tie Rakhis to their brothers. There was so much affection and love. Those cities and places where there were rivers or sea, people used to offer coconuts and milk to the God of Waters 'Varun Devta so that those who were traveling in ships and boats should have a safe and sound journey.

19. Shraadh Just as in India the month of September 'Bado' was meant for Krishna Paksha as Pitar Pakhiya. Any member of the family who had died on particular (tithi) day and date, a Shraadh was offered for the solace of the deceased's soul. The Brahmins were given food and Dakhshna. It is said that Arya Samaj carried out a strong movement against Shraadh, but the Shraadhs continued because of the faith of people since they felt that through this method the deceased members of the family are remembered and all the family members have a good gathering.

20. Nagapanchmi (Gogro) During those days whenever the snake charmer brought snakes, they were given some Dakhshna and also milk for the snakes. Nagpanchami is also called Gogro . It is a folklore from Kutch and Gujarat.

21. Holi The festival of colours in which all the young and old join together to express their joy at the change of season. Some people correlate Holi festival with Holika, the sister of Hirnakashyap, mythological father of Bhagat Prahlad.

Story Telling Festival

A story telling festival is often an annual event that features local, regional and/or nationally known oral story tellers. Each storyteller will have a scheduled amount of time(s) to share a story (or stories) with an audience. The featured storytellers are often professional performing artists, but semi-professional or amateur story tellers may also be included among the events.

A festival may be a single or multiple day event. Depending upon the venue, the festival schedule is organized around blocks of time for the storytellers to share their stories. The storytellers may rotate between smaller venues or the crowds may move from venue to venue. Tents or an amplitheater might be used for outdoor story telling concerts/venues. Auditoriums, theaters, historic buildings, classrooms or gymnasiums might be common indoor venues. Often storytelling festivals will include an open mike event referred to as "story swapping," where amateurs from the audience may share their own stories. Some festivals showcase the winners of story telling contests such as the Young Story teller of the Year.

A tradition at many festivals (including the National Story telling Festival (USA)), paper tickets are substituted by "swatches" of patterned cloth that are pinned on and worn by festival participants. These swatches of cloth have a different/unique pattern each year and various colors may be used to distinguish the level of participation.

Theatre Festival

Theatre festivals amongst the earliest types of festival. Classical Greek theatre was associated with religious festivals dedicated to

Dionysus. The medieval mystery plays were presented at the major Christian feasts. Theatre as an everyday part of life is a comparatively recent phenomenon.

In recent years, theatre festivals have been established to promote various types of theatre, such as the works of William Shakespeare and George Shaw. Many festivals, such as those in the fringe theatre movement promote the work of beginning playwrights and performers.

Wine Festivals

Annual wine festivals celebrate viticulture on most continents and usually occur in October. Many of the festivals carry the Italian name of Vendemmia or Vendimia meaning the harvest of the grapes. In the United States of America festivals are often empowered by Little Italy organizations in support of Italian culture. Other Latin-influenced cultures of Roman origin have also embraced the celebration of wine among the various wine regions of the world.

The grape, and the extraction of the juice to produce wine, have become meaningful parts of mankind's history that is more than a food or drink. It is both rich in flavor, nutrients, and an icon symbolizing virtues used in religion and culture. Although the alcohol content could lead to intoxication, the festivals embody the enlightened spirit of mankind.

Noteble Festivals

Roman festivals (Italian, Spanish, and Mediterranean)

- Wine Festival of Cyprus
- Fiesta Nacional de la Vendimia
- Feria Nacional de San Marcos
- Haro Wine Festival
- Limassol wine festival
- Mendoza Province
- Médanos, Buenos Aires

- Qormi Wine Festival, Malta
- Santiago de Surco

French festivals (fêtes de vendange)

Australian festivals

- Caxton Street Seafood and Wine Festival, Australia
- Kings Cross Food and Wine Festival, Australia
- Melbourne Food and Wine Festival, Australia

United States festivals

- Boston wine festival, Massachusetts, United States
- Maryland Wine Festival, Maryland, United States
- Paso Robles Wine Festival, California, United States
- Temecula Valley Balloon & Wine Festival, California, United States

Other Festivals

- Rheingau Wine Festival, Germany
- Zielona Góra Wine Fest, Poland

Winter Festivals

This is an incomplete list of festivals and holidays that take place during the winter or late autumn in the northern hemisphere. Many festivals of light take place in this period since the shortest day of the year in the northern hemisphere is the Winter Solstice. Holidays are listed in chronological order under each heading.

Andean

- Inti Raymi: Festival of the Sun in Quechua, winter solstice festival in areas of the former Inca empire, still celebrated every June in Cuzco.

Buddhist

- Bodhi Day: 8 December - Day of Enlightenment, celebrating the day that the historical Buddha (Shakyamuni or Siddhartha Guatama) experienced enlightenment (also known as Bodhi).

Celtic

- Samhain: 31 October-1 November - first day of winter in the Celtic calendar (and Celtic New Year's Day)
- Winter Solstice: 21 December-22 December - midwinter
- Imbolc: 1 February - first day of spring in the Celtic calendar

Chinese

- Signature of the Constitution of the Republic of China (Taiwan): 25 December - a secular national holiday, which due to its date is celebrated in some respects like Christmas
- Chinese New Year: (late January - early February) - considered the end of winter in the traditional Chinese calendar

Christian

- All Saints Day: 1 November (in Western Christian churches)
- Advent: four weeks prior to Christmas.
- Saint Nicholas' Day: 6 December
- Christmas Eve: 24 December
- Christmas: 25 December
- 12 Days of Christmas: 25 December through 6 January
- Saint Stephen's Day: 26 December
- Saint John the Evangelist's Day: 27 December
- Holy Innocents' Day: 28 December

- Saint Sylvester's Day: 31 December
- Watch Night: 31 December
- Feast of the Circumcision: 1 January
- Feast of Fools: 1 January
- Saint Basil's Day: 1 January (Christian Orthodox) In Greece, traditionally he is the Father Christmas figure.
- Twelfth Night: Epiphany Eve: 5 January
- Epiphany: 6 January: the arrival of the Three Magi.
- Armenian Apostolic Christmas: 6 January
- Eastern Orthodox Christmas: according to the Julian Calendar, 7 January
- Candlemas: 2 February
- St. Valentine's Day: 14 February

Germanic

- Modranect: or Mothers' Night, the Saxon winter solstice festival.
- Yule: the Germanic winter solstice festival

Hindu

- Navratri:Nine-day celebration worshipping female divinity, in October or November. Culminates in Dussehra.
- Diwali:Known as the Festival of Lights, this Hindu holiday celebrates the victory of good over evil. The five-day festival is marked by ceremonies, fireworks and sweets. Women dress up and decorate their hands with henna tattoos for the melas, or fairs. Many different myths are associated with Diwali, one of which celebrates the return of Lord Rama after a 14-year exile and his defeat of the demon Ravana.

- Pancha Ganapati:Five-day festival in honor of Lord Ganesha, Patron of Arts and Guardian of Culture. December 21–25.
- Bhaubeej

Jewish

- Hanukkah: Starting on 25 Kislev (Hebrew) or various dates in November or December (Gregorian) - eight day festival commemorating the miracle of the oil after the desecration of the Temple by Antiochus IV Epiphanes and his defeat in 165 BCE.
- Tu Bishvat: New Year of the Trees occurring on the 15th of Shevat, January or February.
- Purim: Occurring on 14th or 15th day of Adar, late February to March, commemorating the miraculous deliverance and victory of the Jews of the Persian Empire in the events recorded in the Book of Esther

Muslim

- Eid ul-Adha: Starting on the 10th of Dhul Hijja, a four day holiday commemorating the Prophet Ibrahim's willingness to sacrifice his son, Ismael.

Pagan and Neo-Pagan

- Samhain: 31 October - first day of winter in the Celtic calendar (and Celtic New Year's Day)
- Yule: (Winter Solstice) - Germanic and Egyptian Pagan festival of the rebirth of the Sun
- Imbolc: (Oimelc) (1 February or 2), but traditionally the evening of (31 January)

Persian

- Sadeh: A mid-winter feast to honor fire and to "defeat the forces of darkness, frost and cold". Sadé or Sada Jashn-e

Sada/Sadé, also transliterated as Sadeh, is an ancient Iranian tradition celebrated 50 days before nowrouz. Sadeh in Persian means "hundred" and refers to one hundred days and nights left to the beginning of the new year celebrated at the first day of spring on March 21 each year. Sadeh is a mid winter festival that was celebrated with grandeur and magnificence in ancient Iran. It was a festivity to honor fire and to defeat the forces of darkness, frost, and cold.

- Yalda: The turning point, Winter Solstice (December 21). End of the longest night of the year (Darkness), and beginning of growing of the days (Lights). A celebration of Good over Evil. Shabe Yalda or Shabe Chelle is an Iranian festival originally celebrated on the Northern Hemisphere's longest night of the year, that is, on the eve of the Winter Solstice.
- Chahar Shanbeh Suri: Festival of Fire, Last Wednesday of the Iranian Calendar year. It marks the importance of the light over the darkness, and arrival of spring and revival of nature. Chaha-rshanbe-Su-ri, pronounced Cha-rshanbe-Su-ri is the ancient Iranian festival dating at least back to 1700 BCE of the early Zoroastrian era. The festival of fire is a prelude to the ancient Norouz festival, which marks the arrival of spring and revival of nature. Chahrshanbeh Soori, is celebrated the last Tuesday night of the year.

Polynesian

- Matariki: (Ma-ori New Year, usually early June) - Rising of the Pleiades star cluster before dawn.

Roman

- Saturnalia: the Roman winter solstice festival
- Dies Natalis Solis Invicti (Day of the birth of the Unconquered Sun): late Roman Empire - 25 December

- Lupercalia, the Roman end-of-winter festival - 15 February

Secular

- Halloween: (31 October).
- Thanksgiving (United States): The celebration of the early colonization of the United States and the comradery of the settlers and the Native Americans. Occurs on the fourth Thursday in November.
- Winterval: Secular name for winter festivities coined by Birmingham City Council to encompass all holidays being recognized from October to January.
- Zamenhof Day: (15 December) - Birthday of Ludwig Zamenhof, inventor of Esperanto; holiday reunion for Esperantists.
- Winter Solstice, Yule: (21 December or 22 December) (Late June weekend in Australia) - Celebration of the Winter Solstice.
- Festivus: (23 December) - Holiday celebrating the season without the pressures or commercialism of the other holidays. At first a family holiday, later publicized on the Seinfeld television show, now celebrated independently.
- HumanLight: (23 December) - Humanist holiday originated by the New Jersey Humanist Network.
- Chrismukkah: Slang term for the amalgam of Christmas and Hanukkah celebrated by religiously mixed families and couples.
- Boxing Day: (26 December) - Gift-giving day after Christmas.
- Kwanzaa: (26 December - 1 January) - Pan-African festival
- Yulefest, Midwinter Christmas (around late June or July) - Australian New Zealand winter 'Christmas/Yuletide'.

- New Year's Eve: (31 December) - Last day of the Gregorian year.
- Hogmanay: (Night of 31 December - Before dawn of 1 January) - Scottish New Year's Eve Celebration.
- New Year's Day: (1 January) - First day of the Gregorian year.
- Martin Luther King Day (15 January) - Birthday of American civil rights movement leader, a federal holiday on or near the date.
- Hedgehog Day: 2 February - supposed archaic European version of Groundhog Day, dating back to Roman times.

Fictional

- Chrismahanukwanzakah: the modern-day merging of the holidays of Christianity's Christmas, Judaism's Hanukkah, and the African-American holiday of Kwanzaa.
- Holiday: Around the time of Christmas, Hanukkah, and Kwanzaa, Pastafarians celebrate a vaguely-defined holiday named "Holiday", which doesn't take place on "a specific date so much as it is the Holiday season, itself". Because Pastafarians "reject dogma and formalism", there are no specific requirements for the holiday.
- Wintersday: The annual winter holiday in the MMORPG Guild Wars. This holiday is based on Christmas and Yule and one can obtain festival related drops from monsters and collect gifts in select cities. Special quests are available and at the end players may get Wintersday related headgear.
- Winterval non-religious alternative name for Christmas and Hanukkah, invented by Birmingahm City Council, England, to avoid offence, but quickly abandoned by them.
- Starlight Celebration: The annual winter holiday based on Christmas/Yule/winter solstice in the MMORPG Final

Fantasy XI (aka FFXI). Players can collect various holiday equipment, Mog house furnishings, fireworks, and food.

- Shoe Giving: - quirky holiday famously invented on the show Hyperdrive (TV series).
- Freezingman: - 11 January - A Burning Man inspired event held in Colorado as Winter Arts and Music Festival.
- Feast of Winter Veil: December 15 to January 2 - holiday in the MMORPG World of Warcraft. This holiday is based on Christmas. Cities are decorated with Christmas lights and a tree with presents. Also special quests, items and snowballs are available. It features 'Greatfather Winter' which is modeled after [Santa Claus].
- Kwansolhaneidmas: December 19 - an interdenominational holiday celebrated by people on Facebook.
- Feast of Frith, in the TV series Watership Down.
- Holiday Number 11, in the TV series Quark.
- Xmas, a twisted version of Christmas featuring a murderous robotic Father Christmas in the TV series Futurama.
- Refrigerator Day, in the TV series Dinosaurs.
- Life Day, featured in The Star Wars Holiday Special.
- Agnostica: Agnostic winter festival created by Daren "Gav" Bleuel in the webcomic Nukees and celebrated by many of its fans.
- Alvistide: in the TV series Sealab 2021.
- Frostval: Adventure Quest, Dragonfable, AQworlds etc.

Ancient Egyptian Festivals

Most Ancient Egyptian festivals were religious, but others were not such as one festival established by Rameses III to celebrate his victory over the Libyans. When feasts occurred, they were either determined by lunar cycles or the Egyptian calendar. Festivals were large celebrations with plenty of food available. In one festival in the 12th century BC, 11,341 loaves of bread and 385 jars of beer were given to the public. The Sed festival celebrated the thirtieth year of a pharaoh's rule and then every three (or four in one case) years after that. Iranian traditional festivals: Mehregan festival, Norooz or nuroz festival, qadir festival, Chahar shanbehesori festival. Islamic festivals: EId-ul-Adha festival (biggest Islamic festival), Id-ul-Fiter festival is another Islamic festival (second-biggest)., Ide qadir festival is also an Irano-Islamic festival.

Jacksonville Jazz Festival

The Jacksonville Jazz Festival is a weekend of Jazz that is the "second-largest jazz festival in the nation" according to Superpages and that, according to the Jacksonville Times-Union, has been dubbed by "experts" as "one of the 20 best in the nation." The event in Jacksonville, Florida, USA is sponsored by the city, and the entertainment events take place at Metropolitan Park.

FESTIVAL EVENTS

The festival includes The Great American Jazz Piano competition which takes place at the Florida Theatre on Friday evening of the festival weekend. The winner plays a featured set at Metropolitan Park. During the Art at the Met concert in Metropolitan Park, the audience can view the work of prize-winning artisans and master craftspeople from around the nation while listening. Art mediums can include: Clay, Digital, Drawing, Fiber, Furniture, Glass, Jewelry, Mixed Media, Painting, Sculpture and Wood. The wine tasting event titled 38° Latitude: A Wine Tasting Experience is another favorite pastime at the festival. Patrons may purchase a "Tasting Ticket" for entry to this special experience and receive a souvenir wine glass and eight samplings of more than 50 featured wines. Attendees have an opportunity to speak with winery representatives or to purchase bottles that they may consume at the Park. Food & drink, arts & crafts, souvenirs & music are available for purchase from vendors within the park, and

Sunday Jazz Brunch is available in Metropolitan Park, typically from 11:00am to 1:00pm. When the performers for the upcoming festival are announced, there is also an induction ceremony for the Jacksonville Jazz Festival Hall of Fame to honor people who have made a positive impact on jazz in Jacksonville. An official poster is created each year for the festival.

Past Performers

Over the years the festival has featured such notable artists as Dizzy Gillespie, Miles Davis, George Benson, Al Jarreau, Diane Schuur, Patti Austin, Branford Marsalis, Count Basie Orchestra, Buddy Guy, Robert Cray, Diana Krall, Herbie Hancock, Ramsey Lewis Trio, Chuck Mangione, Chris Botti, Rippingtons, Bela Fleck and the Flecktones, David Sanborn, Pamela Williams, Spyro Gyra, Dianne Reeves, Chick Corea, David Benoit, Boney James, Karrin Allyson, Grover Washington, Jr., Kenny G, Harry Connick, Jr. and Greg Adams, to name a few.

History

In 1980, Jake Godbold was elected Mayor of Jacksonville. He and aide Mike Tolbert founded the jazz festival and envisioned it as an event that would change people's attitudes about Jacksonville. It began as a one-day free concert featuring regional talent and a major headliner at Mayport. The producers expected a few hundred people to show up, but a crowd of several thousand turned out. The following year, attendance was even higher and Mayport could not handle the crowds, so the event moved to the newly opened Metropolitan Park in 1982. Costs were low (Dizzy Gillespie headlined the 1981 show for just $7,500) and sponsors were willing to support it, so it remained a free show.

The production was turned over to public television station WJCT in 1985 and they used it as their primary fund-raising event for many years. In the mid 80's, big name entertainers started raising the rates they charged to perform. The 1986 festival featured Miles Davis for approximately $25,000, more than three times the cost of the headliner five years earlier. Costs began to rise faster than sponsorship money, so the show in 1995 included a $5 admission to help cover the shortfall. Vic DiGenti, who produced the event from 1993 to 2000 stated, "We probably lost some of those people who just want to come and hang out and drink beer." In the late 1990's attendance had risen to 20,000, but that wasn't enough to cover shrinking sponsorships and inflated artists' contracts. After the show in 2000, WJCT announced their withdrawal of sponsorship, citing large losses, resulting in no festival in 2001 and 2002.

The City of Jacksonville resurrected the event in 2003, and named Tony Bennett as the headliner. However, Bennett was the most expensive act in Jazz Festival history. He was paid $100,000 for his 75-minute performance at Metropolitan Park, plus $10,000 for expenses. The festival in 2003 once again did not charge admission. It was a sunny weekend and nearly 60,000 people attended, but the festival's overall profits were half a million dollars short of its expenses. When it rained in 2004, attendance numbers fell to 22,000 and the festival lost another half million dollars. In 2006, the city decided to begin charging admission, but the deficit stayed around $500,000. The 2007-8 budget included significant cuts that required the Jazz Festival to be scaled back. Saturday and Sunday music will be limited to Metropolitan Park whereas in 2007, concerts were also held at the Florida and Ritz theaters.

CHAPTER-7

HAPPENING EVENT TOURISM

A happening is a performance, event or situation meant to be considered as an art, usually as performance art. Happenings take place anywhere (from basements to studio lofts and even street alley ways), are often multi-disciplinary, with a nonlinear narrative and the active participation of the audience. Key elements of happenings are planned, but artists sometimes retain room for improvisation. This new media art aspect to happenings eliminates the boundary between the artwork and its viewer. Henceforth, the interactions between the audience and the artwork makes the audience, in a sense, part of the art.

In the later sixties, perhaps due to the depiction in films of hippie culture, the term was used much less specifically to mean any gathering of interest, from a pool hall meetup or a jamming of a few young people to a beer blast or fancy formal party.

HISTORY

Origins

Allan Kaprow first coined the term happening in the Spring of 1957 at an art picnic at George Segal's farm to describe the art pieces that were going on. The first appearance in print was in Kaprow's famous "Legacy of Jackson Pollock" essay that was published in 1958 but primarily written in 1956. Happening also appeared in print in one issue of the Rutgers University undergraduate literary magazine, Anthologist. The form was imitated and the term was adopted by artists across the U.S., Germany, and Japan. Jack Kerouac referred to Kaprow as "The Happenings man," and an ad showing a woman floating in outer space declared, "I dreamt I was in a happening in my Maidenform brassiere."

"Happenings" are very difficult to describe, in part because each one is unique and completely different from one another. One definition comes from Wardrip-Fruin and Montfort in The New Media Reader, "The term "Happening" has been used to describe many performances and events, organized by Allan Kaprow and others during the 1950s and 1960s, including a number of theatrical productions that were traditionally scripted and invited only limited audience interaction." A "Happening" of the same performance will have a different outcomes because each performance depends on the action of the audience. In New York especially, "Happenings" become quite popular even though many have not seen nor experienced it.

"Happenings" can be a form of participatory new media art, emphasizing an interaction between the performer and the audience. Breaking the fourth wall between "performer" and "spectator", it replaces criticism with support. For some happenings, everyone present is included in the making of the art and even the form of the art depends on audience engagement, for they are a key factor in where the performers' spontaneity leads. Later happenings had no set rules, only vague guidelines that the performers follow based on surrounding props. Unlike other forms of art, "Happenings" that allow chance to enter are ever-changing. When chance determines the path the performance will follow, there is no room for failure. As Kaprow writes in his essay, '"Happenings" in the New York Scene', "Visitors to a Happening are now and then not sure what has taken place, when it has ended, even when things have gone 'wrong'. For when something goes 'wrong', something far more 'right,' more revelatory, has many times emerged"(New Media Reader, pg. 86). The art thrives on an artist's whim, with the comfort of giving their "mistakes" the benefit of the doubt. The art defines itself by the fact that it is a unique, one-time experience that depends on audience response. It cannot be bought or brought home, which entitles every "Happening" artist to a sense of privacy. As Kaprow explains in the aforementioned essay, since the performances are always different, each one of these artists cannot lose their creative drive to a mainstream force.

Kaprow's piece 18 Happenings in 6 Parts (1959) is commonly cited as the first happening, although that distinction is sometimes given to a 1952 performance of Theater Piece No. 1 at Black Mountain College by John Cage, one of Kaprow's teachers in the mid-1950s. Cage stood reading from a ladder, Charles Olson read from another ladder, Robert Rauschenberg showed some of his paintings and played scratched phonograph records, David Tudor performed on a prepared piano and Merce Cunningham danced. All these things took place at the same time, among the audience rather than on a stage. Happenings flourished in New York City in the late 1950s and early 1960s. Key contributors to the form included Carolee Schneemann, Red Grooms, Robert Whitman, Jim Dine Car Crash, Claes Oldenburg, Robert Delford Brown, Lucas Samaras, and Robert Rauschenberg. Some of their work is documented in Michael Kirby's book Happenings (1966). Interestingly, Kaprow claimed that "some of us will become famous, and we will have proven once again that the only success occurred when there was a lack of it."

During the summer of 1959, Red Grooms along with others (Yvonne Andersen, Bill Barrell, Sylvia Small and Dominic Falcone) staged the non-narrative "play" Walking Man, which began with construction sounds, such as sawing. Grooms recalls, "The curtains were opened by me, playing a fireman wearing a simple costume of white pants and T-shirt with a poncholike cloak and a Smokey Stoverish fireman's helmet. Bill, the "star" in a tall hat and black overcoat, walked back and forth across the stage with great wooden gestures. Yvonne sat on the floor by a suspended fire engine. She was a blind woman with tin-foil covered glasses and cup. Sylvia played a radio and pulled on hanging junk. For the finale, I hid behand a false door and shouted pop code words. Then the cast did a wild run around and it ended." Dubbing his 148 Delancey Street studio The Delancey Street Museum, Grooms staged three more happenings there, A Garden, The Burning Building and The Magic Trainride (originally titled Fireman's Dream). No wonder Kaprow called Grooms "a Charlie Chaplin forever dreaming about fire."..'' On the opening night of The Burning Building, Bob Thompson solicited an audience member for a light, since none of the cast had one, and this gesture of spontaneous theater recurred in eight subsequent performances.

Difference between Plays

Happenings emphasize the organic connection between art and its environment. Kaprow supports that "happenings invite us to cast aside for a moment these proper manners and partake wholly in the real nature of the art and life. It is a rough and sudden act, where one often feels "dirty", and dirt, we might begin to realize, is also organic and fertile, and everything including the visitors can grow a little into such circumstances." Secondly, happenings have no plot or philosophy, but rather is materialized in an improvisatory fashion. There is no direction thus the outcome is unpredictable. "It is generated in action by a headful of ideas...and it frequently has words but they may or may not make literal sense. If they do, their meaning is not representational of what the whole element conveys. Hence they carry a brief, detached quality. If they do not make sense, then they are acknowledgement of the sound of the word rather than the meaning conveyed by it." Last, due to the convention's nature, there is no such term as "failure" which can be applied. "For when something goes "wrong", something far more "right", more revelatory may emerge. This sort of sudden near-miracle presently is made more likely by chance procedures." As a conclusion, a happening is fresh while it lasts and cannot be reproduced.

Regarding happenings, Red Grooms has remarked, "I had the sense that I knew it was something. I knew it was something because I didn't know what it was. I think that's when you're at your best point. When you're really doing something, you're doing it all out, but you don't know what it is."

The lack of plot as well as the expected audience participation can be likened to Augusto Boal's Theater of the Oppressed, which also claims that "spectator is a bad word". Boal expected audience members to participate in the theater of the oppressed by becoming the actors. His goal was to allow the downtrodden to act out the forces oppressing them in order to mobilize the people into political action. Both Kaprow and Boal are reinventing theater to try and make plays more interactive and to abolish the traditional narrative form to make theater something more free-form and organic.

Contribution Toward Digital Media

Allan Kaprow's and other artists of the 1950s and 1960s that performed these "Happenings" helped put "new media technology developments into context." It was highly influential in true "intermedia" work and the interactivity in art. The "Happenings" allowed other artists to create performances that would attract attention to the issue they wanted to portray. Digital media examples of "Happenings" could be as simple as artists creating a webpage about their issues or going on to blogs, forumns and other networks that they could send mass art and information through.

Around the world

In 1959 the French artist Yves Klein first performed Zone de Sensibilité Picturale Immatérielle. The work involved the sale of documentation of ownership of empty space (the Immaterial Zone), taking the form of a cheque, in exchange for gold; if the buyer wished, the piece could then be completed in an elaborate ritual in which the buyer would burn the cheque, and Klein would throw half of the gold into the Seine . The ritual would be performed in the presence of an art critic or distinguished dealer, an art museum director and at least two witnesses .

In 1960, Jean-Jacques Lebel oversaw and partook in the first European Happening L'enterrement de la Chose in Venice. For his performance there - called Happening Funeral Ceremony of the Anti-Process - Lebel invited the audience to attend a ceremony in formal dress. In a decorated room within a grand residence, a draped 'cadaver' rested on a plinth which was then ritually stabbed by an 'executioner' while a 'service' was read consisting of extracts from the French décadent writer Joris-Karl Huysmans and le Marquis de Sade. Then pall-bearers carried the coffin out into a gondola and the 'body' - which was in fact a mechanical sculpture by Jean Tinguely - was ceremonially slid into the canal.

Poet and painter Adrian Henri claimed to have organized the first happenings in England in Liverpool in 1962, taking place during the Merseyside Arts Festival. The most important event in London was the Albert Hall "International Poetry Incarnation" on June 11, 1965, where an audience of 7,000 people witnessed and participated in performances by some of the leading avant-garde young British and American poets of the day (see British Poetry Revival and Poetry of the United States). One of the participants, Jeff Nuttall, went on to organize a number of further happenings, often working with his friend Bob Cobbing, sound poet and performance poet.

In Tokyo in 1964, Yoko Ono created a happening by performing her "Cut Piece" at the Sogetsu Art Center. She walked onto the stage draped in fabric, presented the audience with a pair of scissors, and instructed the audience to cut the fabric away gradually until she was naked.

In Belgium, the first happenings were organized around 1965–1968 in Antwerp, Brussels and Ostend by artists Hugo Heyrman and Panamarenko.

In the Netherlands, Provo organized happenings around the little statue "Het Lieverdje" on the Spui, a square in the centre of Amsterdam, from 1966 till 1968. Police often raided these events.

In Germany, HA Schult (b. 1939), together with his muse, Elke Koska, organizes happenings since the late 1960s, thereby primarily working with garbage.

In Australia, the Yellow House Artist Collective in Sydney housed 24-hour happenings throughout the early 1970s.

Behind the Iron Curtain, in Poland, artist and theater director Tadeusz Kantor staged the first happenings starting in 1965. Also, in the second half of 1980s, a student-based happening movement Orange Alternative founded by Major Waldemar Fydrych became known for its much attended happenings (over 10 thousand participants at one time) aimed against the military regime led by General Jaruzelski and the fear blocking the Polish society ever since the Martial Law had been imposed in December 1981.

The non-profit, artist-run organization, iKatun, has reflected the use of "Happenings" influence while in-corporating the medium of internet. They aim is one that "fosters public engagement in the politics of information." Their project entitled "The International Database of Corporate Commands" presents a scrutinizing look at the super-saturating advertisements slogans, and "commands" of companies. "The Institute for Infinitely Small Things uses these commands to conduct research performances-performances in which we attempt to enact, as literally as possible, what the command tells us to do and where it tells us to do it. For example, a user may look at a long list of slogans on the website database section, and may submit, in text, his or her take on the most literal way to act out the slogan/ command. The iKatun team will then act out the slogan in a research-performance related way. This means of performance art draws on the collaboration of the web world and tangible reality to conduct a new, modern "Happening."

MODERN HAPPENINGS

Flash mob

A flash mob (or flashmob) is a large group of people who assemble suddenly in a public place, perform an unusual and pointless act for a brief time, then disperse. The term flash mob is generally applied only to gatherings organized via telecommunications, social media, or viral emails. The term is generally not applied to events organized by public relations firms, protests, and publicity stunts.

Origins

The First Flash Mob

The first flash mob was created in Manhattan in May 2003, by Bill Wasik, senior editor of Harper's Magazine. The origins of the flash mobs were unknown until Wasik published an article about his creation in the March 2006 edition of Harper's. The first attempt was unsuccessful after the targeted retail store was tipped off about the plan for people to gather. Wasik avoided such problems during the second flash mob, which occurred on June 3, 2003 at Macy's department store, by sending participants to preliminary staging areas – in four prearranged Manhattan bars – where they received further instructions about the ultimate event and location just before the event began.

More than 100 people converged upon the ninth floor rug department of the store, gathering around an expensive rug. Anyone approached by a sales assistant was advised to say that the gatherers lived together in a warehouse on the outskirts of New York, that they were shopping for a "love rug", and that they made all their purchase decisions as a group.

Subsequently, 200 people flooded the lobby and mezzanine of the Hyatt hotel in synchronized applause for about 15 seconds, and a shoe boutique in SoHo was invaded by participants pretending to be tourists on a bus trip.

Wasik claimed that he created flash mobs as a social experiment designed to poke fun at hipsters and to highlight the cultural atmosphere of conformity and of wanting to be an insider or part of "the next big thing". The Vancouver Sun wrote, "It may have backfired on him... [Wasik] may instead have ended up giving conformity a vehicle that allowed it to appear nonconforming."

Precursors

Flash mobs began as a form of performance art. While they started as an apolitical act, flash mobs may share superficial similarities to political demonstrations. Flash mobs can be seen as a specialized form of smart mob, which is a term and concept forwarded by author Howard Rheingold in his 2002 book Smart Mobs: The Next Social Revolution.

Literary precedents

In 1973, the story "Flash Crowd" by Larry Niven described a concept similar to flash mobs. With the invention of popular and very inexpensive teleportation, an argument at a shopping mall – which happens to be covered by a news crew – quickly swells into a riot. In the story, broadcast coverage attracts the attention of other people, who use the widely available technology of the teleportation booth to swarm first that event – thus intensifying the riot – and then other events as they happen. Commenting on the social impact of such mobs, one character (articulating the police view) says, "We call them flash crowds, and we watch for them." In related short stories, they are named as a prime location for illegal activities (such as pickpocketing and looting) to take place.

Use of the term

19th century usage

In 19th century Tasmania, the term flash mob was used to describe a subculture consisting of female prisoners, based on the term flash language for the jargon that these women used. The 19th century Australian term flash mob referred to a segment of society, not an event, and showed no other similarities to the modern term flash mob or the events it describes.

21st century usage

The first recorded use of the term flash mob as it is understood today was in 2003 in a blog entry posted in the aftermath of

Wasik's event. The term was inspired by the earlier term smart mob.

Flash mob was added to the 11th edition of the Concise Oxford English Dictionary on 8 July 2004 where it noted it as an "unusual and pointless act" separating it from other forms of smart mobs such as types of performance, protests, and other gatherings. Also recognized noun derivatives are flash mobber and flash mobbing. Webster's New Millennium Dictionary of English defines flash mob as "a group of people who organize on the Internet and then quickly assemble in a public place, do something bizarre, and disperse." This definition is consistent with the original use of the term; however, both news media and promoters have subsequently used the term to refer to any form of smart mob, including political protests; a collaborative Internet denial of service attack; a collaborative supercomputing demonstration; and promotional appearances by a pop musician. The press has also used the term flash mob to refer to a practice being used in China where groups of shoppers arrange online to meet at a store at the same time in order to drive a collective bargain with the store owner.

Notable Flash Mobs

Silent disco

Another example of a well known flash mob was the April 2006 silent disco in London. At various London Underground stations, people gathered with their portable music devices, and at a set time began dancing to their music. It was reported that more than 4,000 people participated at London Victoria station. This had an impact on the regular service of the system enough for the city's police to begin crowd control and slowly clear people. Though no one was arrested, it was reported that the City of London pledged to counter future disruption of the underground system. Since 2006, there have been several flash mobs in the London Underground, including subsequent silent discos comparable in size.

Worldwide Pillow Fight Day

Worldwide Pillow Fight Day (or International Pillow Fight Day) was a pillow fight flash mob that took place on March 22, 2008. Over 25 cities around the globe participated in the first "international flash mob", which was the world's largest flash mob to date. According to The Wall Street Journal, more than 5,000 participated in New York City, overtaking London's 2006 Silent Disco gathering as the largest recorded flash mob. Word spread via social networking sites, including Facebook, Myspace, private blogs, public forums, personal websites, as well as by word of mouth, text messaging, and email. Participating cities included Atlanta, Boston, Budapest, Chicago, Copenhagen, Denver, Dublin, Hamburg, Houston, Huntsville, London, Los Angeles, Melbourne, New York City, Paris, Pécs, Portland, Roanoke, Seattle, Shanghai, Stockholm, Sydney, Székesfehérvár, Szombathely, Vancouver, Washington, D.C. and Zurich.

Response

United States

In April 2009, police used pepper spray to break up a flash mob event at University ofTennessee at Chattanooga, and arrested five people. In December 2009, Old Dominion University campus police pepper-sprayed a flash mob.

In 2009 and 2010 Center City Philadelphia has had at least four incidents where flash mob gatherings have turned violent. During these incidents, teenagers ran through the streets or malls, vandalized property, fought with each other, and attacked passers-by resulting in injuries and arrests. Similar incidents have occurred in Boston, South Orange, Kansas City and Brooklyn. The F.B.I. is assisting Philadelphia police by monitoring social media websites. Philadelphia radio and television stations have recruited hip-hop artists for public service announcements that implore the teenagers to stop the practice.

United Kingdom

In May 2008, police stopped a planned flash mob event over concerns for "public health and safety". In February 2009, the British Transport Police criticized flash mobs, saying "when you get thousands of commuters trying to go home at a very busy station in the middle of rush-hour and then joined by thousands of people who want to dance that can then be a problem."

Germany

The city of Braunschweig, Germany has banned flash mobs. The Association of German Retailers (HDE) filed a legal complaint in Germany's highest court to ban the use of flash mobs during labor disputes, following a Federal Labor Court of Germany ruling that flash mobs are a legitimate form of industrial action.

IMPROVE EVERYWHERE

Improve Everywhere (often abbreviated IE) is a comedic performance art group based in New York City, formed in 2001 by Charlie Todd. Its slogan is "We Cause Scenes."

The group carries out pranks, which they call "missions", in public places. The stated goal of these missions is to cause scenes of "chaos and joy." Some of the group's missions use hundreds of performers and are similar to flash mobs, while other missions utilize only a handful of performers. Improv Everywhere has stated that they do not identify their work with the term flash mob, in part because their site was created two years prior to the flash mob trend.

Improv Everywhere has been profiled by many national and international media outlets including The New York Times, The Today Show, and ABC's Nightline. Todd was interviewed on an episode of This American Life in 2005. While touching briefly on two missions ("No Pants" and "The Moebius"), the show focused on "Best Gig Ever" and "Ted's Birthday", and how they created unintended reactions. Improv Everywhere was also featured in the pilot episode for This American Life's television show on Showtime. In 2007, the group shot a television pilot for NBC.

Background

Todd started the group in August of 2001 after playing a prank in a Manhattan bar with some friends that involved him pretending to be musician Ben Folds. Later that year Todd started taking classes at the Upright Citizens Brigade Theatre in New York City where he first met most of the "Senior Agents" of Improv Everywhere. The owners of the theatre, The Upright Citizens Brigade (UCB), had a television series from 1998–2000 on Comedy Central. While primarily a sketch comedy show, the UCB often filmed their characters in public places with hidden cameras and showed the footage under the end credits. Both the UCB's show and their teachings on improv have been influential to Improv Everywhere. Todd himself currently teaches and performs at the UCB.

Missions

While long-time members of Improv Everywhere often participate in missions, many are open to the public. IE has organized and carried out over 100 missions, from synchronized swimming in a park fountain to repeating a five-minute sequence of events in a Starbucks coffee shop over and over again for an hour, from flooding a Best Buy store with members dressed exactly like the staff to riding the New York City Subway without their pants. All the missions share a certain modus operandi: Members ("agents") play their roles entirely straight, not breaking character or betraying that they are acting. IE claims the missions are benevolent, aiming to give the observers a laugh and an experience.

IE have also performed several 'fake' missions which are staged and uploaded on April fools day as a real mission, causing outrage until the next day when the joke is revealed. Examples include the no underwear subway ride, and the "Best Funeral Ever" prank.

YouTube popularity

Improve Everywhere's videos have been viewed over 117 million times on YouTube and their channel is the 49th most subscribed on the site. IE's most popular YouTube video is "Frozen Grand Central", which has received over 22 million views. The two minute video depicts 200 IE Agents freezing in place simultaneously for five minutes in New York's Grand Central Terminal. The video was listed as number 49 in Urlesque's 100 Most Iconic Internet Videos. Martin Bashir declared on Nightline that the video was "one of the funniest moments ever captured on tape." The prank has been recreated by fans in over 100 cities around the world.

Police intervention

Some IE events have attracted police attention. The annual "No Pants" event involves a large number of people riding the subway, all claiming to have forgotten their pants by accident. During a No Pants mission on 22 January 2006, the New York City Police Department handcuffed eight members of the group while on the subway (according to the group, over 160 people had participated in the city-wide event). The eight handcuffed participants had been riding the 6 train and were taken into custody and issued summonses for disorderly conduct. After appearing in court, the charges were dismissed. Despite the setback, IE continues the tradition each January, and in more recent years, the police have arrived at the event's meeting point not to make arrests, but to serve as friendly escorts. On January 10, 2010, over 3,000 people participated in the No Pants ride in New York, and over 4,000 more participated in 44 additional cities around the world. Todd has stated that No Pants has evolved from a small prank in 2002 into an "international celebration of silliness".

On 21 May 2005 IE staged a fake U2 street concert on a rooftop in New York hours before the real U2 were scheduled to perform at Madison Square Garden. A crowd formed, most of which thought that the people on the rooftop were actually U2. However, just like at the filming of the band's Where the Streets Have No Name video in 1987, the police eventually shut the performance down, but not before IE was able to exhaust their four-song repertoire and get most of the way through an encore repeat of "Vertigo". The crowd, even those who had realized that this was a prank, shouted "one more song!," and then "let them play!" when the police officers arrived. This mission was number 23 on the VH1 countdown of the "40 Greatest Pranks."

During the Best Buy Invasion mission, an 80-person IE team entered a Best Buy store dressed in blue shirts and khaki pants—the uniform colors of Best Buy employees—and answered questions for customers (though denying being an employee of Best Buy if asked). While many of the store's actual employees laughed and took photos of the pranksters, the store's management called the police. After assessing the situation the police informed the Best Buy staff that they could not do anything except ask the IE agents to leave the store as there was nothing illegal about wearing a blue polo shirt with khaki pants.

Performance Art

Performance art refers largely to a performance which is presented to an audience but which does not seek to present a conventional theatrical play or a formal linear narrative, or which alternately does not seek to depict a set of fictitious characters in formal scripted interactions. It therefore will often include some form of action or spoken word which is a form of direct communication between the artist and audience, rather than a script written beforehand.

It often entails a dramatic performer who is directly aware of and in communication with the audience, much the same as a singer or juggler in a concert or variety show might be said to perform directly for an audience, rather than creating a fictitious character who inhabits a fictitious dramatic setting on the stage. Performance art often breaks the fourth wall, meaning that the performance artist does not seek to behave as if unaware of the audience.

Some performance art may utilize a script or create a fictitious dramatic setting, but still constitutes performance art in that it does not seek to follow the usual dramatic norm of creating a fictitious setting with a linear script which follows conventional real-world dynamics; rather, it would intentionally seek to satirize or to transcend the usual real-world dynamics which are used in conventional theatrical plays. In this way, the performance work itself partakes of a form of direct communication with the audience, by relying on the audience's familiarity with nominal dramatic premises and norms, in order to go beyond them or circumvent them, even if the characters within the work themselves do not evince such awareness.

Although performance art could be said to include relatively mainstream forms of performance such as dance, music, and circus-related things like fire breathing, juggling, and gymnastics, these are normally instead known as the performing arts. Performance art is a term usually reserved to refer to a more conceptual art which conveys a content-based meaning in a more drama-related sense, rather than being simple performance for its own sake for entertainment purposes. Furthermore, performance art can include any type of physical stage performance which is not an exhibition of direct artistry such as theater, music or dance, but rather incorporates satirical or conceptual elements; an example of this is Blue Man Group.

In performance art, the actions of an individual or a group at a particular place and in a particular time constitute the work. Performance art can happen anywhere, in any venue or setting and for any length of time. Performance art can be any situation that involves four basic elements: time, space, the performer's body and a relationship between performer and audience. Performance art traditionally involves the artist and other actors, but works like Survival Research Laboratories' pieces, utilizing robots and machines without people, may also be seen as an offshoot of performance art. In some cases,the audience unwittingly becomes part of that performance.

HISTORY

Origins

The first forms of performance art began in the Middle Ages, in the forms of itinerant poets such as minstrels, troubadours, bards, and in some cases jesters. These were artists who often composed and performed their own works. In the case of minstrels, their poems were often composed spontaneously, and bore direct relevance to the audience and their society. thus, they constituted an early form of performance art. This evolved into various forms in various cultures, such as Commedia dell'arte in Italy, pantomime in Great Britain, mime artists (which are quite distinct from pantomime), harlequinade in various European societies, skomorokh in Russia, and folk plays in various countries.

In modern era, there continue to be some paradigmatic roles which fit this function, such as buskers.

Modern development

In the modern era, there have been a variety of new works, concepts and artists which have led to new kinds of performance art. Andy Warhol was noted for staging new types of mass events and performance art in New York, notably with the Velvet Underground and also with the Warhol Superstars. Laurie Anderson's performance art has been staged at a number of major venues, such as Lincoln Center. Modern artistic concepts such as surrealism and dadaism were used by several artists to produce new kinds of performance art.

In the 1960s, an increasing number of artists produced new forms of performance art, including Yves Klein, Allan Kaprow—who coined the term Happenings—Carolee Schneemann, Hermann Nitsch, Yoko Ono, Wolf Vostell, Joseph Beuys, Barbara T. Smith, Vito Acconci, the women associated with the Feminist Studio Workshop and the Woman's Building in Los Angeles, and Chris Burden. But performance art was certainly anticipated, if not explicitly formulated, by Japan's Gutai group of the 1950s, especially in such works as Atsuko Tanaka's "Electric Dress" (1956) . In 1970 the British-based pair Gilbert and George created the first of their "living sculpture" performances when they painted themselves gold and sang "Underneath The Arches" for extended periods. Jud Yalkut, a pioneering video artist, and others, such as Carolee Schneemann and Sandra Binion, began combining video with other media to create experimental works. Guerrilla theater, or street theater, including performances by students and others, have regularly appeared within the ranks of antiwar movements.

The anarchist antiwar group the Yippies, partly organized by Abbie Hoffmann, performed street theater when they dropped hundreds of dollar bills from the balcony of the Stock Exchange in New York. Latino, Latin-American, and other street theater groups, including those like the San Francisco Mime Troupe, that stem from circus and traveling theater traditions, should also be mentioned. Although they may not be not direct antecedents of art-world performance, their influence, particularly in the United States should be noted— as should that of the U.S. conceptual artist Sol Lewitt, who in the early 1960s converted mural-style drawing into an act of performance by others. Performance art, because of its relative transience, had a fairly robust presence in the avant-garde of East Bloc countries, especially Yugoslavia and Poland, by the 1970s.

Western cultural theorists often trace performance art activity back to the beginning of the 20th century. Dada, for example, provided a significant progenitor with the unconventional performances of poetry, often at the Cabaret Voltaire, by the likes of Richard Huelsenbeck and Tristan Tzara. There were also Russian Futurist artists who could be identified as performance artists, such as David Burliuk, who painted his face for his actions (1910-20). However, there are accounts of Renaissance artists putting on public performances that could be said to be early ancestors of modern performance art. Some performance artists and theorists point to other traditions and histories, ranging from tribal to sporting and ritual or religious events. Performance art activity is not confined to European or American art traditions; many notable practitioners can be found in Asia and Latin America.

Performance

In performance art, usually one or more people perform in front of an audience. Performance artists often challenge the audience to think in new and unconventional ways about theater and performing, break conventions of traditional performing arts, and break down conventional ideas about "what art is," a preoccupation of modernist experimental theater and of postmodernism. Thus, even though in most cases the performance is in front of an audience, in some cases, notably in the later works of Allan Kaprow, the audience members become the performers. The performance may be scripted, unscripted, or improvisational. It may incorporate music, dance, song, or complete silence. Art-world performance has often been an intimate set of gestures or actions, lasting from a few minutes to many hours, and may rely on props or avoid them completely. Performance may occur in transient spaces or in galleries, room, theaters or, auditoriums.

Despite the fact that many performances are held within the circle of a small art-world group, RoseLee Goldberg notes, in Performance Art: From Futurism to the Present that "performance has been a way of appealing directly to a large public, as well as shocking audiences into reassessing their own notions of art and its relation to culture. Conversely, public interest in the medium, especially in the 1980s, stems from an apparent desire of that public to gain access to the art world, to be a spectator of its ritual and its distinct community, and to be surprised by the unexpected, always unorthodox presentations that the artists devise."

Allan Kaprow's performance art attempted to integrate art and life. Through Happenings, the separation between life, art, artist, and audience becomes blurred. The Happening allows the artist to experiment with body motion, recorded sounds, written and spoken texts, and even smells. One of Kaprow's earliest Happenings was the "Happenings in the New York Scene," written in 1961 as the form was developing.

Genres

Performance art genres include body art, fluxus, happening, action poetry, and intermedia. Some artists, e.g. the Viennese Actionists and neo-Dadaists, prefer to use the terms live art, "action art", intervention or "manoeuvre" to describe their activities. These activities are also sometimes referred to simply as "actions".

ZOMBIE WALK

A zombie walk (also known as a zombie mob, zombie march, zombie horde, zombie lurch, zombie shamble, zombie shuffle or zombie crawl) is an organized public gathering of people who dress up in zombie costumes. Usually taking place in an urban centre, the participants make their way around the city streets and through shopping malls to a public space (or a series of taverns in the case of a zombie pub crawl) in a somewhat orderly fashion.

Customs

Zombie walks have become relatively common in large cities, especially in North America, often becoming annual traditions, though some are also spontaneous "flash mob" events or performance art. Promoted primarily through word of mouth and online message boards, zombie walks are an underground activity. During the event participants are encouraged to remain in character as zombies and to communicate only in a manner consistent with zombie behavior. This may include grunting, groaning and slurred, moaning calls for 'brains'. Zombie behavior is a hot topic of debate. Purists who draw their definitions from the original Romero Living Dead films will claim that a zombie would never have the ability to call for 'brains' and furthermore that a zombie needs only living or freshly killed flesh for its sustenance, and not the brain in particular.

The complexity and purpose of some zombie walks have grown and changed with their popularity. An advanced technique to heighten interest and realism, some zombie mobs will "eat" victims to create new zombies, in sight of onlookers. The better coordinated zombie mobs will establish a route and an easily recognizable signal, so that other participants can plant themselves, appearing as an otherwise ordinary human, along the route in old, tearable clothes, and as the mob shambles along it can discover and devour new victims. As the zombies surround the new victim to loudly feed, concealing him or her from witnesses' view, they tear clothes and quickly apply makeup and fake blood, to create a new zombie, who then shambles along with the ever-expanding pack to find new victims. Some participants occasionally dress up as soldiers who are called in to contain the outbreak. Some events are staged as spoof political rallies organized "to raise awareness of zombie rights", with participants carrying placards. Many zombie walks have also been staged as "hunger marches" with the intent of raising awareness of world hunger and collecting items for food banks.

History

The earliest zombie walk on record was held in August 19, 2001 in Sacramento, California. The event, billed as 'The Zombie Parade,' was the brain-child of Bryna Lovig, who suggested it to the organizers of The Trash Film Orgy as a way to promote their annual midnight film festival. It was held again in July 2002 and has since become an annual event.

The first zombie gathering run as a non-promotional, public event, and billed as a "Zombie Walk" was held in October 2003, in Toronto, Ontario. It was organized by local horror movie fan, Thea Munster, and had only six participants. In subsequent years the Toronto Zombie Walk grew tremendously in size. One of the first participants in the Toronto Zombie Walk, Heather McDermitt, moved to Vancouver, B.C. and spread the zombie walk tradition to that city. On August 27, 2005 over 400 participants proceeded through Vancouver's Pacific Centre Mall, travelled on the SkyTrain (referred to for the event as the "SkyBrain" or the "BrainTrain") and continued 35 blocks to Mountain View Cemetery.

The mid to late 2000's saw an exponential gain in popularity for zombie walks due largely to the increase of successful zombie films at the time, the Resident Evil movies, 28 Days Later, Zack Snyder's Dawn of the Dead, Shaun of the Dead, George A. Romero's Land of the Dead, and Zombieland being a few examples. Documentation of the phenomenon appeared in mainstream news media and blogs, such as Boingboing. Zombie walks soon spread across North America and to cities around the globe.

On October 15, 2005, the first annual Zombie Pub Crawl was held in Minneapolis, Minnesota. The event consisted of roughly 100-150 zombie-costumed participants moving from bar to bar in the city's Northeast district. It has since grown and been continued annually in different areas of the city. Inspired by Minneapolis, many other cities have started zombie-themed pub crawls of their own, including Chicago and Philadelphia. Philadelphia's zombie pub crawl is held on Easter Sunday in celebration of the world's "most famous zombie." Philadelphia also hosts an annual Zombie Prom in September and a Zombie Beach Party in June.

On October 29, 2006, 894 "zombie walkers" gathered at the Monroeville Mall outside of Pittsburgh, Pennsylvania, which served as the set of George A. Romero's classic zombie film Dawn of the Dead, to participate in Pittsburgh's first annual 'Walk of the Dead.' In addition to setting a Guinness World Record, the event was a benefit for the Greater Pittsburgh Community Food Bank. Pittsburgh's zombie walk has since grown into a annual horror convention called Zombie Fest. Zombie Fest is organized by The It's Alive Show, a local Pittsburgh late night horror and science fiction television program. The festival plays host to the annual 'Walk of the Dead' at Monroeville Mall as well as a zombie ball, costume contest, concerts, and celebrity guest appearances. Zombie Fest also serves as the headquarters of The It's Alive Show's World Zombie Day, a world hunger charity event.

On Halloween weekend in 2007 the group Viking Hats bought to London the largest Zombie Pub Crawl to the Capital, which has now run for 3 years with more zombies joining in year on year and will take place again on Saturday 30th October 2010.

On November 14, 2009, a zombie lurch protest, called the 'Epic Zombie Lurch,' was held in Sydney, Australia.[unreliable source?] The lurch was organized by local video gamers in protest of the lack of an R18+ rating for video games in Australia, which had resulted in the initial rejection of the game Left 4 Dead 2 (although the game was later released in an edited form). The march started in Hyde Park and went around the Sydney central business district area before finishing at Town Hall for a public forum of people's opinions on the lack of the rating. It is estimated that roughly 170 people were in attendance. The walk was repeated on March 27, with about 500 people this time estimated to be in attendance.

World Records

The first zombie walk world record was set on October 29, 2006 at Monroeville Mall outside of Pittsburgh, Pennsylvania during Pittsburgh's first annual 'Walk of the Dead.' Guinness World Records certified that 894 people participated in the walk. The second zombie walk at Monroeville Mall during the 2007 Zombie Fest was also verified by Guinness World Records as the largest gathering of zombies to date (October 28, 2007), with 1,028 participants.

The 2007 Toronto Zombie Walk drew a crowd of over 1,100 zombies, a number confirmed by Toronto Police Services. At the time, this was the largest zombie walk on record.

A zombie march in Brisbane, Australia on May 25, 2008 set an unofficial record of over 1,500 participants according to media reports.

On June 21, 2008, a zombie march took place in Chicago with over 1,550 zombies estimated, setting a new unofficial record.

On October 30, 2008, Grand Rapids, Michigan, became the largest site of zombies anywhere in the world when around 4,000 zombies showed up to a zombie walk organized by Grand Rapids Community College student, Rob Bliss. Bliss organized the walk on Facebook but due to cost and application issues he was unable to get the walk certified by Guinness World Records.

On 31 October 2008, a zombie walk took place in the Old Market Square of Nottingham, United Kingdom with 1,227 attendees. The event was organized by GameCity, and the zombies did dances to zombie-related songs such as Michael Jackson's "Thriller", "Disturbia" and "Ghostbusters". There was also a performance from American singer Jonathan Coulton. The event achieved a new official Guinness World Record for largest zombie walk.

In June 2009, Pittsburgh zombie fans won back the Guinness World Record after Guinness verified that the October 26, 2008 Zombie Fest 'Walk of the Dead' at Monroeville Mall had 1,341 participating walkers.

On July 3, 2009, a zombie walk organized by Fremont Outdoor Movies in Seattle, Washington beat all previous zombie walk records. Guinness World Records officially recorded 3,894 zombies at the 'Red, White and Dead' zombie event, though local news claimed 4,277 participants.

In October 2009 Guinness World Records officially recorded and approved a new record for the largest gathering of zombies. The record was set at 'The Big Chill Festival' in Ledbury, Herefordshire, UK on August 6, 2009. There were 4,026 zombie mob participants.

On October 25, 2009 the biggest recorded gathering of zombies in the Southern Hemisphere occurred in Brisbane, Australia with over 5,000 participants (as reported in various medias). The walk was also a charity event helping to raise awareness and money for the aptly chosen organization, The Brain Foundation of Australia.

On October 30, 2009, zombie walkers in Grand Rapids, Michigan attempted a second run at the zombie mob world record. An estimated 8,000 participates braved rainy weather to gather in Calder Plaza outside of Grand Rapids's City and County buildings. The event was coordinated by Rob Bliss, organizer of Grand Rapids' first zombie walk. Approximately forty to fifty volunteers collected signatures from the crowd. The record is currently unverified by Guinness World Records.

Guinness recognized a new record for zombie gatherings on July 3, 2010 at Seattle, Washington's annual 'Red, White, and

Dead' zombie walk. Guinness recorded 4,200 zombies at the event while organizers claimed almost 5,000 zombies were in attendance.

Charity

Charity work continues to be a common component at many zombie walks. Community service organizations have used zombie walks as demonstrations to raise funds and awareness for local and global issues, such as world hunger.

Both world record walks at Pittsburgh's Zombie Fest have included food drives. In 2008, The It's Alive Show (the organizers of Zombie Fest), initiated World Zombie Day. The It's Alive Show encouraged cities all over the globe to celebrate World Zombie Day by holding zombie walks to raise awareness of global hunger. The first World Zombie Day took place October 26, 2008; the same day as Pittsburgh's Zombie Fest. More than 30 cities worldwide took part in this day of global zombie walking. Food drives for local hunger-related charities took place at each participating city's zombie walk. Pittsburgh's walk alone brought in more than one ton of food to benefit the Greater Pittsburgh Community Food Bank. The second World Zombie Day took place October 11, 2009 with even more participation from cities all over the world.

During Grand Rapids, Michigan's zombie walk on October 30, 2008 over 7,500+ cans of food were collected and donated to a local food bank.

Zombie-Aid, a zombie walk charity organization in Manchester, England has raised thousands of dollars for cancer patients and children since its first walk on July 12, 2009. Future Zombie Aid walks have been planned in multiple UK and American cities.

On August 26, 2009, San Jose based comics publisher SLG Publishing <http://www.slgcomic.com> sponsored a zombie crawl, called the 'Zombie-O-Rama,' to coincide with an outdoor showing of Shaun of the Dead by the San Jose Downtown Association. The event collected canned food for the Second

Harvest Food Bank of Santa Clara County Over 1,000 people participated.

On September 19, 2009, Iowa City's fourth-annual Zombie March raised $1,723 in t-shirt sales to benefit local charity services. The money was given to the charities in memory of University of Iowa student, Christopher McClatchey, who died of necrotizing fasciitis, a skin-eating bacterial disease.

On October 24, 2009, the second annual Houston Zombie Walk collected enough money and food donations to put together 100 care packages for U.S. troops.

Controversy

Due to the spontaneous and naturally chaotic nature of a zombie uprising, some zombie walks have been host to criticism.

On October 31, 2006, a young woman in Bloomington, Indiana reported to police that a group of "zombies" attacked her in her Land Rover and covered the vehicle in "purple goo". The zombies in question turned out to be participants in a small, local zombie walk, and no arrests were made.

At the 2006 Vancouver Zombie Walk, an incident occurred in which an impatient driver attempted to drive his car through a crowd of zombies headed down Robson St. This resulted in some minor injuries among the zombies, severe damage to the car, a number of insurance claims, and coverage on CBC Television.

A zombie walk in Brisbane, Australia on May 25, 2008 saw more than 1,500 participants stopping traffic and shoppers in the central business district. Local newspapers failed to mention the event, in a bid to stop it from continuing, after several businesses complained about minor "zombie damage" and zombies scaring their customers away.

On May 1, 2010, the annual Zombie Shuffle in Melbourne, Victoria saw the largest attendance in its five year history, but some locals complained of the mess that the zombie "gore" left behind as well as the walk's disruption of a play for preschoolers.

SUBWAY PARTY

A subway party is a celebration that occurs on a mass transit system. Generally, people meet at a predetermined station in their city's mass transit system, wait until their numbers have achieved critical mass, and board the train. From there, revelers may engage in many different activities, from playing music and dancing to exchanging gifts.

There are several kinds of subway parties, the two most distinct being the rush hour subway party and the late night subway party.

Rush Hour Subway Parties

The stated goal of the rush hour subway party is to spread joy to commuters, whose daily treks into the center of their metropolis can be long, boring or stressful. Several subway party groups have boarded subway cars dressed in costumes to give presents to commuters, and have been known to play drums, wear wings and sprinkle glitter on the willing.

Critics of these kind of subway parties say that, by introducing chaos, these activities may place the already-crowded subway riders in danger or cause delays. Also, some people are simply annoyed by them.

Late Night Subway Parties

Late night subway parties are for the enjoyment of the attendees. Party-goers don costumes, decorate the subway car, bring musical instruments and sometimes the parties have a theme.

With the advent of email and cellphones, invitations to subway parties can now be distributed electronically. The party usually starts at one subway station and acquires more participants as it proceeds through the system. The instructions often ask people to meet by the last car of the train.

Other Subway Parties

On nights that are especially festive such as New Year's or World Cup victories, a spontaneous subway party may occur. People may already be drinking above ground and decide to board the subway. When this happens, the general feeling of revelry continues below ground.

In 2005, the Toronto Transit Commission declared October "culture month", perhaps inspired by recent subway parties in the city. This campaign included "culture cars", which were randomly-selected cars that contained spontaneous, professional singing, dancing and music.

History of the Subway Party

In 1904, the New York City Subway System opened. Photographs from the event show people dressed in tuxedos and top hats and drinking champagne to celebrate.

In the 1980s, Michael Alig and the Club Kids threw parties on New York City subway trains where they purportedly took the drug ecstasy. The events were promoted through word of mouth and telephones. These parties are detailed in the book Disco Bloodbath.

Today, subway parties are only loosely related to the flash mob phenomenon. The details for subway parties are published on blogs, websites and mailing lists. People assemble seemingly spontaneously in dozens of cities throughout the world.

PILLOW FIGHT FLASH MOB

A pillow fight flash mob is a social phenomenon of flash mobbing and shares many characteristics of a culture jam. The flash mob version of massive pillow fights is distinguished by the fact that nearly all of the promotion is Internet-based. These events occur around the world, some taking the name Pillow Fight Club, a reference to Fight Club by Chuck Palahniuk in which anyone could join and fight as long as they fought by the rules. Both the London and Vancouver Pillow Fight Club's rules reflect that described in the book and feature film.

The trend owes much to uses of modern communications technologies, including decentralised personal networking, known as smartmobbing. Word of the events spreads primarily via digital means, usually on the internet via email, chat rooms and text messaging which result in seemingly spontaneous mass gatherings. Pillows are sometimes hidden and at the exact pre-arranged time or the sound of a whistle, the pillow fighters pull out their pillows and commence pillow fighting. The pillow fights can last from a few minutes to several hours.

The largest pillow fight flash mob was the Worldwide Pillow Fight Day (or International Pillow Fight Day) that took place on March 22, 2008. Over 25 cities around the globe participated in the first "international flash mob", which was the world's largest flash mob to date. According to The Wall Street Journal, more than 5,000 participated in New York City, overtaking London's 2006 Silent Disco gathering as the largest recorded flash mob. Word spread via social networking sites, including Facebook, Myspace, private blogs, public forums, personal websites, as well as by word of mouth, text messaging, and email. Participating cities included Basel, Beirut, Boston, Budapest, Chicago, Copenhagen, Dubai, Dublin, Dundee, Houston, Innsbruck, London, Los Angeles, Melbourne, Monterrey, New York City, Paris, Pécs, São Paulo, Shanghai, San Francisco, Stockholm, Sydney, Tel-Aviv, Toronto, Vancouver, Washington, D.C., and Zurich.

Origins

While ordinary pillow fights have existed for a long time, these events are massive in scale, occur in public and are promoted primarily via the Internet. Many massive pillow fights have been organized in an effort to break Guinness World Records, but the current record is a pillow fight among 10,000 at the Catalyst Conference in Atlanta, Georgia October 6, 2006. Others have been organized by university students around the world for fun.

SILENT DISCO

A silent disco is a disco where people dance to music listened to on headphones. Rather than using a speaker system, music is broadcast via an FM transmitter with the signal being picked up by wireless headphone receivers worn by the partygoers. Those without the headphones hear no music, giving the effect of a room full of people dancing to nothing. Often two DJs compete for listeners. Silent discos are popular at music festivals as they allow dancing to continue past noise curfews. Similar events are "mobile clubbing" gatherings, where a group of people dance to the music on their personal music players.

History

The first silent disco appeared in 1969 in a Finnish science fiction film called Ruusujen Aika (Time of Roses) The concept of a silent disco was then used by eco-activists in the early 90's who utilized headphones at outdoor parties to minimize noise pollution and disturbance to the local wildlife

In May 2000 'BBC Live Music' held a silent disco and gig at Chapter Arts Centre in Cardiff, where the audience listened to the band Rocket Goldstar and various DJs through headphones. Due to noise restrictions, Glastonbury Festival in 2005 held a large-scale silent disco for when the main acts had finished, which triggered an increase of interest in the silent disco. Initially reserved to festivals and club nights, the silent disco has since become popular at weddings and private parties, and home kits are available.

Mobile clubbing

Another type of silent party, known as Mobile Clubbing, involves the gathering of a group of people in an unconventional location to dance to music which they provide themselves via a Portable audio player, such as an MP3 player, listened to on headphones. These flash mob gatherings may involve hundreds of people, transforming public spaces into temporary clubbing areas, in which dancers listen to their personal playlists. To an observer it would appear that the participants are dancing for no apparent reason. Mobile Clubbing events are organized using mass-emails, word-of-mouth and/or social networking websites such as Facebook.

The first event, organised by London-based artists Ben Cummins (also founder of Pillow Fight Club) and Emma Davis, was at London's Liverpool Street Station in September 2003. Over the next five months there were a further five events at other London train stations including Waterloo, Charing Cross and London Bridge.. By the end of 2008 there had been more than twenty of these events at similar venues throughout London, mostly train station concourses or other public spaces that lend themselves to expressive dancing and rapid dispersal.

An event in 2007 at Victoria Station, London involved 4,000 participants. The event was broken up by police two hours later.

Silent Gig

A variant of the silent disco involves live bands competing for the audience. The bands are supplied with electric instruments that are plugged into a transmitter rather than an amplifier, meaning the only sound which can be heard from the band without headphones is light tapping from electric drums and vocals of the singer.

The first silent gig was performed in the Chapter Arts Centre, Cardiff in April 2000 by Rocketgoldstar.

In August 2008, a silent Battle of the Bands was held in Cardiff Barfly. The event featured bands going directly head-to-head with a stage at each end of the venue, allowing gig-goers to choose which one that they wished to listen to. The event was featured on BBC Radio 1 "Introducing" show hosted by Bethan Elfyn, as well as having coverage on S4C.

Philosophy

Kaprow explains that happenings are not a new style, but a moral act, a human stand of great urgency, whose professional status as art is less critical than their certainty as an ultimate existential commitment. He argues that once artists have been recognized and paid, they also surrender to the confinement, rather the tastes of the patrons (even if that may not be the intention on both ends). "The whole situation is corrosive, neither patrons nor artists comprehend their role...and out of this hidden discomfort comes a stillborn art, tight or merely repetitive and at worst, chic." Though the we may easily blame those offering the temptation, Kaprow reminds us that it is not the publicist's moral obligation to protect the artist's freedom, and artists themselves hold the ultimate power to reject fame if they do not want it's responsibilities.

Festivals as happenings

Art and music festivals play a large roll in positive and successful happenings. Some of these festivals include Burning Man and Oregon Country Fair. Along with the famous Allan Kaprow Burning Man frowns on the idea of spectators and stresses the importance of everyone being involved to create something amazing and unique. Both parties embody the "audience" and instead of creating something to show the people, the people become involved in helping create something incredible and spontaneous to the moment. Both of these events are happenings that are recreated and special each year and are always new and organic. These events draw crowds of close to 50,000 people each year and reach more people then just the attendees with their messages and ideals.

Important people

One very important person who has greatly influenced the idea and culture of happenings is Allan Kaprow. Kaprow's influences can be seen in all of his various efforts and art pieces that have spread across the world and have reached the hearts and eyes of many. Kaprow has helped shape a new form and unique art installation that you must be a part of in order to truly understand the significances of the piece.

CHAPTER–8

CONVENTION (MEETING) EVENT TOURISM

A convention, in the sense of a meeting, is a gathering of individuals who meet at an arranged place and time in order to discuss or engage in some common interest. The most common conventions are based upon industry, profession, and fandom. Trade conventions typically focus on a particular industry or industry segment, and feature keynote speakers, vendor displays, and other information and activities of interest to the event organizers and attendees. Professional conventions focus on issues of concern to the profession and advancements in the profession. Such conventions are generally organized by societies dedicated to promotion of the topic of interest. Fan conventions usually feature displays, shows, and sales based on pop culture and guest celebrities. Science fiction conventions traditionally partake of the nature of both professional conventions and fan conventions, with the balance varying from one to another. Conventions also exist for various hobbies, such as gaming or model railroads.

Conventions are often planned and coordinated, often in exacting detail, by professional meeting and convention planners, either by staff of the convention's hosting company or by outside specialists. Most large cities will have a convention center dedicated to hosting such events. The term MICE - meetings Incentives Conventions and Exhibitions - is widely used in Asia as a description of the industry. The Convention ("C") is one of the most dynamic elements in the M.I.C.E. segment. The industry is generally regulated under the tourism sector.

In the technical sense, a convention is a meeting of delegates or representatives. The 1947 Newfoundland National Convention is a classic example of a state-sponsored political convention. More often, organizations made up of smaller units, chapters, or lodges, such as labor unions, honorary societies, and fraternities and sororities, meet as a whole in convention by sending delegates of the units to deliberate on the organization's common issues. This also applies to a political convention, though in modern times the common issues are limited to selecting a party candidate or party chairman. In this technical sense, a congress, when it consists of representatives, is a convention. The British House of Commons is a convention, as are most other houses of a modern representative legislature. The National Convention or just "Convention" in France comprised the constitutional and legislative assembly which sat from September 20, 1792 to October 26, 1795.

Many sovereign states have provisions for conventions besides their permanent legislature. The Constitution of the United States of America has a provision for the calling of a constitutional convention, whereby delegates of the states are summoned to a special meeting to amend or draft the constitution. This process has never occurred, save for the original drafting of the constitution, although it almost happened in several cases. The US Constitution also has provisions for constitutional amendments to be approved by state conventions of the people. This occurred to ratify the original constitution and to adopt the twenty-first amendment, which ended prohibition.

Con is a common abbreviation for convention, and some conventions (such as DEF CON and Gen Con) use it in their names.

Co-located Conventions

When two or more conventions are held at the same place and time they are co-located. Co-located conventions are usually in related industries.

The bulk of the convention industry are driven by associations. Many industry related associations fund their activities with conventions which generally reach from a small gathering to then of thousands (like the Rotary Convention). the association convention industry is monitored by the ICCA who's members are stakeholder in the convention industry.

CONVENTION CENTER

A convention center (American English, conference centre British English) is a large building that is designed to hold a convention, where individuals and groups gather to promote and share common interests. Convention centers typically offer sufficient floor area to accommodate several thousand attendees. Very large venues, suitable for major trade shows, are known as 'exhibition centres'. Convention centers typically have at least one auditorium and may also contain concert halls, lecture halls, meeting rooms, and conference rooms. Some large resort area hotels include a convention center.

EVENT PLANNING

Event planning is the process of planning a festival, ceremony, competition, party, or convention. Event planning includes budgeting, establishing dates and alternate dates, selecting and reserving the event site, acquiring permits, and coordinating transportation and parking. Event planning also includes some or all of the following, depending on the event: developing a theme or motif for the event, arranging for speakers and alternate speakers, coordinating location support (such as electricity and other utilities), arranging decor, tables, chairs, tents, event support and security, catering, police, fire, portable toilets, parking, signage, emergency plans, health care professionals, and cleanup.

Steps to Planning an Event

The first step to planning an event is determining its purpose, whether it is for a wedding, company, birthday, festival, graduation or any other event requiring extensive planning. From this the event planner needs to choose entertainment, location, guest list, speakers, and content. The location for events is endless, but with event planning they would likely be held at hotels, convention centers, reception halls, or outdoors depending on the event. Once the location is set the coordinator/planner needs to prepare the event with staff, set up the entertainment, and keep contact with the client. After all this is set the event planner has all the smaller details to address like set up of the event such as food, drinks, music, guest list, budget, advertising and marketing, decorations, all this preparation is what is needed for an event to run smoothly. An event planner needs to be able to manage their time wisely for the event, and the length of preparation needed for each event so it is a success.

Event Planning as a Career

Event planning is a relatively new career field. There is now training that helps one trying to break into the career field. There must be training for an event planner to handle all the pressure and work efficiently. This career deals with a lot of communication and organization aspects. There are many different names for an event planner such as a conference coordinator, a convention planner, a special event coordinator, and a meeting manager.

Event planners work is considered either stressful or energizing. This line of work is also considered fast paced and demanding. Planners face deadlines and communicating with multiple people at one time. Planners spend most of their time in offices, but when meeting with clients the work is usually on-site at the location where the event is taking place . Some physical activity is required such as carrying boxes of materials and decorations or supplies needed for the event. Also, long working hours can be a part of the job. The day the event is taking place could start as early as 5:00 a.m. and then work until midnight. Working on weekends is sometimes required, which is when many events take place .

Publications and resources

Many business-to-business trade publications exist to help event planning and production professionals become educated about the issues and trends in their industry. Many are controlled circulation publications available at no cost to qualified event professionals. Qualification is based on multiple variables like job title, company type, industry segment or geographic region, and is at the publisher's discretion.

EVENT SCHEDULING

Event scheduling is the activity of finding a suitable time for an event such as meeting, conference, trip, etc. It is an important part of event planning that is usually carried out at its beginning stage.

In general, event scheduling must take into account what impact particular dates of the event could have on the success of the event. When organizing a scientific conference, for example, organizers might take into account the knowledge in which periods classes are held at universities, since it is expected that many potential participants are university professors. They should also try to check that no other similar conferences are held at the same time, because overlapping would make a problem for those participants who are interesting in attending all conferences.

When it is well known who is expected to attend the event (e.g. in the case of a project meeting), organizers usually try to synchronize the time of the event with planned schedules of all participants. This is a difficult task when there are many participants or when the participants are located at distant places. In such cases, the organizers should first define a set of suggested dates and address a query about suitable dates to potential participants. After response is obtained from all participants, the event time suitable for most of participants is selected. This procedure can be alleviated by internet tools.

Meeting and Convention Planner

A meeting and convention planner supervises and coordinates the strategic, operational and logistical activities necessary for the production of events. The planner can be employed or hired ad hoc by corporations, associations, governments, and other organizations.

STANDARDIZATION ISSUES

- Although the Occupational Information Network (O•NET), sponsored by the United States Department of Labor and Employment and Training Administration, identified this occupation as "meeting and convention planner," other titles are more commonly used. These titles include event planner, meeting planner, and meeting manager. In addition, a number of other titles specific to the categories of events produced are used, such as corporate planner and party planner.
- The banquet event order (BEO), a standard form used in the hospitality industry to document the requirements of an event as pertinent to the venue, has presented numerous problems to meeting and convention planners due to the increasing complexity and scope of modern events. In response, Convention Industry Council developed the event specifications guide (ESG) that is currently replacing the BEO.
- Additionally, the Convention Industry Council is spearheading The Accepted Practices Exchange (APEX). By bringing planners and suppliers together to create industry-wide accepted practices and a common terminology, the profession continues to enhance the professionalism of the meetings, conventions and exhibitions industry.

Professional Conference Organiser

A Professional Conference Organiser or Professional Congress Organiser (PCO) is a company which specialises in the organisation and management of congresses, conferences, seminars and similar events.

Role of PCOs

PCOs work as consultants for academic and professional associations. They usually provide full service management for conferences including but not limited to conference design, registration, site and venue selection and booking, audiovisuals, IT support, logistics, leisure management, marketing, printing and web services, sourcing speakers, funding and sponsorship, financial management and budget control.

Other companies offer related services including travel agents and public relations companies. They tend to focus on limited areas such as destination management.

Size of Market Sector

Recent surveys of UK conference venues have found that a third of conference bookings were made by PCOs or venue-finding agencies. In 2006 UK-based conferences generated £7.6 billion in direct sales giving PCOs a central role in some £2.5 billion of revenue generation. The UK is ranked second behind the US for global market share of conferences. Thus, although there is no one source of global statistics for the conference market it appears that PCOs play a central role in several billion dollars worth of revenue generation worldwide.

Meetings, Incentives, Conferencing, Exhibitions

Meetings, Incentives, Conferences, and Exhibitions. The acronym MICE is applied inconsistently with the "E" sometimes referring to events and the "C" sometimes referring to conventions. MICE is used to refer to a particular type of tourism in which large groups, usually planned well in advance, are brought together for some particular purpose. Recently, there has been an industry trend towards using the term "Meetings Industry" to avoid confusion from the acronym.

Most components of MICE are well understood, perhaps with the exception of incentives. Incentive tourism is usually undertaken as a type of employee reward by a company or institution for targets met or exceeded, or a job well done. Unlike the other types of MICE tourism, incentive tourism is usually conducted purely for entertainment, rather than professional or educational purposes.

MICE tourism usually includes a well-planned agenda centered around a particular theme, such as a hobby, a profession, or an educational topic. Such tourism is a specialized area with its own trade shows (IMEX) and practices. MICE events are normally bid on by specialized convention bureaus located in particular countries and cities and established for the purpose of bidding on MICE activities. This process of marketing and bidding is normally conducted well in advance of the actual event, often several years. MICE tourism is known for its extensive planning and demanding clientele.

CHAPTER–9

Competition Event Tourism

Competition is a contest between individuals, groups, nations, animals, etc. for territory, a niche, or a location of resources. It arises whenever two or more parties strive for a goal which cannot be shared. Competition occurs naturally between living organisms which co-exist in the same environment. For example, animals compete over water supplies, food, and mates, etc. Humans compete for water, food, and mates, though when these needs are met deep rivalries often arise over the pursuit of wealth, prestige, and fame. Business is often associated with competition as most companies are in competition with at least one other firm over the same group of customers.

Sizes and levels

Competition may also exist at different sizes; some competitions may be between two members of a species, while other competitions can involve entire species. In an example in economics, a competition between two small stores would be considered small compared to competition between several mega-giants. As a result, the consequences of the competition would also vary- the larger the competition, the larger the effect.

In addition, the level of competition can also vary. At some levels, competition can be informal; more for pride and/or fun. However, other competitions can be extremely serious; for example, some human wars have erupted because of the intense competition between two nations.

DESTRUCTIVE COMPETITION AND CO-OPERATIVE COMPETITION

Destructive Competition

Destructive competition seeks to benefit an individual/group/ organism by damaging and/or eliminating competing individuals, groups and/or organisms; it opposes the desire for mutual survival. It is "winner takes all", the rationale being that the challenge is a zero-sum game; the success of one group is dependent on the failure of the other competing groups. Destructive competition tends to promote fear, a "strike-first" mentality and embraces certain forms of trespass.

Co-operative Competition

Co-operative competition is based upon promoting mutual survival - "everyone wins". Adam Smith's "invisible hand" is a process where individuals compete to improve their level of happiness but compete in a cooperative manner through peaceful exchange and without violating other people. Cooperative competition focuses individuals/groups/organisms against the environment.

Consequences

Competition can have both beneficial and detrimental effects. Many evolutionary biologists view inter-species and intra-species competition as the driving force of adaptation, and ultimately of evolution. However, some biologists, most famously Richard Dawkins, prefer to think of evolution in terms of competition between single genes, which have the welfare of the organism 'in mind' only insofar as that welfare furthers their own selfish drives for replication. Some social Darwinists claim that competition also serves as a mechanism for determining the best-suited group; politically, economically and ecologically.

On the negative side, competition can cause injury to the organisms involved, and drain valuable resources and energy. Human competition can be expensive, as is the case with political elections, international sports competitions, advertising wars and arms races. It can lead to the compromising of ethical standards in order to gain an advantage: for example, several athletes have been caught using banned steroids in professional sports in order to boost their own chances of success or victory. It can also be harmful for the participants, such as athletes who injure themselves when pushing their body past its natural limits, or companies which pursue unprofitable paths while engaging in competitive rivalries. And in the case of an arms race, it can possibly lead to mutually assured destruction.

Economics and Business

Merriam-Webster defines competition in business as "the effort of two or more parties acting independently to secure the business of a third party by offering the most favorable terms".. It was described by Adam Smith in The Wealth of Nations (1776) and later economists as allocating productive resources to their most highly-valued uses. and encouraging efficiency. Later microeconomics theory distinguished between perfect competition and imperfect competition, concluding that no system of resource allocation is more efficient than perfect competition. Competition, according to the theory, causes commercial firms to develop new products, services and technologies, which would give consumers greater selection and better products. The greater selection typically causes lower prices for the products, compared to what the price would be if there was no competition (monopoly) or little competition (oligopoly).

However, competition may also lead to wasted (duplicated) effort and to increased costs (and prices) in some circumstances. For example, the intense competition for the small number of top jobs in music and movie acting leads many aspiring musicians and actors to make substantial investments in training which are not recouped, because only a fraction become successful.

Three levels of economic competition have been classified:

- The most narrow form is direct competition (also called category competition or brand competition), where products which perform the same function compete against each other. For example, one brand of pick-up trucks competes with several other brands of pick-up trucks. Sometimes, two companies are rivals and one adds new products to their line, which leads to the other company distributing the same new things, and in this manner they compete.
- The next form is substitute or indirect competition, where products which are close substitutes for one another compete. For example, butter competes with margarine, mayonnaise and other various sauces and spreads.
- The broadest form of competition is typically called budget competition. Included in this category is anything on which the consumer might want to spend their available money. For example, a family which has $20,000 available may choose to spend it on many different items, which can all be seen as competing with each other for the family's expenditure.

In addition, companies also compete for financing on the capital markets (equity or debt) in order to generate the necessary cash for their operations. An investor typically will consider alternative investment opportunities given his risk profile and not only look at companies just competing on product (direct competitors). Enlarging the investment universe to include indirect competitors leads to a broader peer universe of comparable, indirectly competing companies.

Competition does not necessarily have to be between companies. For example, business writers sometimes refer to internal competition. This is competition within companies. The idea was first introduced by Alfred Sloan at General Motors in the 1920s. Sloan deliberately created areas of overlap between divisions of the company so that each division would be competing with the other divisions. For example, the Chevy division would compete with the Pontiac division for some market segments. Also, in 1931, Procter & Gamble initiated a deliberate system of internal brand-versus-brand rivalry. The company was organized around different brands, with each brand allocated resources, including a dedicated group of employees willing to champion the brand. Each brand manager was given responsibility for the success or failure of the brand, and compensated accordingly. This is known as intra-brand competition.

Finally, most businesses also encourage competition between individual employees. An example of this is a contest between sales representatives. The sales representative with the highest sales (or the best improvement in sales) over a period of time would gain benefits from the employer.

It should also be noted that business and economic competition in most countries is often limited or restricted. Competition often is subject to legal restrictions. For example, competition may be legally prohibited, as in the case with a government monopoly or a government-granted monopoly. Tariffs, subsidies or other protectionist measures may also be instituted by government in order to prevent or reduce competition. Depending on the respective economic policy, pure competition is to a greater or lesser extent regulated by competition policy and competition law.

Competition between countries is quite subtle to detect, but is quite evident in the World economy. Countries compete to provide the best possible business environment for multinational corporations. Such competition is evident by the policies undertaken by these countries to educate the future workforce. For example, East Asian economies such as Singapore, Japan and South Korea tend to emphasize education by allocating a large portion of the budget to this sector, and by implementing programmes such as gifted education. (See separate sub-markets principle).

Law

Competition law, known in the United States as antitrust law, has three main functions. Firstly, it prohibits agreements aimed to restrict free trading between business entities and their customers. For example, a cartel of sports shops who together fix football jersey prices higher than normal is illegal. Secondly, competition law can ban the existence or abusive behaviour of a firm dominating the market. One case in point could be a software company who through its monopoly on computer platforms makes consumers use its media player. Thirdly, to preserve competitive markets, the law supervises the mergers and acquisitions of very large corporations. Competition authorities could for instance require that a large packaging company give plastic bottle licenses to competitors before taking over a major PET producer. In this case (as in all three), competition law aims to protect the welfare of consumers by ensuring business must compete for its share of the market economy.

In recent decades, competition law has also been sold as good medicine to provide better public services, traditionally funded by tax payers and administered by democratically accountable governments. Hence competition law is closely connected with the law on deregulation of access to markets, providing state aids and subsidies, the privatisation of state-owned assets and the use of independent sector regulators, such as the United Kingdom telecommunications watchdog Ofcom. Behind the practice lies the theory, which over the last fifty years has been dominated by neo-classical economics. Markets are seen as the most efficient method of allocating resources, although sometimes they fail, and regulation becomes necessary to protect the ideal market model. Behind the theory lies the history, reaching back further than the Roman Empire. The business practices of market traders, guilds and governments have always been subject to scrutiny and sometimes severe sanctions. Since the twentieth century, competition law has become global. The two largest, most organised and influential systems of competition regulation are United States antitrust law and European Community competition law. The respective national authorities, the U.S. Department of Justice (DOJ) and the Federal Trade Commission (FTC) in the United States and the European Commission's Competition Directorate

General (DGCOMP) have formed international support and enforcement networks. Competition law is growing in importance every day, which warrants for its careful study.

Politics

Competition is also found in politics. In democracies, an election is a competition for an elected office. In other words, two or more candidates strive and compete against one another to attain a position of power. The winner gains the seat of the elected office for a predefined period of time, towards the end of which another election is usually held to determine the next holder of the office.

In addition, there is inevitable competition inside a government. Because several offices are appointed, potential candidates compete against the others in order to gain the particular office. Departments may also compete for a limited amount of resources, such as for funding. Finally, where there are party systems, elected leaders of different parties will ultimately compete against the other parties for laws, funding and power.

Finally, competition also exists between governments. Each country or nationality struggles for world dominance, power, or military strength. For example, the United States competed against the Soviet Union in the Cold War for world power, and the two also struggled over the different types of government (in these cases representative democracy and communism). The result of this type of competition often leads to worldwide tensions, and may sometimes erupt into warfare.

Sports

While some sports (such as fishing or hiking) have been viewed as primarily recreational, most sports are considered competitive. The majority involve competition between two or more persons (sometimes using horses or cars). For example, in a game of basketball, two teams compete against one another to determine who can score the most points. While there is no set reward for the winning team, many players gain an internal sense of pride. In addition, extrinsic rewards may also be given. Athletes, besides competing against other humans, also compete against nature in sports such as whitewater kayaking or mountaineering, where the goal is to reach a destination, with only natural barriers impeding the process. A regularly scheduled (for instance annual) competition meant to determine the "best" competitor of that cycle is called a championship.

While professional sports have been usually viewed as intense and extremely competitive, recreational sports, which are often less intense, are often considered a healthy option for the release of competitive urges in humans. Sport provides a relatively safe venue for converting unbridled competition into harmless competition, because sports competition is restrained. Competitive sports are governed by codified rules agreed upon by the participants. Violating these rules is considered to be unfair competition. Thus, sports provide artificial (not natural) competition; for example, competing for control of a ball, or defending territory on a playing field is not an innate biological factor in humans. Athletes in sports such as gymnastics and competitive diving compete against each other in order to come closest to a conceptual ideal of a perfect performance, which incorporates measurable criteria and standards which are translated into numerical ratings and scores by appointed judges.

Sports competition is generally broken down into three categories: individual sports, such as archery; dual sports, such as doubles tennis, and team sports competition, such as cricket or football. While most sports competitions are recreation, there exist several major and minor professional sports leagues throughout the world. The Olympic Games, held every four years, is usually regarded as the international pinnacle of sports competition.

Education

Competition is a major factor in education. On a global scale, national education systems, intending to bring out the best in the next generation, encourage competitiveness among students through scholarships. Countries such as England and Singapore have special education programmes which cater for specialist students, prompting charges of academic elitism. Upon receipt of their academic results, students tend to compare their grades to see who is better. In severe cases, the pressure to perform in some countries is so high that it can result in stigmatization of intellectually deficient students, or even suicide as a consequence of failing the exams; Japan being a prime example (see Education in Japan). This has resulted in critical re-evaluation of examinations as a whole by educationalists. Critics of competition (as opposed to excellence) as a motivating factor in education systems, such as Alfie Kohn, assert that competition actually has a net negative influence on the achievement levels of students, and that it "turns all of us into losers" (Kohn 1986).

Competitions also make up a large proponent of extracurricular activities in which students participate. Such competitions include TVO's broadcast Reach for the Top competition, FIRST Robotics, Duke Annual Robo-Climb Competition (DARC) and the University of Toronto Space Design Contest. In Texas, the University Interscholastic League (UIL) has 22 High School-level contests and 18 elementary and Junior High in subjects ranging from accounting to science to ready writing.

Literature

Literary competitions, such as contests sponsored by literary journals, publishing houses and theaters, have increasingly become a means for aspiring writers to gain recognition. Prestigious awards for fiction include those sponsored by the Missouri Review, Boston Review, Indiana Review, North American Review and Southwest Review. The Albee Award, sponsored by the Yale Drama Series, is among the most prestigious playwriting awards. Some American writers, such as Gina Ochsner and Jacob Appel, have gained prominence specifically for their active participation in numerous literary competitions.

Charging fees for literary competitions is extremely controversial. Some writers view fees as a form of exploitation that takes advantage of aspiring authors and playwrights. However, fee-based contests also have strong supporters who argue that these competitions offer rare opportunities for young writers to have their voices heard at a time when access to major agents and editors has grown increasingly limited.

Biology and Ecology

Competition within and between species is an important topic in biology, specifically in the field of ecology. Competition between members of a species ("intraspecific") is the driving force behind evolution and natural selection; the competition for resources such as food, water, territory, and sunlight results in the ultimate survival and dominance of the variant of the species best suited for survival. Competition is also present between species ("interspecific"). A limited amount of resources are available, and several species may depend on these resources. Thus, each of the species competes with the others to gain access to the resources. As a result, species less suited to compete for the resources must either adapt or die out. According to evolutionary theory, this competition within and between species for resources plays a critical role in natural selection. For example, a smaller tree will receive less sunlight than an adjacent tree which is larger than it in a rainforest. The larger tree is competing with the smaller one for the same sunlight.

The Study of Competition

Competition has been studied in several fields, including psychology, sociology and anthropology. Social psychologists, for instance, study the nature of competition. They investigate the natural urge of competition and its circumstances. They also study group dynamics, to detect how competition emerges and what its effects are. Sociologists, meanwhile, study the effects of competition on society as a whole. In addition, anthropologists study the history and prehistory of competition in various cultures. They also investigate how competition manifested itself in various cultural settings in the past, and how competition has developed over time.

Competitiveness

Many philosophers and psychologists have identified a trait in most living organisms which can drive the particular organism to compete. This trait, unsurprisingly called competitiveness, is viewed as an innate biological trait which coexists along with the urge for survival. Competitiveness, or the inclination to compete, though, has become synonymous with aggressiveness and ambition in the English language. More advanced civilizations integrate aggressiveness and competitiveness into their interactions, as a way to distribute resources and adapt. Most plants compete for higher spots on trees to receive more sunlight.

However, Stephen Jay Gould and others have argued that as one ascends the evolutionary hierarchy, competitiveness (the survival instinct) becomes less innate, and more a learned behavior. The same could be said for co-operation: in humans, at least, both co-operation and competition are considered learned behaviors, because the human species learns to adapt to environmental pressures. Consequently, if survival requires competitive behaviors, the individual will compete, and if survival requires co-operative behaviors, the individual will co-operate. In the case of humans, therefore, aggressiveness may be an innate characteristic, but a person need not be competitive at the same time, for instance when scaling a cliff. On the other hand, humans seem also to have a nurturing instinct, to protect newborns and the weak. While that does not necessitate co-operative behavior, it does help.

The term also applies to econometrics. Here, it is a comparative measure of the ability and performance of a firm or sub-sector to sell and produce/supply goods and/or services in a given market. The two academic bodies of thought on the assessment of competitiveness are the Structure Conduct Performance Paradigm and the more contemporary New Empirical Industrial Organisation model. Predicting changes in the competitiveness of business sectors is becoming an integral and explicit step in public policymaking. Within capitalist economic systems, the drive of enterprises is to maintain and improve their own competitiveness.

Hypercompetitiveness

The tendency toward extreme, unhealthy competition has been termed hypercompetitiveness. This concept originated in Karen

Horney's theories on neurosis; specifically, the highly aggressive personality type which is characterized as "moving against people". In her view, some people have a need to compete and win at all costs as a means of maintaining their self-worth. These individuals are likely to turn any activity into a competition, and they will feel threatened if they find themselves losing. Researchers have found that men and women who score high on the trait of hypercompetitiveness are more narcissistic and less psychologically healthy than those who score low on the trait . Hypercompetitive individuals generally believe that "winning isn't everything; it's the only thing".

Power and Competition

Power and competition often conflict with each other. Lord Acton said that power corrupts an individual, so absolute power corrupts absolutely. Competition is seeking for first place or the top and when you get the top then you have a degree of power.

CHAPTER-10

The Infrastructure for Event Tourism

Tourism is acknowledged as a 'high growth' industry globally with over 700 million tourist arrival internationally, the sector accounts for more than US $ 500 billion by way of receipt. Besides, the sector possesses immense income, employment and foreign exchange generation potential, thereby, providing a multiplier effect to the economy. The tourism industry is widely regarded as having the ability to generate high levels of economic output with relatively lesser levels of capital investment.

The potential and benefits of the tourism sector become more relevant especially for developing economies like India, where capital availability is scarce and need for economic and employment generation activity is high. With a mere 0.4% share of international tourist arrivals and a large volume of domestic travellers – mainly in the religion/ pilgrimage segment – the sector still accounts for 5.6% of GDP while providing direct employment to 20 million people. However, compared to global averages, the industry has not scaled up to its full potential. Geographical smaller countries have managed successfully to generate much higher levels of revenue from this industry . This is borne out by the fact that globally, the industry contributes approximately 11.6% to the GDP.

Delhi, the capital of India, has its origin from 1450 B.C. and has been in continuous existence for over a thousand years now. It is a site of many historic capital cities, traces of ten of which survive even today. The city is significant for the role it has played throughout history, having been the centre of an empire for the majority of this millennium. It is an important city in the Indian subcontinent and comparisons have often been made to other great cities of the world. However, very few cities carry with them, to such an extent, the weight of several layers of continuous history. In spite of this rich and diverse cultural heritage, Delhi is used only as a gateway for travelling to Jaipur, Agra and other cities of tourist interest. Though, Delhi has the highest number of tourist arrivals, it is only used as entry point to the country.

Delhi being National Capital Territory, receives 62% of foreign travellers and NRI visiting India. There has been no concerted effort to project Delhi as a Tourism Destination, with attractions to provide the visitors 2 – 3 night stays. There is an emergent need to make Delhi a historical city, a convention center, environmental and eco friendly destination and cultural destination and to spread awareness among tourists as well as its citizens regarding its glorious past. To achieve above goals, there is a need to develop the basic infrastructure, accessibility to the tourist destination, local facilities and identification of thrust areas of tourism promotion. The schemes, which are to be taken up under the major head, "TOURISM INFRASTRUCTURE" are as under:

1. Water Sports Tourism Complex at Bhalswa

Delhi Tourism is in possession of Bhalswa Lake Over the past decade; Delhi Tourism has developed facilities for outdoor leisure by undertaking water sports and allied activities in the lake. Such recreational activities have added to the civic life of capital. Recreational-boating through pedal boats, hovercraft, water scooter, shikara and sports boats like kayaking, canoeing and rowing has already been introduced by the Corporation. In the recent past DTTDC has constructed an earthen bandh around the lake and fixed sluice gate between the lake and supplementary drain to maintain the water level in the lake. Indian Kayaking and Canoeing Association has given proposal to organize national and international level competition at this lake. At present the facilities for tourists/ visitors are very limited. DTTDC proposed to add some facilities like open shed, change room, water cooler for drinking water for visitors/tourists .

Besides, the Government of NCT of Delhi has a plan to develop this area as an integrated tourist complex by creating infrastructure facilities like water sports, golf course, amusement rides and various other adventure activities. It is an ambitious project and could be developed as a centre-point for sports lovers from all over the world.

2. Establishment of Wayside Amenities

At present, the arrival of foreign tourists in Delhi is approximately 13 lacs annually with the growth rate of 5% p.a. With the introduction of modern techniques of dissemination of tourists information identification of new destinations, better marketing and services, it is contemplated that growth rate shall be progressively stepped up and by the year 2008, number of tourists visiting Delhi shall be approx. 25 lacs. In addition, domestic tourists shall be double within the next five years.

In the present scenario, no wayside amenities are available at the national highways around the city. The nearest wayside amenities provided by the adjoining states are at a distance of 40 km or more from the entry point of Delhi. The Corporation is in possession of land measuring 2.08 acres at Delhi-Jaipur Road, National Highway No. 8. The Corporation has a plan to provide these amenities to the tourists and commuters through developing this site into a unique project.

The concept/ design of the project has been finalized. The construction work of the project will start soon. However, the boundary wall, earth work and boring of two tube wells, have been done.

3. Development of Dilli Haat type projects in different parts of Delhi.

The Corporation has set up a Dilli Haat at INA, Sri Aurobindindo Marg, which is an upgraded version of traditional part offering a delightful amalgam of craft, food and cultural activities with a major difference-while the Village haat is a mobile, flexible arrangements, here it is the craftsmen who are mobile and ever changing there by offering ponaramic view of the richness and diversity of Indian handicrafts and artifacts. The project has already won heritage and cultural award i.e. PATA gold awards.

In view of its wide success and in pursuance of govt. policy of promoting and preserving our immense heritage of human skills, the Corporation has decided to set up more Haats in the Capital. The Corporation is in the process of identifying the sites for the purpose. The DDA has been approached by DTTDC for identification of suitable sites to set up these projects.

One site measuring 7.2 acres at Pitampura near TV Tower has been allotted to DTTDC for this purpose.

4. Restoration of Denotified Monuments

Delhi, being a city of monuments consisting historical importance, rich heritage and religious tradition and culture, attracts a large flow of tourists towards it. There is a series of denotified monuments that have remained neglected, unknown and unvisited due to absence of proper maintenance, hygienic conditions, publicity and better accessibility. Since 1996, Delhi Tourism has undertaken the restoration of such denotified monuments through INTACH. A study has been conducted by INTACH in the area and identified over 80 monuments. The Corporation has restored 34 denotified monuments in Mehrauli area and the work at 4 more monuments is in full swing.

5. Refurbishment of monuments

Delhi being a city of monuments has rich cultural heritage and its glorious past. There is an emergent need to make aware the tourists visiting capital territory about these buildings/ monuments through wide publicity, more accessibility and providing infrastructure facilities like drinking water, public conveniences, food kiosks, telephone facilities, souvenir shop, tourists information counter, path ways, land scrapping, hark system etc.

6. Signage at monuments and other historical places for identification and awareness of tourists.

There is lack of information and awareness amongst the tourists and residents of Delhi for the cities with historic past. There are a large number of monuments in the Maurauli heritage area and other parts of the city that has tremendous historical significance but unveiled. In order to provide more detailed information on the rich architecture of the buildings, their historic importance and other aspects, DTTDC proposes installation of signage aesthetically designed at these monuments. Department of tourism, Government of India has sanctioned a scheme for installation of signage at monuments/ historical buildings in Delhi.

7. Accessibility to Destination Through Trail etc.

Integrated conservation and landscape development of Mehrauli is a project that attempts to consolidate the scattered ruins of the settlement into a comprehensive scheme to preserve the monuments and potential archaeological sites and provide the city populace with a meaningful, multifaceted recreation space following the image of an ideal 'City Forest'. The management of the natural and historic environment being the prime objectives, the proposal aims at developing a series of pathways for access and maintenance, suitably treated to uphold historic authenticity and serving to heighten the perception of the complex natural setting for an enhanced interpretation of the site. With the stretch around the Jamali Kamali being the present focus and scope of the project, the process once initiated would go for a long way to reintegrate the historic area through positive intervention with the socio-cultural and economic processes of the city so as to make it an active part of the system, imparting it a new relevance within the contemporary scenario.

8. Illumination of Monuments

Many tourists are visiting Delhi from India and abroad. There is much to see during daytime but hardly any thing for the evenings. To enhance the beauty of Delhi during evenings proposed to illuminate the ancient monuments, which are visible from the roads while driving.

9. Development of Lakes

In spite of having more than 30 big ancient lakes, Delhi does not offer sufficient outdoor leisure facilities for tourists and its residents, as most of the lakes have been disappeared due to change in use of land and non-retention of water. Delhi, acrossing range of Aravali hills, particularly in Mehrauli area of South Delhi had underground water level at 50 feet. Now, the water level has drastically gone down to 200 feet deep, which is not only disastrous from agricultural point of view but also for tourism potential. Water bodies with recreational facilities provide ample attraction to the tourists. These facilities have added to the civic life of capital. For the purpose, infrastructure for various types of amusement could also be developed on the embankment of the lakes. There is an emergent need for development, preservation and maintenance of existing water bodies to beautify the city and to keep it at par with the other major cities of the world and to cater to the widening demands.

Recently Delhi Tourism has taken over the possession of Sanjay Lake at Mayur Vihar and Shahdara Lake for recreational water sports activities through Boats, water scooter, Jetty, Shikara, bungee jumping, etc. the Hovercraft facilities at Sanjay Lake & Bhalaswa Lake are also being considered and battery operated eco-friendly boats at Nazafgarh drain at Chhawla and Kanganheri .

Setting up of soft adventure park with Bungee Tower at Sanjay Lake – Trans Yamuna Area

Sanjay lake is one of the biggest lake of Delhi and is abound 2.5 k.m. long. The lake is mainly rain fed. leisure boating activities at Sanjay Lake are available since September 2004. There is a huge scope for setting up of soft adventure park at Sanjay lake consisting of obstacle courses, spider web, tarzan rope, Burma bridge, trampoline, zapping. The area has scope for construction of high bungee tower made of concrete structure. It is also proposed to construct a restaurant at the top of Bungee tower. This Bungee tower will also support an artificial rock climbing wall.

Soft Adventure Park at Purana Quila

Purana Quila is situated at main Mehrauli Road and is surrounded by important land marks of Delhi like Delhi Zoo and Trade Fair ground. Leisure boating activity at Purana Quila and is also provided and it is proposed to develop soft adventure park in the land around Purana Quila .

10. Development of Coffee Homes in Different Parts of Delhi.

Coffee Homes at Connaught Place, Laxmi Nagar, R.K. Puram and Ajmal Khan Park were set up to provide clean hygenic wholesome food to Delhi ties/visitors at reasonable rates. These coffee homes have become very popular and propose to extend these facilities in other parts of the city.

11. Installation of Sport Climbing Wall

Delhi, being an urban city, the government has more emphasis to spread awareness through education in all spheres of life like social economical political, technical, to educate every citizen of the city. Besides, tourism and its various streams like Adventure Tourism has become an important activity to promote tourism potential, revenue generation, and employment generation among the youth of Delhi. To promote the adventure activities, DTTDC intends to install four Rock Climbing

Walls atleast in four corners to the city to facilitate the students and youth during 10th five-year plan. Recently, DTTDC has set up an artificial (Fibre) Rock Climbing Wall at Azad Hind Gram. It has been observed that small school children a slightly scared to climb the Fibre Rock Climbing Wall. It is proposed to put up two inflated Rock Climbing Wall at Azad Hind Gram specially for small children. These walls can also be carried out for demonstration to various schools of Delhi.

12. Setting up of Night Bazaar

The life at National Capital Territory has become more and more busier day by day. The Delhites have no time of amusement, entertainment and to cater the daily needs as per demand of progressive living standard. Moreover, the tourists visiting the city stay two or three nights in Delhi as they use this city only as an entry point to the country by them. To facilities these visitors, DTTDC intends to set up Night Bazaar in Delhi to keep Delhi at par with the world's most popular cities.

Delhi Tourism proposes to organize Night Bazaar on the corridors of the State Emporiums commencing from Gram Ship Emporium up to Phulkaari Emporium at Baba Kharak Singh Marg. Bazaar is proposed to be organzed on weekends instead of weekdays. The timing of the Bazaar will be from 8.00 P.M. to 04.00 A.M. The objective for holding Bazaar is to showcase the rich art, culture and heritage of India and to provide quality leisure time to the tourists (foreign as well as domestic) and Delhities along with the shopping experience. It has been proposed to have stalls of easily dismantable items such as, Octonorm exhibition panels or fabric walls. Stalls shall display Handloom and Handicraft items, souvenir, Boutiques, books on culture and heritage of India etc. Toys, traditional/ ethnic jewellery, Indian food especially from Walled City, Puppet show, Magic show, classical music and dance performances and performance of folklore of India etc.

13. Consultancy of Tourism Projects Tourism Research and Development

Many agencies are involved in promoting tourism in city through its various roles. The thrust areas of tourism potential are identified for establishment of tourism projects. Due to lack ness at various corners, these projects have not attained success at requisite level. Therefore, the proficiency and technical expertise are required while identifying the thrust areas and conducting techno-feasibility study of the tourism projects.

14. IT APPLICTION

The potential of Information Technology for promotion of the tourism is only limited by the imagination. The world is in the midst of an Information and Technological revolution and the opportunities for the Government are enormous. it is not enough to simply automate their current ways of doing business. With the new tools of a networked society, Delhi Tourism is rethinking and engineering its IT infrastructure. By taking full advantage of the information revolution, we can both provide better services to the tourists and use our unique position to promote competition and innovation-thus improving the quality of services for the tourists. Delhi Tourism may like to produce more information material on the electronic media such as interactive, theme based and Virtual walkthrough based CDs. Besides Delhi Tourism may like to extend and expand the computer networks by way of new technology and software systems. The frontiers of Internet are to be explored further for better information dissemination and facilitation.

15. Chhawla & Kanganheri Project

The Corporation identified two sites measuring 2.77 and 11.44 acres at Chhawla and Kanganheri on Najafgarh Drain respectively for setting up of Adventure Sports Complex and Eco Park with leisure facilities. Memorandum of Understanding is being finalised with Irrigation and Flood Department to transfer the land to DTTDC. The preparation of concept/design of the project is under process and soon after the approval of GNCTD. the project may go ahead with the preliminary work like Development of site and other services i.e. construction of boundary wall, earth work, levelling and dressing of site etc.

16. Adventure Park at Azad Hind Gram

DTTDC owns around six acres of land on National Highway No. 10 at Tikri Kalan on Rohtak Road before Bahadurgarh Border. DTTDC has already set up a museum and smark on Netaji Subhash Chandra Bose at Azad Hind Gram. Public convenience, snack bar, restaurant, banquet facilities are already in existence in this complex.The process of setting up an artificial rock climbing wall is already completed. In the remaining portion of this complex, DTTDC plans to set up a permanent adventure park where tourist would be given courses in soft and hard adventure. The tourist will also be provided with night stay after completion of their soft and hard adventure games.

BASIC INFRASTRUCTURE

Transport

The following modes of transport are in vogue in the parlance of the tourism industry:

Air Transport : It is used mostly for going abroad, or for travelling from one place to another in a large country. Air tickets have to be booked at least 21 days in advance.

Sea Transport: It involves steamers, cruise liners, ferries and large ships. It can be used for long-distance travel as well as for short-distance excursions. Sea tickets must be procured at least 30 days in advance. Steamers, motorboats and ferries are used to carry passengers from one tourist spot to another or from the mainland to an island of tourist interest. For example, tourists can go from the main island of Singapore to Santosa aboard a motorboat. Tourists can take a trip through the canals and waterways of Venice by gondolas. Finally, a local oarsman can take an oar-boat through the backwaters of Kerala to let the tourist enjoy the beauty of flora and fauna of these backwaters.

Road Transport: These are used mostly for moving within a region or country as bookings are done quickly and time is not wasted in other formalities. Some package tour operators use buses extensively to facilitate quick movements of their customers to popular hill resorts, lakes, hotels, motels, forts, palaces, museums etc. These buses cover nearly 300- 400 km per day of 72 hours. These are also cheaper than air transport and quite convenient.

Air conditioned luxury coaches with public address systems and other amenities are used by most of travel operators. These are also used by tour agencies to show the cities, and tourist spots to tourists. The tour guide addresses the tourists on the PA system and tells them about the historical monument or place while the coach passes by the same. Tickets for luxury coaches and buses have to be booked at least 3 days in advance. If a bus or luxury coach has to be used to move from one country to another, then bookings have to be done at least 30 days in advance. The tour operator is responsible for such bookings, if he has been allocated the responsibility of surface travel of the tourist. The example of travel from Singapore to Kuala Lumpur (Malaysia) is prominent in this context.

Cable Ropeway Transport : These are available at popular tourist sites. These cannot be used to move from one country to another or from one city to another. These take tourists from a station or terminal and transport them in the cable car to a tourist spot. Example : The cable rope-way of Genting Heights is the longest cable rope way in the world.

Rail Transport : It is very much popular in India. Trains are also popular in western Europe, Malaysia, Singapore, Japan, Siberia and South America. The trans-Siberian Railway is the longest railway route in the world. Trains are also used for intra-city transport. The prominent examples of metropolitan railways of India are the Metro Rail systems of Delhi and Kolkata. In the West, the speeds of trains are very high, just like these are in Japan. Tourists enjoy the high speed of the Euro Rail that takes them to different countries of Europe. Meglev trains are operating in Japan and China. A Meglev train can have a speed of up to *480 km per hour.*

Hotels

A tourist is a not a native of the place he visits. So, he has to stay in a rented accommodation at such a place. For this purpose, government agencies and private firms construct places of temporary residence at or near many famous tourist spots.

Consequently, hotels, motels, highway inns and rest houses have been constructed at almost all the tourist destinations of the world. Even those visitors, who visit new places for the purpose conducting business transactions, stay at such hotels and motels. The rooms of most of these hotels are double rooms or suites, though these can also be rented out to visitors on a single occupancy basis. In many *sarais,* large halls are constructed in which, *20-30* beds are laid. Several tourists can take rest in such *sarais* during the night at very cheap rates. In India, these *sarais* used to be popular resting places for tourists and travellers during the ancient times. Even in modern times, some *sarais* are operating in our country. Further, many professional organisations get their rest houses constructed in popular cities and at famous tourist spots. These places of residence are not available for the *hoi polloi* of tourist markets; these are exclusively reserved for those employees of these firms who come either for excursion, or for getting training. Thus, these employees almost always combine work with tourist activities. In fact, their employers promote such visits so that these employees could have a change from the routine activities of their offices.

Guest houses, drive-in hotels, inns and *dharamshalas* are also common in India. *Dharamsdhalas* are very cheap, if we consider the costs of stay in such residential complexes. These are managed by religious organisations charitable trusts or communities in most of the cases. For example, *dharamshalas* of Haridwar are famous. These are good places for staying for longer journeys. Poor and middle-income families find them to be very much suitable simply because these are cheap. These *dharamshalas* provide only the rooms for night stay and do not serve food. However, tea, coffee and snacks are served in all types of hotels, motels, guest houses and dharamshalas. Five-star hotels have good infrastructure and facilities. The owners and managers of such hotels ensure that their hotels are free from dirt, chaos and other nuisances that usually bother a tourist. Five-star hotels are, in fact, luxury hotels. Intercontinental hotels are above these hotels in terms of facilities provided and costs. Four-star hotels are also nice places to stay in; but these are also costly. Most of the middle-income tourists prefer three-star hotels, which may lack many facilities. Two-star hotels are good enough for single tourists, youngsters and businessmen who are always on the move. One-star hotels are fit for operative staff, workers, transport operators and people from the lower strata of the society.

Communication

Every professional tourist agency is connected to Internet, the information superhighway of the world. Besides, many tour operators and travel agencies are connected to the global network of the IATA, which keeps them updated on the bookings of various airlines. Bookings can be done online. Seats can be reserved in any airline without paying for them. This is called Seat Holding. The travel agent can hold a seat for at least *14 days* from the date of online booking. Further, telephones, cellular phones, SMS messages, radio paging systems, fax messages and E-mail messages are used by tour operators, tour guides and tour managers. The staff members of travel agencies, who contact embassies or high commissioners for completing visa formalities of customers, also keep in touch with their respective offices through cellular phones and pagers. In the USA, the data transfer rates of *128 kbps* are common (over the Net). But in India, the data transfer rate is only *56 kbps,* though new technologies and hardware are entering India at a much quicker pace. Cellular phones are being used extensively and in all parts of the world by the members of tourist organisations, hotels, travel agents and tour guides. Satellites, optical cable networks, radio frequency transmitters and land lines (of telephones) are used to ensure successful completion of tours. Besides, there are PCO and STD booths that help tourists communicate with people located in any part of the world. They can also send and receive E-mail in Internet cafes that have mushroomed in all the parts of the world. Even the hotels they check in are able to provide them such services like Internet Relay Chat (IRC), Internet newsgroups, E-mail exchange services etc. Tourists can surf through various web sites and download information from the same. Fax transmissions can also be effected.

But the visitors have to pay for such services. In most of the hotels, they may have to pay more whereas they would always be able to surf through Internet web sites in local Net cafes at much cheaper rates.

Natural Sites

Many tourists visit natural spots simply because they want to spend some time in the lap of nature. Lakes, parks, bird sanctuaries, wild-life sanctuaries, mountains, ponds etc. are a part of these spots. These must be maintained by authorities responsible for their upkeep, lest these should be spoiled by tourists. These spots are spoiled due to vehicular pollution, large numbers of tourists, polytheism bags, chemicals, human excreta, industrial wastage and things spread or thrown by tourists. Hence, these lose their charm over a period of time. Many natural spots have already become redundant with the passage of time. For example, the famous Juhu-Chaupati Beach in Mumbai was once a hot tourist destination. But filth, garbage, polytheism bags, chemicals and pollutants of the air have converted this beautiful spot into a hell. Ironically, the administration is neither taking care of it nor preventing local residents or visitors from contaminating or polluting it. If these trends were to continue, people would not like to visit the Juhu-Chaupati beach in the times to come.

Historical Importance

These are the vital assets for the tourism industry of any country. Most often, these monuments are controlled and maintained by the governments of those nations in which, these are located. Besides, there are some World Heritage Sites, which are deemed the property of the mankind. Global-level efforts are made to preserve and repair these Heritage Sites. Due to incessant inflow of visitors, such historical monuments are destroyed or damaged. The governments or agencies responsible for their maintenance have to spend millions of Dollars to preserve them. Historical monuments include forts, palaces, towers, *baolis* (small water tanks), minarets, mosques, temples etc.

Artificial Spots

Several man-made tourist destinations have been built by man to facilitate tourist traffic to those destinations. Genting Heights, in Malaysia, is one such spot. Several artificial lakes have also been made around the world. These attract large numbers of tourists. For example, the Sukhna Lake, in Chandigarh, is one such spot. Billions of Dollars are spent to construct and maintain such spots. Tickets are sold to tourists, who enjoy games, joyrides, theme parks, amusement parks, dances in disco clubs and other such facilities as are provided at such spots. These spots also have shops, which sell souvenirs, crockery, leather goods, electronics goods, gifts for children and apparel.

Human Power

In the tourism industry, manpower plays a major role. We can divide tourism staff into the following categories.

Owners of Diverse Agencies

These are the owners of tour agencies, hotels, travel agencies or tourist resorts. They remain abroad for most of the time of the year. They are achievers and professionals in the world of tourism and travel. They are quite effluent. They want results from their subordinates. Normally, they are directors, CVPs, CEOs, COOs and Presidents of their firms.

The Authorities

They are general managers, senior managers and travel consultants. They either work in large firms like SOTC, Cox & Kings, Thomas Cook or are Self-Employed Professionals (SEPs) who operate from their offices/homes. Nowadays, the concept of Small Office Home Office (SOHO) is catching up at a fast pace. Such professionals are finding it easier to use their expertise (in travel and tourism operations) by working as independent consultants. The concept of SOHO has also been promoted by SOHONET, a web portal dedicated to the needs of SEPs. We have noted, after meeting many such professionals, that they start their businesses as one-man shows. But later, they employ skeletal staff to from private limited or public limited firms. Many of these professionals handle corporate clients too. Senior hotel managers, F&B managers, lobby managers, front office managers, flight captains, security chiefs and head chefs also fall under this category.

STAFFING

Junior Staff

These are the people who actually run the tourism and travel industry. They are :

(a) airline booking and ticketing staff;

(b) marketing staff;

(c) bell captains in hotels;

(d) hotel supervisors;

(e) personnel who get the passports stamped for visas (from embassies/high commissions);

(f) staff that handle or converts foreign exchange;

(g) captains of aircraft and ships/cruises;

(h) resort supervisors;

(i) flight stewards or pursers;

(j) travel/tour guides;

(k) air hostesses; and

(l) security officers at various hotels and resort sites who actually show the sites/monuments to tourists/visitors.

Nature of Staff

These are the people who carry out manual tasks to keep the tourism and travel industry chugging along. These include :

(a) office boys and peons;

(b) couriers

(c) salesmen;

(d) delivery boys;

(e) trainee cooks;

(f) cleaners and in-house laundry staff in a hotel;

(g) drivers of buses, coaches, vans etc.;

(h) drivers of cruises, small boats, large boats/ferries, ships etc.;

(i) resort operatives and cleaners;

(j) bar-men;

(k) waiters and waitresses;

(l) trainee air hostesses;

(m) trainee flight stewards;

(n) doormen at hotels/restaurant; and

(o) security staff (operatives) at various hotels and resorts.

Religious Places

Such places are visited by religious tourists. Popular places include Mecca, Medina, the church of Bom Jusus, the Holy See, Shri Harmandir Sahib, the wailing wall at Jerusalem, Betheleham, the dargah of Hadrat Nizammuddin Aulia, the shrine of Vaishno Devi, Meenakshi Temple, Jagannath Temple, the dargah of Salim Chishti, Angkor Wat, Reclining Buddha and many other religious shrines of the world. Some religious places are meant to be visited only by the followers of those faiths; others may not be allowed to visit such places. But most of religious places are visited by followers of all the religious sects due to their curiosity to know more about the religious customs and norms prevailing at such places. Religious tourism was popular in the world even two thousand years ago. In the new era, its methodology has changed due to the advent of modern technologies. For example, many hajis travel to Mecca (in

Saudi Arabia) by air; during the ancient times, they used to travel either by foot or by sea. Further, at some religious shrines, visitors can take photographs of deities; this was not possible nearly 150 years ago because gadgets of photography were not available during those times.

Air Communication

The growth of the airlines industry, in the parlance of tourism administration, was witnessed only after the late fifties of the previous century. Currently, most of the major cities of the world are on the air maps of the popular airlines. Air travel offers the following advantages to a tourist : (a) Speed, (b) Luxury, (c) Saving of Time, (d) Possibility of visiting a large number of places within a short duration of time.

If we want to go from one country to another, we invariably use aircraft. Even within a large country like the USA, people use aircraft, helicopters and chartered flights quite often. Interestingly, people as well as tourists of the United States have lost interest in rail travel. Air travel offers them speed, comfort and luxury of a high order. For most of the international tourists, time is the major consideration. So, they do not mind spending more on air tickets because they save a lot of time if they fly by air. Further, surface travel over a large distance like *1000 km* is not practically feasible. Surface transport companies do not offer such services as extend beyond a distance *of 200-600 km.* Air travel is, therefore, most suitable for long-distance tourism activities. Each airline offers economy class, executive class and royal executive class seats in its aircraft. Cost-conscious travelers can choose from among these classes according to the financial resources at their command.

Railways Communication

Millions of tourists travel by railways every year. Within a region, which is known as a tourist destination or region, railway networks provide access to spots of tourist interest. For example, the Palace on Wheels takes tourists through the countryside of Rajasthan. This luxury train is known for its cuisine, grandeur and hospitality. It gives thrilling experiences to its passengers at the railway station where the train halts. It is a part of the package tour during which, historic sites are also visited by passengers. The Euro Rail is another travel/tour system that helps international tourists visit important tourist sites of Europe. Other examples in this context are the Royal Orient and Indrail, the latter being a type of pass that allows travellers to travel through any part of India in trains (at nominal prices).

Road Communication

Luxury coaches, vans and ordinary buses are used by tourists to travel to important tourist sites. Some sites are not linked to railway networks. Hence, it becomes necessary to connect these sites through extensive road networks. Buses and air conditioned coaches take tourists from the nearest large city or town and transport them to those sites. Some travellers may prefer only road transport due to personal reasons. Some others may use their own vehicles. In hilly areas, it is not possible to construct railway tracks. Hence, roads are used in most of the hilly tracks to facilitate movements of tourists. All the tourist spots are well connected through road networks, though many of these may not be connected through rail networks. This type of travel is popularly called surface transport in the parlance of tourism administration. Local and state governments of many countries provide facilities for transport for transporting tourists to many a popular tourist spot. Finally, travel within a city is also easier if the tour operator uses buses and luxury coaches. That is because tourists prefer to move according to flexible schedules (keeping their convenience in view). However, railway trains do not abide by their departure schedules in most of the cases (because these have rigid departure timings). Thus, surface transport is a vital element of the entire gamut of tourism.

Computers and Networks

Advanced computer systems and networks are required to book tickets online. Internet is used to send E-mail messages to those hotels that need to be booked. Travel agents and associates are also contacted through E-mail messages. Further, travel agencies send SMS messages to their clients (on their cellular phones). Thus, these agencies must have computer networks connected to the Net. Most of these agencies use Pentium systems having CPU speeds of up to *2.4 Mhz*. These agencies as well as travel agents use web sites like pc2phone.com and sms.ac. in to send SMS messages to cellular phones (of their clients) en masse. Advanced computer systems, networks and printers are a necessity in the tourism industry of today. The client of a travel agency needs fast and efficient service; if he does not get it from the agency he contacts, he switches over to another. All the schedules of travel, local sightseeing and local tours are time bound. Obviously, computers play a vital role in executing tour programmes. It is mandatory for the airlines booking staff and marketing personnel of a travel agency to learn computer operations due to this very reason.

Varied Departments

The governments of various countries have formed departments and/or ministries of tourism in their respective countries. Such departments/ministries help tour operators and agencies working within their geographical boundaries. The ministries of external affairs look into visa formalities, baggage rules, import restrictions, export formalities, customs, customs regulations, various levies and other such rules as are related to international travel. Further, airport authorities of all the nations define airport customs formalities, taxes or levies to be imposed on imported goods, airport taxes, immigration rules, emigration formalities, rules with respect to import of precious items such as diamonds, gold and jewellery, baggage rules, check-in procedures at airports and other such rules as are related to national and international travel. Further, these rules could be different for domestic tours and travel. The ministry of external affairs coordinates the embassies, consulates and high commissions of various nations (located in its own country) and delineates procedures for issuing tourist visas to citizens of its own country. Several thousand people work in such offices and facilitate movements of tourists and travellers. Many private tour operators get details of changes in rules or visa fees from these government departments and/or ministries from time to time. So, these departments and/or ministries are also a vital part of the vast global infrastructure of tourism.

Finally, the embassies, high commissions and consulates also assist the nationals of their countries when they face problems in the countries chosen by them for the purpose of tour and travel. For example, a tourist may lose his passport, or he may be manhandled by the native or hooligan of the country that is being visited by him. He contacts the embassy or high commission of his country in that country. He can get all types of support from this embassy or high commission. In many cases, the tourist loses his wallet and hence, all of his money. So, he can get an air ticket, through the high commission or embassy of his country located (in the country being visited by him), so that he may be able to go back to his country without any hassles. Such crises do surface while people travel to unknown areas or countries. Thus, they are assisted, through a set of international travel protocols, by the embassies and high commissions of their own countries that are located in countries visited by them. Hence, we can conclude that these high commissions, embassies and consulates are also a vital part of the infrastructure of tourism.

Important Organisations

These are also a part of the infrastructure of tourism. Globally recognised organisations, namely the WTO, PATA, IATA, IOTO, UFTAA, FHRAI AND ICAO provide data and technical support to travel agencies, tour operators, airlines, hotels, resorts and other such persons as are associated with the travel and tourism industry. But such firms must be the members of these organisations so that the latter could take care of the interests of the former. For example, a travel agency must have recognition from IATA, if it wishes to book air tickets for its customers. Normally, a customer or traveller-to-be would not contact a travel agency that is not recognised by the IATA.

Tourist Resources

These are used by tourists while they travel to foreign countries. These elements or resources include :

(a) credit cards;

(b) debit cards;

(c) recommendations of their employees and/or letters/ invitations to conferences and seminars;

(d) still cameras and video cameras;

(e) personal effects used in tourism activities;

(f) automobiles (two-wheelers and four-wheelers and)

(g) food items, beverages, liquor etc. carried by tourists during their tours.

These sundry elements also help tourists complete their tours without problems. The needs of individuals vary in this context.

Local Facilities

At the tourist spot, the following facilities must be provided to tourists on a continuous basis :—

(a) Electric power.

(b) Sewage and waste disposal facilities.

(c) Water.

(d) Medical attention by qualified doctors (whenever the need arises) and medicines.

(e) Safety and security equipment.

(f) Local telephones, PCOs for STD and ISD calls, fax machines, cellular phones, walkie-talkies etc.

(g) Language translators (interpreters of languages or books that should be easily available).

(h) Maps, tour guides and booklets (in printed formats).

CHAPTER–11

Transport : The Basic Infrastructure of Event Tourism

Transport or transportation is the movement of people and goods from one location to another. Modes of transport include air, rail, road, water, cable, pipeline, and space. The field can be divided into infrastructure, vehicles, and operations.

Transport infrastructure consists of the fixed installations necessary for transport, and may be roads, railways, airways, waterways, canals and pipelines, and terminals such as airports, railway stations, bus stations, warehouses, trucking terminals, refueling depots (including fueling docks and fuel stations), and seaports. Terminals may be used both for interchange of passengers and cargo and for maintenance.

Vehicles traveling on these networks may include automobiles, bicycles, buses, trains, trucks, people, helicopters, and aircraft. Operations deal with the way the vehicles are operated, and the procedures set for this purpose including financing, legalities and policies. In the transport industry, operations and ownership of infrastructure can be either public or private, depending on the country and mode.

Passenger transport may be public, where operators provide scheduled services, or private. Freight transport has become focused on containerization, although bulk transport is used for large volumes of durable items. Transport plays an important part in economic growth and globalization, but most types cause air pollution and use large amounts of land. While it is heavily subsidized by governments, good planning of transport is essential to make traffic flow, and restrain urban sprawl.

MODE

A mode of transport is a solution that makes use of a particular type of vehicle, infrastructure and operation. The transport of a person or of cargo may involve one mode or several modes, with the latter case being called intermodal or multimodal transport. Each mode has its advantages and disadvantages, and will be chosen for a trip on the basis of cost, capability, route, and speed.

Human-powered

Human powered transport is the transport of people and/or goods using human muscle-power, in the form of walking, running and swimming. Modern technology has allowed machines to enhance human-power. Human-powered transport remains popular for reasons of cost-saving, leisure, physical exercise and environmentalism. Human-powered transport is sometimes the only type available, especially in underdeveloped or inaccessible regions. It is considered an ideal form of sustainable transportation.

Although humans are able to walk without infrastructure, the transport can be enhanced through the use of roads, especially when enforcing the human power with vehicles, such as bicycles and inline skates. Human-powered vehicles have also been developed for difficult environments, such as snow and water, by watercraft rowing and skiing; even the air can be entered with human-powered aircraft.

ANIMAL-POWERED

Animal-powered transport is the use of working animals for the movement of people and goods. Humans may ride some of the animals directly, use them as pack animals for carrying goods, or harness them, alone or in teams, to pull sleds or wheeled vehicles. Animals are superior to people in their speed, endurance and carrying capacity; prior to the Industrial Revolution they were used for all land transport impracticable for people, and they remain an important mode of transport in less developed areas of the world.

Air

A fixed-wing aircraft, commonly called airplane, is a heavier-than-air craft where movement of the air in relation to the wings is used to generate lift. The term is used to distinguish from rotary-wing aircraft, where the movement of the lift surfaces relative to the air generates lift. A gyroplane is both fixed-wing and rotary-wing. Fixed-wing aircraft range from small trainers and recreational aircraft to large airliners and military cargo aircraft.

Two things necessary for aircraft are air flow over the wings for lift and an area for landing. The majority of aircraft also need an airport with the infrastructure to receive maintenance, restocking, refueling and for the loading and unloading of crew, cargo and passengers. While the vast majority of aircraft land and take off on land, some are capable of take off and landing on ice, snow and calm water.

The aircraft is the second fastest method of transport, after the rocket. Commercial jets can reach up to 875 kilometres per hour (544 mph), single-engine aircraft 175 kilometres per hour (109 mph). Aviation is able to quickly transport people and limited amounts of cargo over longer distances, but incur high costs and energy use; for short distances or in inaccessible places helicopters can be used. WHO estimates that up to 500,000 people are on planes at any time.

Rail

Rail transport is where a train runs along a set of two parallel steel rails, known as a railway or railroad. The rails are anchored perpendicular to ties (or sleepers) of timber, concrete or steel, to maintain a consistent distance apart, or gauge. The rails and perpendicular beams are placed on a foundation made of concrete, or compressed earth and gravel in a bed of ballast. Alternative methods include monorail and maglev.

A train consists of one or more connected vehicles that run on the rails. Propulsion is commonly provided by a locomotive, that hauls a series of unpowered cars, that can carry passengers or freight. The locomotive can be powered by steam, diesel or by electricity supplied by trackside systems. Alternatively, some or all the cars can be powered, known as a multiple unit. Also, a train can be powered by horses, cables, gravity, pneumatics and gas turbines. Railed vehicles move with much less friction than rubber tires on paved roads, making trains more energy efficient, though not as efficient as ships.

Intercity trains are long-haul services connecting cities; modern high-speed rail is capable of speeds up to 350 km/h (220 mph), but this requires specially built track. Regional and commuter trains feed cities from suburbs and surrounding areas, while intra-urban transport is performed by high-capacity tramways and rapid transits, often making up the backbone of a city's public transport. Freight trains traditionally used box cars, requiring manual loading and unloading of the cargo. Since the 1960s, container trains have become the dominant solution for general freight, while large quantities of bulk are transported by dedicated trains.

Road

A road is an identifiable route, way or path between two or more places. Roads are typically smoothed, paved, or otherwise prepared to allow easy travel; though they need not be, and historically many roads were simply recognizable routes without any formal construction or maintenance. In urban areas, roads may pass through a city or village and be named as streets, serving a dual function as urban space easement and route.

The most common road vehicle is the automobile; a wheeled passenger vehicle that carries its own motor. Other users of roads include buses, trucks, motorcycles, bicycles and pedestrians. As of 2002, there were 590 million automobiles worldwide.

Automobiles offer high flexibility and with low capacity, but are deemed with high energy and area use, and the main source of noise and air pollution in cities; buses allow for more efficient travel at the cost of reduced flexibility. Road transport by truck is often the initial and final stage of freight transport.

Water

Water transport is the process of transport a watercraft, such as a barge, boat, ship or sailboat, makes over a body of water, such as a sea, ocean, lake, canal or river. The need for buoyancy unites watercraft, and makes the hull a dominant aspect of its construction, maintenance and appearance.

In the 1800s the first steam ships were developed, using a steam engine to drive a paddle wheel or propeller to move the ship. The steam was produced using wood or coal. Now most ships have an engine using a slightly refined type of petroleum called bunker fuel. Some ships, such as submarines, use nuclear power to produce the steam. Recreational or educational craft still use wind power, while some smaller craft use internal combustion engines to drive one or more propellers, or in the case of jet boats, an inboard water jet. In shallow draft areas, hovercraft are propelled by large pusher-prop fans.

Although slow, modern sea transport is a highly effective method of transporting large quantities of non-perishable goods. Commercial vessels, nearly 35,000 in number, carried 7.4 billion tons of cargo in 2007. Transport by water is significantly less costly than air transport for trans-continental shipping; short sea shipping and ferries remain viable in coastal areas.

Other

Pipeline transport sends goods through a pipe, most commonly liquid and gases are sent, but pneumatic tubes can also send solid capsules using compressed air. For liquids/gases, any chemically stable liquid or gas can be sent through a pipeline. Short-distance systems exist for sewage, slurry, water and beer, while long-distance networks are used for petroleum and natural gas.

Cable transport is a broad mode where vehicles are pulled by cables instead of an internal power source. It is most commonly used at steep gradient. Typical solutions include aerial tramway, elevators, escalator and ski lifts; some of these are also categorized as conveyor transport.

Spaceflight is transport out of Earth's atmosphere into outer space by means of a spacecraft. While large amounts of research have gone into technology, it is rarely used except to put satellites into orbit, and conduct scientific experiments. However, man has landed on the moon, and probes have been sent to all the planets of the Solar System.

Suborbital spaceflight is the fastest of the existing and planned transport systems from a place on Earth to a distant other place on Earth. Faster transport could be achieved through part of a Low Earth orbit, or following that trajectory even faster using the propulsion of the rocket to steer it.

ELEMENTS

Infrastructure

Infrastructure is the fixed installations that allow a vehicle to operate. It consists of both a way, terminal and facilities for parking and maintenance. For rail, pipeline, road and cable transport, the entire way the vehicle travels must be built up. Air and water craft are able to avoid this, since the airway and seaway do not need to be built up. However, they require fixed infrastructure at terminals.

Terminals such as airports, ports and stations, are locations where passengers and freight can be transferred from one vehicle or mode to another. For passenger transport, terminals are integrating different modes to allow riders to interchange to take advantage of each mode's advantages. For instance, airport rail links connect airports to the city centers and suburbs. The terminals for automobiles are parking lots, while buses and coaches can operates from simple stops. For freight, terminals act as transshipment points, though some cargo is transported directly from the point of production to the point of use.

The financing of infrastructure can either be public or private. Transport is often a natural monopoly and a necessity for the public; roads, and in some countries railways and airports are funded through taxation. New infrastructure projects can involve large spendings, and are often financed through debt. Many infrastructure owners therefore impose usage fees, such as landing fees at airports, or toll plazas on roads. Independent of this, authorities may impose taxes on the purchase or use of vehicles.

Vehicles

A vehicle is any non-living device that is used to move people and goods. Unlike the infrastructure, the vehicle moves along with the cargo and riders. Vehicles that do not operate on land, are usually called crafts. Unless being pulled by a cable or muscle-power, the vehicle must provide its own propulsion; this is most commonly done through a steam engine, combustion engine, electric motor, a jet engine or a rocket, though other means of propulsion also exist. Vehicles also need a system of converting the energy into movement; this is most commonly done through wheels, propellers and pressure.

Vehicles are most commonly staffed by a driver. However, some systems, such as people movers and some rapid transits, are fully automated. For passenger transport, the vehicle must have a compartment for the passengers. Simple vehicles, such as automobiles, bicycles or simple aircraft, may have one of the passengers as a driver.

Operation

Private transport is only subject to the owner of the vehicle, who operates the vehicle themselves. For public transport and freight transport, operations are done through private enterprise or by governments. The infrastructure and vehicles may be owned and operated by the same company, or they may be operated by different entities. Traditionally, many countries have had a national airline and national railway. Since the 1980s, many of these have been privatized. International shipping remains a highly competitive industry with little regulation, but ports can be public owned.

Function

Relocation of travelers and cargo are the most common uses of transport. However, other uses exist, such as the strategic and tactical relocation of armed forces during warfare, or the civilian mobility construction or emergency equipment.

Passenger

Passenger transport, or travel, is divided into public and private transport. Public is scheduled services on fixed routes, while private is vehicles that provide ad hoc services at the riders desire. The latter offers better flexibility, but has lower capacity, and a higher environmental impact. Travel may be as part of daily commuting, for business, leisure or migration.

Short-haul transport is dominated by the automobile and mass transit. The latter consists of buses in rural and small cities, supplemented with commuter rail, trams and rapid transit in larger cities. Long-haul transport involves the use of the automobile, trains, coaches and aircraft, the last of which have become predominantly used for the longest, including intercontinental, travel. Intermodal passenger transport is where a journey is performed through the use of several modes of transport; since all human transport normally starts and ends with walking, all passenger transport can be considered intermodal. Public transport may also involve the intermediate change of vehicle, within or across modes, at a transport hub, such as a bus or railway station.

Taxis and Buses can be found on both ends of Public Transport spectrum, whereas Buses remain the cheaper mode of transport but are not necessarily flexible, and Taxis being very flexible but more expensive. In the middle is Demand responsive transport offering flexibility whilst remaining affordable.

International travel may be restricted for some individuals due to legislation and visa requirements.

Freight

Freight transport, or shipping, is a key in the value chain in manufacturing. With increased specialization and globalization, production is being located further away from consumption, rapidly increasing the demand for transport. While all modes of transport are used for cargo transport, there is high differentiation between the nature of the cargo transport, in which mode is chosen. Logistics refers to the entire process of transferring products from producer to consumer, including storage, transport, transshipment, warehousing, material-handling and packaging, with associated exchange of information. Incoterm deals with the handling of payment and responsibility of risk during transport.

Containerization, with the standardization of ISO containers on all vehicles and at all ports, has revolutionized international and domestic trade, offering huge reduction in transshipment costs. Traditionally, all cargo had to be manually loaded and unloaded into the haul of any ship or car; containerization allows for automated handling and transfer between modes, and the standardized sizes allow for gains in economy of scale in vehicle operation. This has been one of the key driving factors in international trade and globalization since the 1950s.

Bulk transport is common with cargo that can be handled roughly without deterioration; typical examples are ore, coal, cereals and petroleum. Because of the uniformity of the product, mechanical handling can allow enormous quantities to be handled quickly and efficiently. The low value of the cargo combined with high volume also means that economies of scale become essential in transport, and gigantic ships and whole trains are commonly used to transport bulk. Liquid products with sufficient volume may also be transported by pipeline.

Air freight has become more common for products of high value; while less than one percent of world transport by volume is by airline, it amounts to forty percent of the value. Time has become especially important in regards to principles such as postponement and just-in-time within the value chain, resulting in a high willingness to pay for quick delivery of key components or items of high value-to-weight ratio. In addition to mail, common items send by air include electronics and fashion clothing.

History

Humans' first means of transport were walking and swimming. The domestication of animals introduces a new way to lay the burden of transport on more powerful creatures, allowing heavier loads to be hauled, or humans to ride the animals for higher speed and duration. Inventions such as the wheel and sled helped make animal transport more efficient through the introduction of vehicles. Also water transport, including rowed and sailed vessels, dates back to time immemorial, and was the only efficient way to transport large quantities or over large distances prior to the Industrial Revolution.

The first forms of road transport were horses, oxen or even humans carrying goods over dirt tracks that often followed game trails. Paved roads were built by many early civilizations, including Mesopotamia and the Indus Valley Civilization. The Persian and Roman empires built stone-paved roads to allow armies to travel quickly. Deep roadbeds of crushed stone underneath ensured that the roads kept dry. The medieval Caliphate later built tar-paved roads. The first watercraft were canoes cut out from tree trunks. Early water transport was accomplished with ships that were either rowed or used the wind for propulsion, or a combination of the two. The importance of water has led to most cities, that grew up as sites for trading, being located on rivers or at sea, ofter at the intersection of two bodies of water. Until the Industrial Revolution, transport remained slow and costly, and production and consumption were located as close to each other as feasible.

The Industrial Revolution in the 19th century saw a number of inventions fundamentally change transport. With telegraphy, communication became instant and independent of transport. The invention of the steam engine, closely followed by its application in rail transport, made land transport independent of human or animal muscles. Both speed and capacity increased rapidly, allowing specialization through manufacturing being located independent of natural resources. The 19th century also saw the development of the steam ship, that sped up global transport.

The development of the combustion engine and the automobile at the turn into the 20th century, road transport became more viable, allowing the introduction of mechanical private transport. The first highways were constructed during the 19th century with macadam. Later, tarmac and concrete became the dominant paving material. In 1903, the first controllable airplane was invented, and after World War I, it became a fast way to transport people and express goods over long distances.

After World War II, the automobile and airlines took higher shares of transport, reducing rail and water to freight and short-haul passenger. Spaceflight was launched in the 1950s, with rapid growth until the 1970s, when interest dwindled. In the 1950s, the introduction of containerization gave massive efficiency gains in freight transport, permitting globalization. International air travel became much more accessible in the 1960s, with the commercialization of the jet engine. Along with the growth in automobiles and motorways, this introduced a decline for rail and water transport. After the introduction of the Shinkansen in 1964, high-speed rail in Asia and Europe started taking passengers on long-haul routes from airlines.

IMPACT

Economic

Transport is a key necessity for specialization—allowing production and consumption of products to occur at different locations. Transport has throughout history been a spur to expansion; better transport allows more trade and a greater spread of people. Economic growth has always been dependent on increasing the capacity and rationality of transport. But the infrastructure and operation of transport has a great impact on the land and is the largest drainer of energy, making transport sustainability a major issue.

Modern society dictates a physical distinction between home and work, forcing people to transport themselves to places of work or study, as well as to temporarily relocate for other daily activities. Passenger transport is also the essence of tourism, a major part of recreational transport. Commerce requires the transport of people to conduct business, either to allow face-to-face communication for important decisions or to move specialists from their regular place of work to sites where they are needed.

Planning

Transport planning allows for high utilization and less impact regarding new infrastructure. Using models of transport forecasting, planners are able to predict future transport patterns. On the operative level, logistics allows owners of cargo to plan transport as part of the supply chain. Transport as a field is studied through transport economics, the backbone for the creation of regulation policy by authorities. Transport engineering, a sub-discipline of civil engineering, and must take into account trip generation, trip distribution, mode choice and route assignment, while the operative level is handles through traffic engineering.

Because of the negative impacts made, transport often becomes the subject of controversy related to choice of mode, as well as increased capacity. Automotive transport can be seen as a tragedy of the commons, where the flexibility and comfort for the individual deteriorate the natural and urban environment for all. Density of development depends on mode of transport, with public transport allowing for better spacial utilization. Good land use keeps common activities close to peoples homes and places higher-density development closer to transport lines and hubs; minimize the need for transport. There are economies of agglomeration. Beyond transportation some land uses are more efficient when clustered. Transportation facilities consume land, and in cities, pavement (devoted to streets and parking) can easily exceed 20 percent of the total land use. An efficient transport system can reduce land waste.

Too much infrastructure and too much smoothing for maximum vehicle throughput means that in many cities there is too much traffic and many—if not all—of the negative impacts that come with it. It is only in recent years that traditional practices have started to be questioned in many places, and as a result of new types of analysis which bring in a much broader range of skills than those traditionally relied on—spanning such areas as environmental impact analysis, public health, sociologists as well as economists who increasingly are questioning the viability of the old mobility solutions. European cities are leading this transition.

Environment

Transport is a major use of energy, and burns most of the world's petroleum. This creates air pollution, including nitrous oxides and particulates, and is a significant contributor to global warming through emission of carbon dioxide, for which transport is the fastest-growing emission sector. By subsector, road transport is the largest contributor to global warming. Environmental regulations in developed countries have reduced the individual vehicles emission; however, this has been offset by an increase in the number of vehicles, and more use of each vehicle. Some pathways to reduce the carbon emissions of road vehicles considerably have been studied. Energy use and emissions vary largely between modes, causing environmentalists to call for a transition from air and road to rail and human-powered transport, and increase transport electrification and energy efficiency.

CHAPTER–12

Principle of Tour and Travel

Travel is the movement of people between relatively distant geographical locations for any purpose and any duration, with or without any means of transport. Travel also includes relatively short stays between successive movements. Movements between locations requiring only a few minutes are not considered as travel. As an activity, "travel" also covers all the activities performed during a travel (movement).

Travel may be local, regional, national (domestic) or international. In some countries, non-local internal travel may require an internal passport, while international travel typically requires a passport and visa.

Travel can be for recreational purposes, for tourism, to visit people, for business or for commuting, and may occur for numerous other reasons, such as to obtain health care, migration, fleeing war, etc. Travel may occur by human-powered transport such as walking or bicycling, or with vehicles, such as airplanes, private transport, public transport, automobiles and trains.

A round trip is a particular type of travel whereby a person moves from his/her usual residence to one or several locations and returns. A trip can also be part of a round trip.

The word originates from the Middle English word travailen ("to toil"), which comes from the Old French word travailler ("travail"). A person who travels is called a traveler (U.S.) or traveller (UK).

TRAVEL ADVISORY

A travel advisory is a public notice issued by a government agency to provide information about the relative safety of travelling to or visiting one or more specific destinations. The purpose is to enable travelers make an informed decision about a particular travel destination, and to help travellers prepare adequately for what may be encountered on their trip.

Travel advisories may relate to issues such as inclement weather, security matters, civil unrest or disease.

Travel agency

A travel agency is a retail business, that sells travel related products and services to customers, on behalf of suppliers, such as airlines, car rentals, cruise lines, hotels, railways, sightseeing tours and package holidays that combine several products. In addition to dealing with ordinary tourists, most travel agencies have a separate department devoted to making travel arrangements for business travelers and some travel agencies specialize in commercial and business travel only. There are also travel agencies that serve as general sales agents for foreign travel companies, allowing them to have offices in countries other than where their headquarters are located.

Origins

The British company Cox & Kings is sometimes said to be the oldest travel agency in the world, but this rests upon the services that the original bank, established in 1758, supplied to its wealthy clients. The modern travel agency first appeared in the second half of the 19th century. Thomas Cook, in addition to developing the package tour, established a chain of agencies in the last quarter of the 19th century, in association with the Midland Railway. They not only sold their own tours to the public, but in addition, represented other tour companies. Other British pioneer travel agencies were Dean and Dawson, the Polytechnic Touring Association and the Co-operative Wholesale Society. The oldest travel agency in North America is Brownell Travel; on July 4, 1887, Walter T. Brownell led ten travelers on a European tour, setting sail from New York on the SS Devonia.

Travel agencies became more commonplace with the development of commercial aviation, starting in the 1920s. Originally, travel agencies largely catered to middle and upper class customers, but the post-war boom in mass-market package holidays resulted in travel agencies on the main streets of most British towns, catering to a working class clientèle, looking for a convenient way to book overseas beach holidays.

Operations

As the name implies, a travel agency's main function is to act as an agent, that is to say, selling travel products and services on behalf of a supplier. Consequently, unlike other retail businesses, they do not keep a stock in hand. A package holiday or a ticket is not purchased from a supplier unless a customer requests that purchase. The holiday or ticket is supplied to them at a discount. The profit is therefore the difference between the advertised price which the customer pays and the discounted price at which it is supplied to the agent. This is known as the commission. A British travel agent would consider a 10-12% commission as a good arrangement. In Australia, all individuals or companies that sell tickets are required to be licensed as a travel agent.

In some countries, airlines have stopped giving commission to travel agencies. Therefore, travel agencies are now forced to charge a percentage premium or a standard flat fee, per sale. However, some companies still give them a set percentage for selling their product. Major tour companies can afford to do this, because if they were to sell a thousand trips at a cheaper rate, they still come out better than if they sell a hundred trips at a higher rate. This process benefits both parties.

Other commercial operations are undertaken, especially by the larger chains. These can include the sale of in-house insurance, travel guide books and timetables, car rentals, and the services of an on-site Bureau de change, dealing in the most popular holiday currencies.

The majority of travel agents have felt the need to protect themselves and their clients against the possibilities of commercial failure, either their own or a supplier's. They will advertise the fact that they are surety bonded, meaning in the case of a failure, the customers are guaranteed either an equivalent holiday to that which they have lost or if they prefer, a refund. Many British and American agencies and tour operators are bonded with the International Air Transport Association (IATA), for those who issue air tickets, Air Travel Organisers' Licensing (ATOL) for those who order tickets in, the Association of British Travel Agents (ABTA) or the American Society of Travel Agents (ASTA), for those who sell package holidays on behalf of a tour company.

A travel agent is supposed to offer impartial travel advice to the customer. However, this function almost disappeared with the mass-market package holiday and some agency chains seemed to develop a 'holiday supermarket' concept, in which customers choose their holiday from brochures on racks and then book it from a counter. Again, a variety of social and economic changes have now contrived to bring this aspect to the fore once more, particularly with the advent of multiple, no-frills, low-cost airlines.

Commissions

Most travel agencies operate on a commission-basis, meaning that the compensation from the airlines, car rentals, cruise lines, hotels, railways, sightseeing tours and tour operators, etc., is expected in form of a commission from their bookings. Most often, the commission consists of a set percentage of the sale.

In the United States, most airlines pay no commission at all to travel agencies. In this case, an agency usually adds a service fee to the net price.

Types of agencies

There are three different types of agencies in the UK: Multiples, Miniples and Independent Agencies. The former comprises a number of national chains, often owned by international conglomerates, like Thomson Holidays, now a subsidiary of TUI AG, the German multinational. It is now quite common for the large mass-market tour companies to purchase a controlling interest in a chain of travel agencies, in order to control the distribution of their product. (This is an example of vertical integration.) The smaller chains are often based in particular regions or districts.

In the United States, there are four different types of agencies: Mega, Regional, Consortium and Independent Agencies. American Express and the American Automobile Association (AAA) are examples of mega travel agencies.

Independent Agencies usually cater to a special or niche market, such as the needs of residents in an upmarket commuter town or suburb or a particular group interested in a similar activity, such as sporting events, like football, golf or tennis.

There are two approaches of travel agencies. One is the traditional, multi-destination, out-bound travel agency, based in the originating location of the traveler and the other is the destination focused, in-bound travel agency, that is based in the destination and delivers an expertise on that location. At present, the former is usually a larger operator like Thomas Cook, while the latter is often a smaller, independent operator.

Consolidators

Airline consolidators and other types of travel consolidators and wholesalers are high volume sales companies that specialize in selling to niche markets. They may or may not offer various types of services, at a single point of access. These can be hotel reservations, flights or car-rentals, for example. Sometimes the services are combined into vacation packages, that include transfers to the location and lodging. These companies do not usually sell directly to the public, but act as wholesalers to retail travel agencies. Commonly, the sole purpose of consolidators is to sell to ethnic niches in the travel industry. Usually, no consolidator offers everything, they may only have contracted rates to specific destinations. Today, there are no domestic consolidators, with some exceptions for business class contracts.

CRITICISM AND CONTROVERSY

"Racking"

Travel agencies have been accused of employing a number of restrictive practices, the chief of which is known as 'racking'. This is the practice of displaying only the brochures of those travel companies whose holidays they wish to sell, the ones that pay them the most commission. Of course, the average customer tends to think that these are the only holidays on offer and is unaware of the possible alternatives.

Conversely, by limiting the number of companies that a travel agency represents, this can bring a better and more profitable, working relationship between the agency and its suppliers. Travel agencies can then obtain special benefits for their customers, from a supplier, by concentrating their bookings with that supplier. Some examples of these special benefits would be room upgrades or the waiver of change and cancellation fees.

The Internet threat

With general public access to the Internet, many airlines and other travel companies began to sell directly to passengers. As a consequence, airlines no longer needed to pay the commissions to travel agents on each ticket sold. Since 1997, travel agencies have gradually been disintermediated, by the reduction in costs caused by removing layers from the package holiday distribution network. However, travel agents remain dominant in some areas such as cruise vacations where they represent 77% of bookings and 73% of packaged travel.

In response, travel agencies have developed an internet presence of their own by creating travel websites, with detailed information and online booking capabilities. Several major online travel agencies include: Expedia, Voyages-sncf.com, Travelocity, Orbitz,

CheapTickets, Priceline, CheapOair and Hotwire.com. Travel agencies also use the services of the major computer reservations systems companies, also known as Global Distribution Systems (GDS), including: SABRE, Amadeus CRS, Galileo CRS and Worldspan, which is a subsidiary of Travelport, allowing them to book and sell airline tickets, hotels, car rentals and other travel related services. Some online travel websites allow visitors to compare hotel and flight rates with multiple companies for free. They often allow visitors to sort the travel packages by amenities, price, and proximity to a city or landmark.

Travel agents have applied dynamic packaging tools to provide fully bonded (full financial protection) travel at prices equal to or lower than a member of the public can book online. As such, the agencies' financial assets are protected in addition to professional travel agency advice.

All travel sites that sell hotels online work together with GDS, suppliers and hotels directly to search for room inventory. Once the travel site sells a hotel, the site will try to get a confirmation for this hotel. Once confirmed or not, the customer is contacted with the result. This means that booking a hotel on a travel website will not necessarily result in an instant answer. Only some hotels on a travel website can be confirmed instantly (which is normally marked as such on each site). As different travel websites work with different suppliers together, each site has different hotels that it can confirm instantly. Some examples of such online travel websites that sell hotel rooms are Expedia, Orbitz and WorldHotel-Link.

The comparison sites, such as Kayak.com, TripAdvisor and SideStep search the resellers site all at once to save time searching. None of these sites actually sell hotel rooms.

Often tour operators have hotel contracts, allotments and free sell agreements which allow for the immediate confirmation of hotel rooms for vacation bookings.

Mainline service providers are those that actually produce the direct service, like various hotels chains or airlines that have a website for online bookings. Portals will serve a consolidator of various airlines and hotels on the internet. They work on a commission from these hotels and airlines. Often, they provide cheaper rates than the mainline service providers as these sites get bulk deals from the service providers. A meta search engine on the other hand, simply culls data from the internet on real time rates for various search queries and diverts traffic to the mainline service providers for an online booking. These websites usually do not have their own booking engine.

Careers

With the many people switching to self-service internet websites, the number of available jobs as travel agents is decreasing. Most jobs that become available are from older travel agents retiring. Counteracting the decrease in jobs due to internet services is the increase in the number of people travelling. Since 1995, many travel agents have exited the industry, and relatively few young people have entered the field due to less competitive salaries. However, others have abandoned the 'brick and mortar' agency for a home-based business to reduce overheads and those who remain have managed to survive by promoting other travel products such as cruise lines and train excursions or by promoting their ability to aggressively research and assemble complex travel packages on a moment's notice, essentially acting as a very advanced concierge.

TRAVEL DOCUMENT

A travel document is an identity document issued by a government or international treaty organization to facilitate the movement of individuals or small groups of persons across international boundaries. Travel documents usually assure other governments that the bearer may return to the issuing country, and are often issued in booklet form to allow other governments to place visas as well as entry and exit stamps into them. The most common travel document is a passport, which usually identifies the bearer as a citizen of the issuing country. However, the term is sometimes used only for those documents which do not bear proof of nationality, such as the Refugee Travel Document.

Passport

In general, a passport is a travel document that also serves as proof of citizenship from the issuing country. Although generally accepted by the majority of countries in the world, some issuing countries expressly exclude the validity of passports from nations that are not recognized by their governments.

Laissez-Passer/Emergency passports

A laissez-passer (from the French let pass) is a travel document issued by a national government or certain international organizations, such as the United Nations, European Union and the International Committee of the Red Cross (ICRC). A laissez-passer is often for one-way travel to the issuing country for humanitarian reasons only. Some national governments issue laissez-passers to their own nationals as emergency passports. Others issue them to people who are stateless, or who are unable to obtain a passport from their own government, or whose government is not recognized by the issuing country.

Historically, laissez-passers were commonly issued during wartime and at other periods, literally acting as a pass to allow travel to specific areas, or out of war zones or countries for various officials, diplomatic agents, other representatives or citizens of third countries. In these contexts, a laissez-passer would frequently include quite specific and limited freedom of movement. The form and issuing authority would be more or less standardized, depending on the circumstances.

An example is when in the early 1950s, the Iraqi government granted permission to its 120 thousand Jewish citizens to leave (Operation Ezra and Nehemiah), conditional on their renouncement of their citizenship and leaving behind all their properties and assets. The travel document that was issued was the laissez-passer, since an Iraqi passport was no longer possible.

UN Travel Documents

The United Nations (and the International Labour Organization) issue a laissez-passer to officials and members of the UN and other specialized agencies as well as to several international organizations. The laissez-passer is also issued to their families for official use. The United Nations Laissez-Passer is similar to a passport, and is generally recognized worldwide, although some countries will not accept the document as sufficient to gain entry. It does not generally confer diplomatic immunity, but may confer limited immunities and privileges.

Between 2000 and 2010, the United Nations Interim Administration Mission in Kosovo (UNMIK) issued travel documents to residents of Kosovo as they were often not able to obtain a passport through other channels.

Aliens and Refugees

- Refugee travel document (formally: 1951 Convention travel document) are passport-like booklets issued by national governments to refugees under the 1951 Convention Relating to the Status of Refugees.
- 1954 Convention travel documents are similar documents issued to stateless persons under the 1954 Convention Relating to the Status of Stateless Persons. The document is the successor of the (now defunct) League of Nations' Nansen passport.
- Alien's passports and certificates of identity are passport-like booklets issued by national governments to resident foreigners, other than those issued under the 1951 and 1954 conventions mentioned above. However, some governments issue certificates of identity to their own nationals as emergency passports.

Other Documents as Travel Documents

Several other groups of documents issued for a different purpose officially serve as travel documents, generally for a limited set of countries. Such documents (when allowing full border crossing - exiting one country, and entering another- only) are discussed below:

National Identity Card

Identity cards are generally issued as a means of identification within a country, but can often also be used as a travel document. For example, complying National Identity Cards of the European Union can be used unrestricted in more than 20 countries. Also the U.S. passport card can be regarded an identity card fit for international travel.

Driver's Licence

Driver's licenses are generally not considered travel documents, since they bear no information on nationality and conditions which would lead to refusal of a travel document have generally not been tested. However, in several provinces of Canada and U.S. states, nationals/citizens can -upon payment of an extra fee and additional information regarding- receive an Enhanced Drivers License which enables border crossing between Canada and the U.S. by land.

De facto Travel Documents

De facto travel documents are documents which in practice will be sufficient to cross borders legally, but with no legal status as a travel document. Within the Border Controls in the Common Travel Area, travel between Ireland, the United Kingdom, the British Crown Dependencies, Isle of Man and Channel Islands, no travel documents is required by British or Irish citizens. As this requirement does not hold for others, these citizens have to establish the presumption of having this nationality, which requires in practice some form of identification. The documents used for this purpose (most notably: driver's license) are thus de facto travel documents.

TRAVEL JOURNAL

A travel journal, also called road journal or travelogue, is a record made by a voyager. Generally in diary form, a travel journal

were his stated reasons for going. In the mid 15th century, Gilles le Bouvier, in his Livre de la description des pays, gave us his reason to travel and write:

Because many people of diverse nations and countries delight and take pleasure, as I have done in times past, in seeing the world and things therein, and also because many wish to know without going there, and others wish to see, go, and travel, I have begun this little book.

In 1589, Richard Hakluyt (c. 1552–1616) published Voyages, a foundational text of the travel literature genre.

Other later examples of travel literature include accounts of the Grand Tour. Aristocrats, clergy, and others with money and leisure time travelled Europe to learn about the art and architecture of its past. One tourism literature pioneer was Robert Louis Stevenson (1850–1894).

Travel literature also became popular during the Song Dynasty (960–1279) of medieval China. The genre was called 'travel record literature' (youji wenxue), and was often written in narrative, prose, essay and diary style. Travel literature authors such as Fan Chengda (1126–1193) and Xu Xiake (1587–1641) incorporated a wealth of geographical and topographical information into their writing, while the 'daytrip essay' Record of Stone Bell Mountain by the noted poet and statesman Su Shi (1037–1101) presented a philosophical and moral argument as its central purpose.

In the 18th century, travel literature was commonly known as the book of travels, which mainly consisted of maritime diaries. In 18th century England, almost every famous writer worked in the travel literature form. Captain James Cook's diaries (1784) were the equivalent of today's best sellers.

Travelogues

The Americans, Paul Theroux, Bill Bryson and William Least Heat-Moon, Welsh author Jan Morris and Englishman Eric Newby are or were widely acclaimed as travel writers although Morris is also a historian and Theroux a novelist.

Travel literature often intersects with essay writing, as in V. S. Naipaul's India: A Wounded Civilization, where a trip becomes the occasion for extended observations on a nation and people. This is similarly the case in Rebecca West's work on Yugoslavia, Black Lamb and Grey Falcon.

Sometimes a writer will settle into a locality for an extended period, absorbing a sense of place while continuing to observe with a travel writer's sensibility. Examples of such writings include Lawrence Durrell's Bitter Lemons, Deborah Tall's The Island of the White Cow and Peter Mayle's best-selling A Year in Provence and its sequels.

Travel and nature writing merge in many of the works by Sally Carrighar, Ivan T. Sanderson and Gerald Durrell. These authors are naturalists, who write in support of their fields of study. Charles Darwin wrote his famous account of the journey of HMS Beagle at the intersection of science, natural history and travel.

Literary travel writing also occurs when an author, famous in another field, travels and writes about his or her experiences. Examples of such writers are Samuel Johnson, Charles Dickens, Mary Wollstonecraft, Robert Louis Stevenson, Hilaire Belloc, D. H. Lawrence, Rebecca West and John Steinbeck.

Fiction

Fictional travelogues make up a large proportion of travel literature. Although it may be desirable in some contexts to distinguish fictional from non-fictional works, such distinctions have proved notoriously difficult to make in practice, as in the famous instance of the travel writings of Marco Polo or John Mandeville. Many "fictional" works of travel literature are based on factual journeys – Joseph Conrad's Heart of Darkness and presumably, Homer's Odyssey (c. 8th cent. BCE) – while other works, though based on imaginary and even highly fantastic journeys – Dante's Divine Comedy, Jonathan Swift's Gulliver's Travels, Voltaire's Candide or Samuel Johnson's The History of Rasselas, Prince of Abissinia – nevertheless contain factual elements.

Jack Kerouac's On the Road (1957) and The Dharma Bums (1958) are fictionalized accounts of his travels across the United States during the late 1940s and early 1950s.

One contemporary example of a real life journey transformed into a work of fiction is travel writer Kira Salak's novel, The White Mary, which takes place in Papua New Guinea and the Congo and is largely based on her own experiences in those countries.

Travel literature in criticism

The systematic study of travel literature emerged as a legitimate field of scholarly inquiry in the mid-1990s, with its own conferences, organizations, journals, monographs, anthologies, and encyclopedias. Among the most important, pre-1995 monographs are: Abroad (1980) by Paul Fussell, an exploration of British interwar travel writing as escapism; Gone Primitive: Modern Intellects, Savage Minds (1990) by Marianna Torgovnick, an inquiry into the primitivist presentation of foreign cultures; Haunted Journeys: Desire and Transgression in European Travel Writing (1991) by Dennis Porter, a close look at the psychological correlatives of travel; Discourses of Difference: An Analysis of Women's Travel Writing by Sara Mills, an inquiry into the intersection of gender and colonialism during the nineteenth century; Imperial Eyes: Travel Writing and Transculturation (1992), Mary Louise Pratt's influential study of Victorian travel writing's dissemination of a colonial mind-set; and Belated Travelers (1994), an analysis of colonial anxiety by Ali Behdad.

The study of travel writing developed most extensively in the late 1990s, encouraged by the currency of Foucauldian criticism and Edward Said's postcolonial landmark study Orientalism. This growing interdisciplinary preoccupation with cultural diversity, globalization, and migration is expressed in other fields of literary study, most notably Comparative Literature. The first international travel writing conference, "Snapshots from Abroad", organized by Donald Ross at the University of Minnesota in 1997, attracted over one hundred scholars and led to the foundation of the International Society for Travel Writing (ISTW). The first issue of Studies in Travel Writing was published the same year, edited by Tim Youngs. Annual scholarly conferences about travel writing, held in the USA, Europe and Asia, saw an unprecedented upswing in the number of published travel literature monographs and essay collections, as well as a proliferation of travel writing anthologies.

Major directions in recent travel writing scholarship include: studies about the role of gender in travel and travel writing (e.g. Women Travelers in Colonial India: The Power of the Female Gaze [1998] by Indira Ghose); explorations of the political functions of travel (e.g. Radicals on the Road: The Politics of English Travel Writing in the 1930s [2001] by Bernard Schweizer); postcolonial perspectives on travel (e.g. English Travel Writing: From Pilgrimages to Postcolonial Explorations (2000) by Barbara Korte); and studies about the function of language in travel and travel writing (e.g. Across the Lines: Travel, Language, and Translation [2000] by Michael Cronin). Tim Youngs is a driving force behind the growth of the field, notably through the journal Studies in Travel Writing, through his two co-edited volumes of essays on travel writing, Cambridge Companion to Travel Writing (2002), co-edited with T. Hulme, and Perspectives in Travel Writing (2004), co-edited with G. Hooper. Youngs also co-organized the 2005 travel writing conference, "Mobilis in Mobile", in Hong Kong. Kristi Siegel is another prolific editor of travel writing scholarship, having edited Issues in Travel Writing: Empire, Spectacle and Displacement (2002), as well as Gender, Genre, and Identity in Women's Travel Writing (2004).

TRAVEL WEBSITE

A travel website is a website on the world wide web, that is dedicated to travel. The site may be focused on travel reviews, the booking of travel, or a combination of both. Approximately seventy million consumers researched travel plans online in July 2006. Travel bookings are the single largest component of e-commerce, according to Forrester Research.

Travelogues

Many travel websites are online travelogues or travel journals, usually created by individual travellers and hosted by companies that generally provide their information to consumers for free. These companies generate revenue through advertising or by providing services to other businesses. This medium produces a wide variety of styles, often incorporating graphics, photography, maps, and other unique content. Some examples of websites that use a combination of travel reviews and the booking of travel are TripAdvisor, Virtualtourist, GLOBOsapiens, IgoUgo, and Cruise Critic. TripAdvisor allows travelers to view, contribute to, and edit the online travel "guide books", containing over 25 million travel reviews on more than 33,000 destinations worldwide, as of July 2009. IgoUgo offers a place to store and share trip stories, pictures, opinions, tips, and experiences. Similarly, Cruise Critic is an interactive virtual community of avid and first-time cruisers who plan, research, and share their experiences online.

Service Providers

Individual airlines, hotels, bed and breakfasts, cruise lines, automobile rental companies, and other travel-related service providers often maintain their own web sites providing retail sales. Many with complex offerings include some sort of search engine technology to look for bookings within a certain timeframe, service class, geographic location, or price range.

Online Travel Agencies

An online travel agency (OTA) specializes in offering planning sources and booking capabilities. Major OTAs include:

- Voyages-sncf.com - revenue €2.23 billion (2008)
- Expedia, Inc., including Expedia.com, Hotels.com, Hotwire.com, and others - revenue US$2.937 billion (2008)
- Sabre Holdings, including Travelocity, lastminute.com, and others - revenue US$2.9 billion (2008)

- Opodo - revenue €1.3 billion (2008)
- Priceline.com - revenue US$1.9 billion (2008)
- Orbitz Worldwide, Inc., including Orbitz.com, CheapTickets, ebookers, and others - revenue US$870 million (2008)

Fare Aggregators and Metasearch Engines

The average consumer visits 3.6 sites when shopping for an airline ticket online, according to PhoCusWright, a Sherman, CT-based travel technology firm. Yahoo claims 76% of all online travel purchases are preceded by some sort of search function, according to Malcolmson, director of product development for Yahoo Travel. The 2004 Travel Consumer Survey published Jupiter Research noted that "nearly two in five online travel consumers say they believe that no one site has the lowest rates or fares." Thus a niche was created for aggregate travel search which seek to find the lowest rates from multiple travel sites, obviating the need for consumers to cross-shop from site to site.

Metasearch engines are so named conduct searches across multiple independent search engines. Metasearch engines often make use of "screen scraping" to get live availability of flights. Screen scraping is a way of crawling through the airline websites, getting content from those sites by extracting data from the same human-readable HTML feed (rather than a Semantic Web or database feed designed to be machine-readable). Metasearch engines usually process incoming data to eliminate duplicate entries, but may not expose "advanced search" options in the underlying databases (because not all databases support the same options).

Fare aggregators redirect the users to an airline, cruise, hotel, or car rental site or Online Travel Agent for the final purchase of a ticket. Aggregators' business models include getting feeds from major OTAs, then displaying to the users all of the results on one screen. The OTA then fulfills the ticket. Aggregators generate revenues through advertising and charging OTAs for referring clients. Examples of aggregate sites are Cheapflights, Dohop,

Kayak.com, Mobissimo, Momondo, CheapOair, Ixigo.com, SideStep, and Skyscanner.

The difference between a "fare aggregator" and "metasearch engine" is unclear, though different terms may imply different levels of cooperation between the companies involved.

In 2008, Ryanair threatened to cancel all bookings made on Ryanair flights made through metasearch engines, but later allowed the sites to operate as long as they did not resell tickets or overload Ryanair's servers.

Bargain sites

Travel bargain websites collect and publish bargain rates by advising consumers where to find them online (sometimes but not always through a direct link). Rather than providing detailed search tools, these sites generally focus on offering advertised specials, such as last-minute sales from travel suppliers eager to deplete unused inventory; therefore, these sites often work best for consumers who are flexible about destinations and other key itinerary components.

Bibliography

- Ahang S. and A.B. Markman, 'Processing Product Unique Features: Alignability and Involvement in Preference Construction', Journal of Consumer Psychology, 11, 1 (2001), 13–27.

- Andrew Smith , REIMAGING THE CITY, The Value of Sport Initiatives, Annals of Tourism Research, Vol. 32, No.1, pp. 217–236, 2005

- Anderson, N. : *Work and Leisure,* Routledge and Kegan Faul, London, 1961.

- Ansell, G.B. Hawthrone J. N. and R.M.C. Dawson : *Functions of Phospholipids,* Elsevier, New York, 1973.

- Asli D. A. Tasci and Metin Kozak Journal of Vacation Marketing, Vol. 12, No. 4, 299-317 (2006)

- Asli D. A. Tasci (2006). Destination brands vs destination images: Do we know what we mean? , Journal of Vacation Marketing, Vol. 12, No. 4, 299-31

- Auld, T. & McArthur, S. (2003) Does event-driven tourism provide economic benefits? A case study from the Manawatu region of New Zealand. Tourism Economics, 9 (2) pp.191-201

- Bramwell B., 'Strategic Planning Before and After a Mega-Event', Tourism Management, 18, 3 (1997), 167–76.